MULTIPLE INTELLIGENCES, HOWARD GARDNER AND NEW METHODS IN COLLEGE TEACHING

CLYDE COREIL, PH.D., EDITOR

ANDREW MOULTON, ASSISTANT EDITOR

A PUBLICATION OF NEW JERSEY CITY UNIVERSITY

Book design by Ronald Bogusz, Director of Publications and Special Programs, New Jersey City University.

Photograph of Dr. Clyde Coreil on the back cover is by Mr. Bill Wittkop. Author's photographs were submitted by the authors.

Additional copies may be ordered through the distributor:
Bastos Educational Books
P.O. Box 770-433
Woodside, New York 11377
Voice: 800-662-0301
Fax: 718-997-6445

ISBN: 1-883514-07-X

CONTENTS

For any human undertaking, it is necessary for an incredibly large number of contributions to be made—some large, some small. If we consider the proverb about the battle that was lost because of a loose horseshoe, we realize that the size of the contribution make little difference—what is important is that it was made.

The conference on which this book is based was considered successful. It is natural to feel gratitude. It is equally important, however, to realize how easy it would have been for failure to replace success. We ask that all of the people not mentioned here feel our sincere gratitude for what they have done.

High on the list of those to be mentioned is Howard Gardner himself. For a man so well and widely known to share his time with people he did not even know is an indication of character. Another interesting lesson in care and attention to detail is known by very few.

In his public address, he made reference to the difficulty his driver had in finding something as big as the Mariott Hotel in Newark. He made no reference, however, to coming to our University the night before the conference to make certain that his electronic devices and our electronic devices matched and worked. He was here for at least one hour, making sure that his illustrated remarks would seem easy and effortless. Because of that extra effort, everything worked and went as planned.

There is a somewhat profound lesson in his effort that we—and certainly every public speaker—should take very much to heart. That lesson is this: take every event seriously and do your best to return the respect an audience has shown in showing up. If we wonder why Dr. Gardner is successful, let us find a first reason in the sincerity and humility of that attitude.

A similar lesson in conviction is in the self-confidence of Dr. Ansley LaMar, then serving as Dean of the College of Arts and Sciences. His sincere interest and generosity made things happen. It is Dr. LaMar who founded the annual Urban Mission Conference which focuses on civic and educational contributions that can be made by institutions of higher education. For her open-hearted and high-minded cooperation in the publication of this book, the present Dean, Dr. Lisa Fiol-Matta, is truly deserving of gratitude, as is Dr. Jo Bruno, Associate Vice President for Academic Affairs.

There immediately comes to mind the complete commitment, enormous effort and unfailing good nature of Mr. Andrew Platizky and of his secretary, Mrs. Judy Kuchler, who has a serious aversion to leaving things undone. Dr. Annette Lesiege, then Assistant Dean, is as quiet as she is efficient. Other officials and assistants whose efforts are much appreciated are Ms. Ann McGovern, Mr. Ron Bogusz, Ms. Annette Winns, and Ms. Hilda Merchan. One could not ask for a better natured, more responsible colleague than Mr. Andrew Moulton, whose role in this publication was assistant editor. He has my sincere appreciation.

ACKNOWLEDGMENTS

It is virtually always the case that the persons heading an organization share responsibility for the excellent service of their team. It is with respect and appreciation that we wish to acknowledge the trust and cooperation of President Carlos Hernández and Dr. Larry Carter, Vice President of Academic Affairs. To Dr. Carter we are especially grateful and deeply appreciative of the confidence and generous support that helped to make this publication possible.

Most of us need someone to ease the concerns of a major project—such has been my fortune. I wish to thank my wife, Vivian Tsao, who is always there, ready to listen or to share the silence.

Dr. Clyde Coreil, Executive Committee Member
Fifth Urban Mission Conference

This book started life as the planned digest of proceedings of the 5th Urban Mission Conference, held on October 26, 2001, at New Jersey City University. The theme was "Innovative Teaching in Higher Education," and the keynote speaker was Dr. Howard Gardner of Harvard University. Those of us who organized the Urban Mission Conference were initially interested mainly in contemporary reflections on college teaching. In our invitations to some 35 presenters, we informed them—almost in passing— that Dr. Gardner would be delivering the keynote and that their presentations would be published if they were later written as papers. We had not anticipated that Gardner's Multiple Intelligences Theory (MI) would prove to be a rich, unifying central theme. It has. Neither had we anticipated that 30 of the presenters would put pen to paper. They did. And we thank them deeply for it.

All of the contributors were concerned that their professional expressions meet the highest standards. In an effort to render their texts fully comprehensible to readers from different areas, however, I sometimes suggested simplifications that caused them to wince. Wherever possible, they agreed. For that and for their generous and enthusiastic spirit of cooperation, I am truly grateful. In my opinion, our joint effort has matured from a "digest of proceedings" into a full and careful consideration of college teaching at its best.

Most of the following articles make specific and pointed reference to MI as constituting the direction of pedagogical change in higher education. As you go through the 30 pieces, you will see that they are not simply predictions of possible movement, but descriptions of changes that are well underway. So that one more unintended feature of this book is that it serves as a cross-section of new and different teaching techniques in Canada and the USA at the beginning of the new millennium.

Gardner is best known for his theory that intelligence is not limited to the skills in mathematics and language that are measured by the traditional IQ test, but is much broader and includes reference to art, music, space, physical movement, interpersonal and intrapersonal relations, and the ability to perceive and evaluate differences between things. These ideas seem to have had far more influence on Kindergarten through secondary education (K-12) than those of any other researcher or writer of the 20th century.

It seems probable that because the teachers of K-12 seized upon MI as a valuable way forward, and because of a certain reluctance of professors to discuss teaching methods, Gardner's influence has remained centered in pre-college education. It is time, however, to acknowledge that MI also provides important approaches to problems faced by higher education at the turn of the millennium. It is with critical issues such as the following that the essays in this volume deal, either explicitly or indirectly:

PREFACE: A MAGICAL TRANSFORMATION

CLYDE COREIL

- Are there levels of education past which Gardner's notions do not apply?
- Why have so few college teachers been taught how to teach?
- Has the role of the professor changed over the past 30 years?
- Can students actually be expected to learn from other students?
- Has education moved past the idea of a physical classroom shared by a professor and students in a specific location?
- Why is teaching for tests considered so profoundly pathetic and hopelessly misguided by so many teachers?
- Should professors in higher education look to elementary and secondary teachers for help in classroom methodology?

It may come to pass that K-12 will become K-16, in which pre-school, elementary, secondary and higher education will be conceived as a single continuum. If so, one would expect that each sector will examine the methods and directions of the others. The dubious assumption that value trickles from top to bottom—that is, from college to pre-school—might well be replaced by one of mutual sharing at all levels. That is a possibility that is within our grasp as we begin the new millennium. In such an attitude of open receptiveness, professors would be as eager to use new methods as they are to share discoveries and approaches introduced in the university.

Gardner not only holds that intelligences are multiple in nature, but that in each individual person, they are combined in a different fashion. As a result, students would seem to construct their own knowledge through unique configurations of intelligences. These theories tend to objectively affirm the integrity of diversity. It is, however, not primarily the diversity of cultures. Instead, the focus shifts to the individual person and to the way in which consciousness—and presumably, conscience— develop. In my opinion, it is in contexts such as these that Gardner's contribution can be contemplated quite meaningfully.

Editing these writings has been ever so slightly like peeking under the thick canvas of the Big Top and seeing the circus performers as they begin their magical transformation. I trust that at some point in your reading, you will pause and say, "You know, in a way, he was right. The show is a grand one, and we've got ringside tickets."

In 1983, when Howard Gardner published *Frames of Mind*, nobody would have imagined the educational implications that the theory was going to have. Most of these implications have been felt in elementary and secondary education. Largely because of efforts such as the conference at New Jersey City University, it is becoming apparent that Gardner's Multiple Intelligences Theory (MI) is also relevant at the post-secondary level.

Although it is not often discussed, there seems to be a correspondence between (1) the unique combination of skills and abilities that students have before they ever set foot in a classroom, and (2) the skills and abilities that they will use to pursue advanced studies in post-secondary education. Ideally, if teachers along the way are aware of and respect these abilities, then each student's journey through elementary and secondary school will be based on his or her well established areas of strength.

It is of critical importance that the existence of special abilities and talents be recognized at all levels including kindergarten and college. Such recognition provides for a wide, harmonious and continuous development of human interests. In such an environment, each student senses the teacher's welcoming acceptance and approval. There emerges a confidence on the part of the student who can then find or create a set of activities and interests that has a deep and personal meaning for him or her. These activities should be nurtured and developed to the fullest extent possible.

On the other hand, a broader and more inclusive approach on the part of the teacher will promote a richer and more fulfilling development of the skills that are so valuable at higher levels. Post-secondary teaching should not be considered as inherently different from the lower levels. Although the material is more complex, the students have not put away the psycho-dynamic structure of approaches and attitudes that made them unique individuals in their youth. In the essays in the book, again and again, we see teachers who are courageous enough to operate according to the principles that constitute MI Theory. The effect seems obvious and perfectly predictable—students are more interested, learn more and are very probably less inclined to leave the university. In fact, though it would be difficult to measure, data might well be kept on the relation between teaching style and retention.

Such parallels of interest and ability might seem obvious, but quite often they are neglected. Education designed without such an awareness will very likely be narrow, disconnected and inefficient. One example of this occurs if we accept the belief that I.Q. scores are sufficient and dependable indicators of the general ability to learn. A person who makes a low score often suffers from it during all of the years of study and even later in the career to which he is guided. This is quite unfortunate, considering that what the traditional I.Q. test measures is limited to ability in mathematics and language. In itself, this is quite

FOREWORD: CORRELATING KINDERGARTEN WITH COLLEGE

LOLA PRIETO AND CARMEN FERRÁNDIZ

useful. But these tests say little or nothing of the individual's ability to relate to other persons or to the self, of the architect's ability to perceive and work with space, of the artist's ability to find relationships between color and form that human beings will perceive as pleasing and beautiful, of the musicians ability to find different progressions of chords that resonate in the human mind and emotions. In short, they are about those things that we consider dear to us as feeling human beings.

In methodology that is broad and intended to include different abilities and talents, children tend to respond in terms of their own talents and abilities and to become more involved in the activities of the classroom. It is a win-win situation. They feel more fulfilled as children and are more productive as adults. There is a place for each of them in our society, and it is our responsibility to help them find it. All people have the right to lead lives in which they are aware of what they do well, and hopefully can be employed in those areas.

If a man like Beethoven or Shakespeare scores relatively low on an I.Q. test, does this mean that his life will be narrow and uninteresting? Hardly. However, outrageous tragedies of frustration and feelings of low self-esteem will occur if we attempt to apply the results of the traditional I.Q. scores to areas where they have no meaning. In this book, a wonderful thing is done. Specific subjects taught in the university such as history, statistics, language, art, biology, music, and education itself are dealt with from points of view that focus on the student's individual combination of skills and abilities, as well as from deep respect of the academic field.

As we suggested above, the phenomena of multiple intelligences does not vanish after elementary school, but remains as an integral part of the lifelong intellectual and personality profile of a person. Through a high level of personal commitment, each contributor to this book shows a high respect—not only for the different fields of study—but for the perspectives of the learner and of his of her human potential. This is being done more and more in pre-university education. There is a time for all things, and the time for the application of Multiple Intelligences Theory to post-secondary education is here.

For the above reasons, we welcome the efforts being made by the contributors to this anthology. In university classrooms and faculty lounges, methodology is not often spoken of. These writer/professors, however, have demonstrated here the courage, not only to talk about techniques that might work, but to discuss in detail the practices and principles they are following with their students today. This approximates a paradigm shift in higher education from the widespread preoccupation with the lectern and the lecture. We applaud their noble and productive efforts. They show us how we can make university education a broader and more fulfilling experience for all students. We also salute the attempt to cooperate in the transformation of college-level teaching methods being made by New Jersey City University in the USA. They are, by example, doing a much-needed and innovative service for higher education in all countries.

A VERY BRIEF INTRODUCTION TO MULTIPLE INTELLIGENCES

Gardner assumes that intelligence is multi-dimensional and that people have different cognitive potentials, which implies different cognitive styles. He has identified the existence of eight intelligences or capacities required for problem solving or for making products which area valued in a cultural context. These intelligences are Linguistic, Mathematical/Logical, Musical, Spatial, Bodily-Kinesthetic, Interpersonal, Intrapersonal, and Naturalistic. One aim of Multiple Intelligences Theory (MI) is to assess and identify the strengths of students in different learning areas. For that purpose, a set of instruments, measurements and procedures have been designed to evaluate abilities, knowledge and attitudes implicit in the learning process. The most important is related to observation. The best way to evaluate MI is to observe the child while he/she learns by manipulating materials. MI includes a set of tasks which, when per-

formed, allow the child to express his/her cognitive competence within specific curriculum areas such as math, writing, reading, and science.

Assessment is a dynamic process for obtaining information about individual potential, with the aim of achieving useful data about the cognitive profile of the pupils. The difference between this kind of assessment and the test is that in the former, we include all kinds of information derived from the teaching-learning process within the classroom context. The project offers teachers a portfolio assessment, whose objective is to design the cognitive profile of children.

MI AND THE CURRICULUM

MI has made a great contribution to education because it offers a large repertoire of techniques, strategies and tools for teaching the eight intelligences throughout the curriculum as well as at all school levels. The psycho-pedagogical roots of MI theory are in Maria Montessori, Decroly and Dewey, who defend the school centered on the individual. Montessori believed that children learn through the senses. She designed a set of materials to develop the children's awareness of their ability to make sense of their experience. In order to do this, Montessori designed didactic materials to prepare the children to acquire learning in such areas as writing, reading and math. She was also interested in the child's abilities and strategies for every-day life.

Decroly based his teaching methods on the active experience of the child, who learns through his/her own interests. For him, the globalization of education is important. This will take place through the "interest centers," which are complex thematic units where the diverse contents of subjects are grouped, with some relations between them. One "interest center" could include some notions of language, natural sciences, social sciences, and maths, all of which could be studied at different levels according to the interests and capacities of the child. Observation is the tool which, according to Decroly, is used to awake the child's interest in learning.

The influence of Decroly in Gardner's work is clear because he includes and uses Decroly's "interest centers" as a way of organizing the classroom, so that all the children explore the materials of the eight intelligences. Gardner uses Decroly's ideas and proposes "learning centers" as a way of creating learning spaces, organized around learning domains, where a set of materials in which each of the intelligences is manifest, are included. Dewey's concepts of learning by doing, instruction centered on the individual as well as cooperative learning, are present in the instructional principles of MI theory. Both Gardner and Dewey believed that the child has to interact with the learning materials and his/her peers, discovering and building through social interaction.

In short, in MI Theory Gardner includes the following New School principles: a) the classroom is a pedagogical laboratory where the child learns by doing; b) in the classroom, work is organized according to the children's interests and capabilities in such a way as to awake their creativity; c) the classroom activities are centered on the individual and his/her diversity; d) cooperative learning is encouraged; and e) the school prepares the child to be a future citizen.

MI THEORY AND TEACHERS

There are a large number of teaching and assessment strategies which go beyond traditional methods of instruction:
a) The identification of the strengths and weaknesses that the children show while learning.
b) The development of the identified strengths, so that they can be used to reduce weaknesses during the teaching-learning process.
c) The teaching of children to transfer the experiences involving their strengths to other curriculum contents where they could have weaknesses.

To achieve these aims, the teacher has a wide variety of materials and instructional strategies for each of the eight intelligences.

MI AND SPECIAL EDUCATION

In the MI school, there many interesting initiatives with respect to educational innovation. An important aspect that must be highlighted is the attention given to children with special needs in the ordinary classroom (both children with learning difficulties and gifted children). The findings of MI theory take into account the fact that everybody has strengths and weaknesses within the eight intelligences. For this reason, it offers a much wider and more natural context in which to understand the teaching learning process. In this sense, we all have weaknesses in some intelligence: the MI Theory works within the parameters of a growth paradigm versus a deficit paradigm. Some points of interest are: a) the establishment of new and more efficient collaborative teaching and learning models; b) the avoidance of labels; c) the use of materials, strategies, and activities for different intelligences; and d) the improvement of the instructional process to facilitate the development of personal and social interaction.

A PROJECT IN MURCIA

Some years ago, a field of research was begun in Murcia (in the South of Spain) whose aim was to validate MI Theory in the classroom. The aim of the Spectrum

Project is to develop an innovative approach to assessment and curriculum for the preschool and early primary years. The work was based on the conviction that each child exhibits a distinctive profile of different abilities, or spectrum of intelligences. The following procedure was used: first, the Spectrum Project's materials was translated and adapted for Preschool and Primary children; secondly, the cognitive competence of 237 children was evaluated using eleven activities from the Spectrum Project; thirdly, an IQ test to measure cognitive profiles was used; finally the data was analyzed using the statistic procedure employed by Krechevsky and Gardner (1990).

Throughout this study, we have highlighted the innovations of the MI model, pointing out the richness of the data and information when it comes to evaluating competence in the students. Although this evaluation supposes an alternative to psychometrics, in our empirical study we have used it complementarily to contrast the two types of information: quantitative and qualitative. The MI evaluation model permits us to design the classroom profile, detecting the strong points and gaps in basic abilities which make up each of the intelligences.

The procedure suggested by MI to assess students' ability, knowledge, attitude, and work habits can be adjusted quite well to the teaching-learning process that occurs inside the classroom. It is a very useful procedure, especially for assessing exceptional students. What distinguishes this type of evaluation with respect to psychometrics is that techniques are used to extract information about the use that students make of their abilities and knowledge during the teaching-learning process. Based on our experience, we would like to highlight some of the repercussions of MI Theory.

ON OUR SCHOOLS:
- It allows the creation of efficient schools centred on the development of thinking.
- It focuses inclusive classroom where all kind of intelligences and ways of learning have a place.

ON OUR STUDENTS:
- It instills in them the necessity and curiosity to discover.
- It teaches them to think by exploring different alternatives, using all the information processing channels.

ON OUR TEACHERS:
- It trains them in methodology focused on exploiting the hidden potential of the students, especially those who need tutorial learning.
- It offers them strategies and resources for teaching the children a wide spectrum of learning areas.

ON OUR CURRICULUM:

- MI theory allows us to design strategies for the transfer of knowledge and skills beyond the classroom.
- MI theory enriches the curriculum and favours the multimodal teaching, through which any content can be learnt through all the processing information channels.

ON OUR PARENTS:

- They are involved in MI teaching, because they can help their children and the teachers to develop different skills.
- It teaches them to observe how the different intelligences are shown in an everyday context.

This book offers a wide range of experiences and reflections on MI Theory that are taking place in the USA. Throughout the chapters, diverse strategies are presented to apply the theory to the classroom and the curriculum. The derivation of the model for the study or reading biology, statistic, music, inter- and intra-skills development, and creativity are also discussed. The authors try to adapt MI theory to individual cases throughout teaching-learning process. In each chapter the authors present constructivism philosophy from which this model emanates.

REFERENCES

Decroly, O. (1929). *La function de globalization et son application a l'enseignment*. Paris: Lamertin.

Dewey, J. (1906). *The School and the Child*. London: J. J. Findlay.

Krechevsky, M. and Gardner, H. (1990). "The Emergence and Nurturance of Multiple Intelligences: The Project Spectrum Approach" in *Encouraging the Development of Exceptional Skills and Talents*. (221-244) M.J.A., Howe (comp.). Leicester: The British Psychological Society.

Montessori, M. (1964). *The Montessori Method*. London: Schocken Books.

Recently, I was reading over notes I had taken several years ago in the heat of some insight or other. When I wrote them, I was not thinking at all of Howard Gardner and his Multiple Intelligences, and only vaguely of innovative teaching in higher education. However, as usual, serendipity seems to have been at work. Several of the questions I jotted down were, in effect, taken up by the gentleman from Harvard in his visit to New Jersey City University (NJCU). My first question had been in relation to the Equal Opportunity Fund Program (EOF), which is available to students who are financially disadvantaged and who, because they are academically under-prepared, cannot meet our regular admission standards. In other words, students whose future in academia is grim.

Yet about 15% more EOF students graduate than regular admits. So that, without fanfare, we are able to educate and award Bachelor degrees to these students, and by doing so enrich their personal lives, make them more productive members of their community, and perhaps, by some unspecified social dynamic, enhance the lives of their closest associates. Any one of these EOF graduates constitutes one of the near-miracles that go almost unnoticed in an urban institution of higher learning.

How did we manage to do this? First, let's consider what EOF does. It provides financial aid, an on-going skills workshop, specially trained advisors, and, before classes begin, an intense six-week-long academic boot camp. The students live in a dormitory, get up at 7:00 a.m. sharp, and follow a tight schedule of study, classes, meals, relaxation, and lights out. As might be expected, a strong sense of community develops. This is undoubtedly very important to the program.

ENTER SERENDIPITY

The crucial element, however, seems to be a tight focus on pedagogical innovation. The EOF instructors continuously try new methods of teaching, assess the impact of these innovations, and are flexible enough to change the methodologies accordingly. When I studied these areas of innovation more closely, it seemed as if each made a close fit with one or another of Gardner's eight Multiple Intelligences. This insight was validated by the 5th annual Urban Mission Conference, which had as its theme, "Innovative Methods of Teaching in Higher Education."

The purpose of the Conference was to expose the members of the academy to new metaphors of teaching and to begin a dialogue on the pedagogy of higher education. The Conference took place on October 26, 2001 and featured Dr. Howard Gardner as the keynote speaker, followed by thirty-five individual presentations. Dr. Gardner's remarks and twenty-nine of the papers are published in this anthology.

Gardner argued for two educational paradigms that have just begun to enter the discussion of post-secondary teaching; constructivism and multiple intelligences. Briefly,

INTRODUCTION

ANSLEY LaMar

constructivism refers to the notion that, regardless of what is taught, ultimately, a student's understanding of the subject matter is strongly influenced by his prior knowledge and experiences. The Multiple Intelligences Theory is Gardner's idea that traditional IQ tests measure only a part of a student's capabilities and say little or nothing about his or her abilities in art, music, personal relations and the other aptitudes that make us human. Taking these "non-academic" aptitudes into account enriches the learning environment and assists the student in developing an understanding of the subject matter.

These two paradigms provide a broad intellectual framework for many of the papers that follow. Others referenced Freirean pedagogy, feminist pedagogy and multiculturalism. Few papers sought to use the reflexive practitioner's model, a pedagogical orientation that encourages faculty to discover and critically examine the assumptions they bring to the classroom as a starting point. Experiential education—the belief that learning takes place when students are encouraged to reflect on and process relevant experience—while never overtly identified, did serve as a guiding paradigm for many of the pieces.

Of great importance to each innovative method treated in this book are (1) viewing the student as an active learner; (2) viewing the professor as a facilitator who orchestrates the construction of an understanding; (3) creating a psychologically safe classroom that encourages students to express their ideas fully; and (4) believing that through active exploration of the subject matter and informed discourse, the students' understanding will become broader, deeper, and increasingly sophisticated.

A CONCERN AND A CAVEAT

I enjoyed reading and being inspired by each of the papers, but I kept wondering to what extent the innovations were more effective than conventional methods of instruction. Perhaps I am being unduly influenced by my background as an administrator or my training as a social psychologist, but outcomes must continue to be measured and the efficacy of the approaches must continue to be evaluated. However, recent research in neuropsychology and cognitive psychology provide a good deal of empirical support, and there is ample anecdotal evidence for these innovations.

A viable pedagogy of innovative instruction in higher education must have as its foundation a research program that asks three questions: given the cost of the innovation (1) do students learn more, (2) do they retain more of what they learned, and (3) are they better able to use the knowledge acquired in one context to more effectively solve problems that emerge in another context? (I think that this ability is precisely what Gardner was referring to at the University when he said that students must be encouraged to "perform their understanding.")

And finally this research program must be designed to identify those elements of the instructional environment that result in the student having a broader, deeper and more sophisticated understanding of the subject matter. Perhaps we will learn that certain techniques work better with certain students or subject matter, or that it is simply the amount of time spent on task, or that it is the teacher and not the technique.

Someone once said that ideas we read about strike us as being twice as valid if we have—however fleetingly—entertained them before. I like to think that that's why Howard Gardner and his Multiple Intelligences seem so well grounded to us. It is quite possible that we have engaged some of them before, but certainly not in the concentrated yet clear manner you will find them presented in the essays that follow. I think it is important that you read Gardner's piece first, although you might have encountered him before. The things he says about teaching for understanding and about Multiple Intelligences are echoed and reinforced in the writings that follow—writings by teachers from very different areas of higher education.

THE STANDARD OF INNOVATION

I hope that you feel an irresistible urge to make your own notes as you go through those pages. Suggest to yourself ways in which thc ideas presented might be applied to different fields and classrooms. At some point in the past, the lecture was "standard fare" in college. Some professors and students are still quite comfortable with this protocol, which can be excellent. It seems, however, that the singular message of Gardner and of this book is that "the times, they are a-changing." There is no longer a "standard fare" in the classroom. The new standard of innovation knows no limits,

but rather always leads to another door that can be opened by the professor, the students, or by whatever it is that is on the other side.

I think that the most distinctive value of this book is that it brings to all of us the spirit, enthusiasm and knowledge that Gardner took to his plenary and that the presenters gave to each of their audiences. As a rule, conferences are intellectually stimulating and bring us into contact with persons we will never forget. The Conference at our University last year certainly did that—and more. Teaching methodology in higher education had been addressed before, but very possibly never with the focus, depth, vigor and expertise we were fortunate to welcome. One of the contributors to this volume called it a "national leadership conference." I doubt that any of us who helped organize it would have been so bold. But New Jersey City University will gladly consider this a challenge made and accepted. Whenever possible, we will cooperate to further the cause of innovation in the methodology of teaching in higher education. We invite you to join us in flying this banner and in the worthwhile pursuit it represents.

I was asked a couple of years ago what I thought was the greatest invention of the last 2,000 years. It's a good question. You might take 10 seconds to think about what you would have said. Anyway, the answer I gave was admittedly a strange one. I said that I thought that classical music was the greatest invention of the last 2,000 years. Now, I happen to love classical music. I love the music of Mozart—I hope that you do as well—but I have to admit that one of the reasons I gave that answer was that I wanted to be quoted. I mean, if I'd said, the battery or contraceptives or Windows or whatever came out yesterday, I would have said what other people said. Nobody else said classical music.

But I think there's a better answer. The one that I would give as a scholar, as an academic, is: The Disciplines, The Academic Disciplines. Disciplines like science and history and mathematics and the various art forms. The problem is that those of us who are in the academy—those of us who teach—take the disciplines for granted. They are part of what we breathe every day, and we forget that, in fact, the disciplines were invented over the last few thousand years. Many of them began in classical times. Some of them like mathematics started in the Arab world a thousand years ago; science, in Western Europe after the Renaissance.

But they are human inventions, and we could have very well have gone till today as human beings without having those disciplines. Yet they have become our mental furniture. We can't really think without the disciplines. We can't think about the past without thinking historically or biologically. We can't think about the physical world without thinking in terms of forces and matter and, if we are more current, relativity or quantum mechanics.

It seems to me that the disciplines are human beings' ways of understanding the world—the physical world, the biological world, the world of human beings, the world of artifacts including artistic artifacts. Now, this isn't to say that we couldn't think about these things without the disciplines, but we would think about them in very primitive, simplistic and naive ways. If you can develop a system that transmits breathtaking views of the rings around Jupiter, you have indeed ascended new heights successfully on your bootstraps. It's that way with all of the disciplines: they are hard-earned victories against intuitive forms of knowledge.

THE ARGUMENT FOR THE DAY

I'm going to argue today that the major purpose of liberal education and certainly education through secondary if not post-graduate life, is to understand the disciplines which help us to answer fundamental questions such as these: What's the world made of? What does it mean to be a human being? What is beautiful? and What is true?

If you think about it, education has other purposes like keeping kids off the street. But we could do that a lot more cheaply than sending them to school for 12 or 16

Note: This publication is based on a transcription of an informal oral presentation. It has been edited only in the interests of clarity.

HOW TO TEACH FOR UNDERSTANDING: CHALLENGES AND OPPORTUNITIES

DR. HOWARD GARDNER

years, and we could probably teach them to get along relatively well with one another less expensively (and more successfully) than we do now. So when it comes down to it, I guess I would say the literacy that we need to understand the disciplines is certainly necessary, but the disciplines themselves are, to my way of thinking, the major educational goal.

A PERFORMANCE OF UNDERSTANDING

When I talk about understanding, which is in the title of my talk and also a theme of this conference, I have something specific in mind. Understanding is very different from parroting back. If you've got a book and you've read it, or you've got a teacher who lectures and you can repeat what you've read or heard, you might understand, but you might just have a good memory. If, however, you can take something that you've learned and you can apply it appropriately to something new, something that you haven't encountered before, then you are executing what I call *a performance of understanding*. You are showing that you can make use of what it is that you allegedly learned.

Alfred North Whitehead, the great philosopher, talked about "inert knowledge"—and it's a very good term. A lot of us have inert knowledge, but unless we can activate the inert knowledge and use it, about the only thing it might be good for is doing well in one of those television quiz shows where they say, "What is the capital of X ?" or What is the atomic weight of Y?" But if you don't understand what a capital is or how atomic weights are computed and why

1

they matter, then the knowledge is inert: that is, you can't use it. Indeed, a good kind of litmus test for understanding is to go over the day's newspaper with students or *Time* magazine or your favorite television news hour, and see whether the *students* can explicate or whether *you* can explain what's going on.

We read about Anthrax, which most of us have probably not thought about ever in our life before. Then the question is: to what extent does what we learned about biology help us understand the risks and what we can do about them? You know, we read about terrorism and we ask to what extent are there examples from other realms of life or from other historical eras that can help us understand this? And again, if you can mobilize what you've learned before, that's the sense that it's not all been in vain. But if you never think to apply what you learned about Northern Ireland or about Basques or about the founding of the State of Israel to what's going on nowadays in the Middle East and in this country, then essentially that knowledge was wasted. It's not doing you any good.

A Non-Postmodern Claim

In a book called *The Disciplined Mind* which came out a couple of years ago, I made a distinctly, non-postmodern claim. I claimed that the understandings that we would like people to have are understandings of what's *true* or *not true*. We get the basis for making this judgment from science, math, history as well as folk knowledge, what's *beautiful* and *ugly*, or what's kitsch. (If you don't know what kitsch is, next time you're in a hotel look at the decorations in your room and you'll probably get a good exemplar of kitsch.) And you know, understanding is in the arts but it's also in beauty—and in nature. You know, there *is* beauty in nature.

Most important, I would say, are *good* and *evil*: not just understanding the difference, but in being able to act in a good and not an evil way. I said non-postmodern because, as many of you will know, part of postmodernism is to attack these notions of truth, beauty and goodness as having any coherence at all. Indeed, just last week, Stanley Fish, a very well known and well respected literary critic, wrote an article in *The New York Times*. He basically claimed that postmodernism had not been refuted by terrorism, that there was still no way of talking about good and evil or truth and lying which could encompass our world and the world of—I would use a most non-postmodern phrase— the world of ourselves and our enemies.

I was moved to write a letter to the *Times* and, as is not usually the case, they printed it. I called Fish's argument either incoherent, inconsistent or self-refuting. If I wanted to take Fish's position, I would say, "Look, we're never going

to have an uncontested notion of truth, beauty and goodness." But if I would want to take the Gardner position, which is what I believe in, I would say that even though we never reach them, these ideals are something we have to aim for. Indeed, I was going to sign my letter to the *Times* "Howard Gardner, formerly of the Flat Earth Society." (But because I didn't want to sound impertinent, I didn't.) But you know, the more you think like a scientist, the more the notion that there are no truths seems bizarre.

Truth, Beauty and Morality

This is all pretty theoretical. In *The Disciplined Mind*, I take three examples deliberately chosen because they are parts of curricula everywhere. In the area of truth, I look at a science example, the theory of evolution, not because it's been proved true in every regard—that's not the way science works—but rather because it's the only non-faith based explanation we have of where human beings come from.

As a beauty dimension, I chose the work of Mozart; and as an example of morality and immorality, I chose the Holocaust. Without question, those are big topics. And so I didn't just focus on evolution, I focused on what I call *Darwin's finches*. Darwin's finches constitute a very interesting puzzle. If you go to the Galapagos Islands where Darwin went, on each island there is a different species of finch. It was thinking about this question that got Darwin to think about the survival of the fittest among species that are fighting to survive in a particular ecological niche. So I focused on Darwin's finches. Maybe only one out of ten kids could get interested in *evolution* if you just used that word. But it's different if you actually go to the Galapagos or you look at films of it and you ask the question: "Why do all the finches have big beaks on this island and smaller beaks on that island?" Most kids can get into that.

The Holocaust

The Holocaust, of course, is also a vast topic. So I take a historical incident, what is called the Wanssee Conference, which took place in January of 1942. That is the conference at which Hitler's henchmen actually began to implement the Final Solution. There are two interesting things about that conference: One is there is no record, which says that this is where the Final Solution was first implemented. Yet historians all agree that it was. The trains to Auschwitz began the next day, and within a year, a million and a half people were killed. So it's pretty high circumstantial evidence.

It's also interesting—and this gets to the morality issue—that there were 14 persons, all men, at the Wanssee Conference in Berlin. Eight of them had doctorates from Central European universities so having a high degree is no guarantee that you're going to be behaving the way that most of us think is defensible.

The examples I used are ones that I felt competent to write about. I'm not at all saying everybody should study evolution, Mozart and the Holocaust, but everybody should study topics that are rich and through *whose study*—a very important phrase—through whose study one can begin to acquire disciplined habits of mind. If you really understand evolution, you learn to think like a scientist. If you really understand the music of Mozart, you can think artistically. If you really understand the Holocaust, you begin to think historically. And only if you can think historically, artistically, mathematically, scientifically and so on, are you thinking in a disciplined way.

AN INSIGHT CONCERNING FACTS

An insight I had some years ago is that facts have no disciplinary status at all. A fact is just a proposition. It's only when you can put facts together into some kind of a tapestry of explanation, of causality, of sense making, that the facts acquire any kind of meaning.

That is what is deeply wrong, not only with those television shows but with a lot of the standardized testing that goes on. Such a practice is very fact oriented, but it never looks at whether you can put the stuff together and make some kind of sense.

UNDERSTANDING AS A PERFORMANCE

I could have chosen examples from physics like relativity. I could have chosen examples from the visual arts, Chinese ink and brush painting. I could have chosen an example of somebody from the positive end of morality, somebody whom I very much admire, Mahatma Gandhi. In short, the examples could be changed, but the concept of the understanding as a performance stands. Intellectual understanding can be thought of as a performance by a brilliant actor or actress. When he or she is given a script to interpret and contextualize, then and only then does the performer perform in a charismatic genius. Only then does the dancer become spellbindingly inextricable from the dance.

This was a big insight that a number of us had at Project Zero about a dozen years ago. We tend to think of understanding as a little thing that goes on between the ears and, of course, I do recommend that you keep whatever you have between your ears. It is needed to keep your skull in place. But unless you can perform your understanding, unless you can actually take the knowledge and use it publicly, neither you nor other people will have a sense of whether you understand or not. Indeed, we all know this because we've all gone to lectures—in my case, it was almost always in mathematics—where we understood it

perfectly when we were in the room—or so we thought. But as soon as we walked out and somebody asked us about the central point, we realized that our understanding was extremely tenuous. Only then did it dawn on us that we had allowed our understanding to be lulled into a mild hypnosis. Instead of performing, our heads had been metaphorically nodding.

People often say to me, "Howard, has your teaching at Harvard been changed by multiple intelligences theory?" The answer is not as much as I would have hoped—I'll talk about that later. But my notions about understanding have really been radically changed. Now in all of my classes we're doing performances all of the time, and that's the way in which we can see whether or not understanding has taken place.

CURRENT STATUS OF UNDERSTANDING

There are two other closely related points I would like to take up. Of course understanding begins from day one of life, way before anybody ever meets a discipline. But if we want to assess understanding, we have to look at *disciplinary* understanding. Do students understand the physical world, the social world, the human world, the artistic world and so on? The bad news is that understanding is very difficult to achieve as well as to assess. Why is it so difficult to achieve? Why is it so difficult to (1) develop these ways of thinking from the disciplines, and then (2) apply them appropriately in new situations? That's the real enigma.

Here are some answers to why it's hard to educate for understanding. These are sociological answers: these are things we could change about our society. We wouldn't have to use short answer assessments, although I imagine many people here do. They would probably say, "What choice do I have? I have so many students?" We could talk about that. Many people use the text, and then give a test on the text. Again, I understand why we do that, but as I said earlier, you can get a very high performance as long as you have a good memory. *Unless you're asked to take what's in the text and apply it to something new, we don't know whether you're understanding it or not.*

The correct-answer compromise—I commit it every day but I'm not proud of it—the correct answer compromise is the following: "Students, if you don't push me too hard, I won't push you too hard." We get through the day, but understanding suffers because understanding is never total. Indeed, Socrates correctly pointed out that he was ahead of other people because he *knew* all the stuff he didn't understand, whereas most of us walk around with the illusion that we understand lots of things. But if we really push ourselves, we understand that our understanding is tenuous, but that it can be improved. It's rather like truth:

we'll never get to the ultimate truth, but why shouldn't we try? We'll never get to ultimate understanding, but why shouldn't we use our precious time on earth to understand as much as we can?

TEACH A LIMITED NUMBER OF THINGS IN DEPTH

The worst problem that most of us face is the pressures for coverage. The amount of information in the world increases enormously. It increases the amount of understanding that is required. So we're in an impossible position. We're aware of all this accumulated stuff, and so we feel guilty if we don't try to disperse it.

And yet, I believe—and here is where I am at odds with almost every policy maker in this country—that if you try to cover a lot of stuff, you will not have understanding. I also think that the best way to get understanding is to cover a limited number of things in depth. But that is not a popular point of view. You will not get elected to office if you take that point of view.

Cognitive freudianism was named after Piaget, the cognitivist, and Freud, the Freudian—though there are other freudians like Anna Freud. Cognitive freudianism is a term that I coined some years ago and it is, I think, the nonsociologic reason why understanding is difficult. It is the deep biological, psychological, epistemological reason, to wit: When we're young, we develop very powerful theories about the world, theories of how the physical world works, like the bigger thing falls more quickly to the ground than a smaller thing, or the world is flat because it looks flat or theories about the biological world. "If it's moving it's alive; if it's not moving, it's dead. If it's on a monitor or other screen, who can tell? It might be alive, it might be dead."

These are very common sense notions that kids develop when they're very young, and that nobody has to teach. They just pick the notion up themselves. But while some of these notions are true and many of them are charming, most of them fall flat in the face of the discipline. They just are not backed up by disciplinary insights. *And yet, for evolutionary reasons which we could talk about, these early ideas which I call early conceptions or early engravings, are very difficult to change.* They are very entrenched. It is as if during the first five to ten years of life we had a very powerful engraving in our mind/brain—not because of teaching but just because of living in the world. When we go to school, school is like powder. The powder gets poured in those engravings and it accumulates because people say, "Oh great, look at all the powder. Our kids know so much."

A DISCIPLINED ENGRAVING

The problem is that powder is basically non-disciplinary factual information. One day kids leave school, and depending on how good the memory is, the powder evaporates quickly or not so quickly, and then what is left? That same initial engraving. The nondisciplined theory has never changed. What is needed to happen—and later I'll tell you how I think it happens—is that we've got to rub away that early engraving. We have to smooth it, and then we have to construct a new engraving, a disciplined engraving, which is a more sophisticated way of thinking. We have to construct a disciplined way of thinking.

EIGHT-YEAR-OLD CREATIONISTS

An interesting finding from a psychologist at the University of Toledo named Margaret Evans. If you talk to eight-year-olds all over this country—and I would assume all over the world—you would find that they are all creationists. Every eight-year-old, whether the child grows up in a fundamentalist home or a free thinking home, the home of a Darwinian scholar or the home of somebody who's never studied biology—all eight-year-olds are creationists. Basically, all eight-year-olds believe the world was created at a certain moment, and all the creatures were created at that moment and things have never changed. This is not because of reading the Bible: it is because at the age of eight, kids realize that kids have origins and a default assumption is everything started at the same time.

That is why Darwin's ideas are so deeply difficult to understand: Darwin teaches us that human beings didn't always exist, that monkeys didn't always exist, that fish didn't always exist. It goes back to before the amoeba. So it takes a long time to really understand those ideas. Even if you want ultimately to disagree with him, it takes a long time to understand them because—this is another evolutionary argument—*our mind didn't evolve to think in a disciplined way, it evolved basically to avoid getting eaten before you have a chance to reproduce.* I mean that's the long and the short of it.

THE FLAT PART UNDERNEATH

So it's hard work to undo those things. I have an example some of you will have heard me use. When my son Benjamin was five, I asked him what the shape of the world was. He said, "That's easy, Dad, it's round." I said, "Benjamin, that's very good." And I said to myself, "Does he have a misconception?" So I said, "Benjamin, that's great but tell me, where are you standing?" He said, "That's easy. I'm standing on the flat part underneath." Kids can learn to tell us what they think we want to hear, but it's really making them understand that even though Cambridge looks reasonably flat, that if you go far enough away and you walk long enough you'll discover that, in fact, the earth is spherical.

Understanding Algorithms

So in a book called *The Unschooled Mind*, I went through the various areas of the curriculum: science, mathematics, social studies, arts, humanities. I showed that in each area, young children developed these powerful misconceptions or stereotypes or what I called "rigidly applied algorithms." The latter term is from mathematics. It refers to a principle in which you memorize the formula, and if somebody tells you to plug numbers into the formula, you know what to do. So it looks like you can understand the mathematics.

However, the algorithm is rigidly applied. Consider these two situations. You are walking down the street, and you recognize a situation where a trigonometric equation would be relevant. Similarly, you are trying to figure out a financial statement and you see something where a quadratic equation would be relevant. There's nothing really wrong with these pictures, other than that they are rather thin. It's much more difficult to decide whether to use a trigonometric formula or a geometric formula or a calculus derivative procedure if you're asked to use it where you weren't trained to. Why? Because then you really have to understand what it was meant to do. Indeed, mathematicians I've discovered are not people with particularly good memories. They are people who, when they forget the formulas, can derive it because they've understood it. I think most of us know what it's like *not* to be in that position. If you forget the formula, you are in deep trouble.

So I hope I've convinced you that the disciplinary knowledge is not there simply for the asking. I'm a cognitive scientist, a cognitive psychologist, and I think by far the most important demonstration from cognitive psychology for education is the pervasiveness of these early theories. No matter what area you look in—physical science, social science, arts, mathematics, humanities—you find these very powerful misconceptions or scripts.

Critical Decisions

I'll now say something which will be sensitive. In the United States we have a tendency to think with a five-year-old mind about foreign policy, and every five years we have a new bad guy. Now we've got a real bad guy called bin Laden, but the notion that if we got rid of bin Laden, somehow our problems would be solved is very naive. Indeed, if we got rid of him and it came out that we did, we would create many more bin Ladens

But the point is not bin Laden. There's also Sadaam Hussein, Fidel Castro, Muramar Kadaffi, Manuel Noriega— It's kind of like *Newsweek,* "Where are they now?" Some of them are now our allies, right? Because Hussein and Kadaffi might be able to help us with bin Laden. Again, it's not to say bin Laden's a good guy. Remember, I'm not a postmodernist: I know evil when I see it. But it's simplistic to think that one person is solely responsible for an organization with thousands of people in it and millions of people supporting it. It doesn't work that way. There have to be very complex supporting forces which essentially have to be convinced, not neutralized, if the current terrorist threat is going to end.

Recommendation

So if you want to have disciplinary understanding, here are the things that I recommend. First, you have to decide what's really important in the discipline—which ideas and which ways of thinking are central. Second, you have to make a commitment to spend time on this material and to cover it. Third, if you make those two commitments, *then* you can make use of the fact that we have different ways of representing the world, different kinds of intelligence.

If you only had an hour to teach your subject, what would you teach? Now, that's kind of intimidating because most of us don't feel we have enough hours even if we meet our class several times a week. On the other hand, if three years after taking your course your student still remembers an hour's worth of stuff, you should jump in the air and click your heels, right? That's a terrific thing.

But if you can decide what are the things that are most important, and you could teach them in an hour, and then you spend a whole term going into them—if you could do that, you will really have understanding. But if you try to get, as the old saying goes, from Plato to NATO in 36 weeks, you'll have a lot of inert knowledge there but very little that can be mobilized.

Multiple Intelligences

So we come to Multiple Intelligences. What is an intelligence? An intelligence is a word that I pluralized some years ago. It's a potential in mind/brain to process certain kinds of information in the world. I think of the mind/brain as a bunch of computers—that is the metaphor I use—and these computers either solve problems or make things. The contrasting notion of general intelligence is that there's only one computer, and it's either strong or weak. The idea of multiple intelligence is that we have a bunch of computers in our mind/brain. We've all got them, but some computers are going to be stronger than others at any historical moment, and some computers are going to be easier to change and strengthen than others. So it's a very different way of thinking about intelligence. In research conducted twenty years ago, I came up with a list of intelligences.

A LIST OF INTELLIGENCES
> **Linguistic**
> **Mathematical/Logical**
> **Musical**
> **Spatial**
> **Bodily-Kinesthetic**
> **Interpersonal**
> **Intrapersonal**
> **Naturalistic**

In each case, the most efficient way to communicate what an intelligence is, is to talk about an individual or a role that exemplifies a lot of that intelligence. So linguistic intelligence is the intelligence of a poet. This is a famous Chinese poet named Li Po. Poets think in words. That is their medium: that is, their chosen form of mental representation. The second form of intelligence is mathematical/logical. It is the intelligence of the scientist, the logician, the mathematician, the computer programmer. I don't have to tell you that in schools throughout the world and especially in Western schools, linguistic and logical intelligence are at a premium. That's not controversial. Kids who are very good in language and logic do well in school, and as long as they stay in school, they think they're smart. If they were ever to venture onto the Jersey Turnpike, then they would discover that those intelligences won't help them very much.

Language logic is really the mind of a law professor. It's the mind of Bill and Hillary Clinton, who are very smart in a scholastic way. What do we do with students whose strengths are not in language/logic? [Not every student is going to have that law professor mind.] We can give up and tell them that they're dumb. Or we can say we're going to make you into language/logic people, which may work in some cases. Or we can say we're going to try to use the intelligences which are stronger as a way of helping you to attain valued educational virtues.

Musical intelligence is, of course, the ability to think musically, to represent the world in music. Spatial intelligence, the ability to imagine large spaces like a pilot or more circumscribed spaces like an architect or a sculpture or a chess player. Bodily kinesthetic intelligence is the intelligence of a dancer, the athlete, the surgeon, the crafts person, the actor, anybody who uses the whole body or parts of the body to make things or to solve problems.

INTELLIGENCES RELATED TO OTHER PEOPLE

Two forms of intelligence are related to other people: *Interpersonal Intelligence* and *Intrapersonal intelligence*. Interpersonal Intelligence is understanding other people; it is the intelligence of the teacher, the sales person, the religious leader, the politician. Intrapersonal Intelligence, on the other hand, is the ability to understand yourself. The latter, Intrapersonal Intelligence, is tremendously important in a world where we have to make decisions about where to live, whom to live with, what work to pursue, what to do if we want to change careers, homes, or spouses.

An intelligence which I only began to write about recently is "Naturalist Intelligence." It is the intelligence that someone like Charles Darwin had being able to make fine discriminations in the world of nature. Most of us are not farmers or fisherman or hunters any more, but we use our naturalist intelligence to tell one sneaker from the another, one automobile from another. We make the same kind of distinctions and discriminations that were so useful to survival in pre-historic times.

So the claim is that all of us have these intelligences. That is what makes us human. That is extremely important for teachers to know because it means you can count on every one of your students to have linguistic intelligence, logical intelligence, musical intelligence and all the rest. The complementary point is that no two people, not even identical twins, have exactly the same combination and strengths of intelligences. We look different from one another, we have different personalities and temperaments, and we now have scientific evidence that even identical twins, because their experiences are different, have different profiles of intelligences.

If you teach only one way, you're only going to reach one kind of student. Most of us teach the language/logic way because that's what worked for us: we're good for those particular young men and women. But for students who have other strengths, school is very, very difficult. Moreover, once they pick up the notion they can't learn because they can't learn the language-logic way, then you have an additional obstacle to deal with, which is a loss of self-efficacy. *So here are the two big cognitive ideas of today. First, we have many intelligences, many ways of representing and understanding the world . Second, our initial understandings are very powerful, often wrong, and difficult to change.*

ENTERING THE TOPIC

I want to return now to the three examples from the beginning. I'm going to give you the basic argument of the talk. If you want students to understand and if you're willing to spend time on topics, you can take advantage of MI, of multiple intelligences. You can do this in three ways. The first way is how you approach the topic, how you enter the topic. For example, getting at evolution through Darwin's finches. That's an entry point.

ANALOGIES AND METAPHORS

Number two involves the analogies, metaphors and comparisons you use. Everything that we don't understand can only be understood initially with reference to something we understand better. We're always making comparisons or drawing analogies or using metaphors. Once you open up the treasure box of multiple intelligences, you can draw the analogies and metaphors and comparisons from many different domains.

Evolution is about species, but you can also talk about the evolution of fashion or the evolution of a theme in a work of art. In some ways, that metaphor will be very powerful; in other ways, not. With the metaphor or analogy, you have to always show where it works and where it doesn't. But anything new has to be approached through metaphors. So if you never heard about multiple intelligences before, I might use the metaphor of different personality types because most people know about different personality types. Again, it's not a perfect metaphor but it's a way of opening the conversation.

DIFFERENT REPRESENTATIONS

The third way to take advantage of multiple intelligences is really important, but you've got to read *The Disciplined Mind* because I can't do it in five minutes. *Any set of ideas, any set of concepts that are important can be thought about in a number of different languages, in a number of different ways of representing.* Let us take something like evolution: you can think about it linguistically, you can think about it logically, you can think about it dramatically, you can think about it cinematically. There are many ways of thinking about evolution and a person who understands a topic well can think about it in lots of ways, can capture it in many forms of intelligence. Anything you know well—yourself, your family, your home, your job, your discipline—you can think about in more than one way.

The point is that our multiple intelligences can be great allies in broaching and enhancing understanding if we're willing to spend time on things. Let's say you're studying one of these three topics that I mentioned: the Holocaust, evolution, or Mozart. Or choose your own. You want to enter that point in a way that reaches students. Here are six or seven ways in which you can do it.

SIX WAYS TO REACH STUDENTS:

1. THROUGH STORIES

Many students like stories. That's a linguistic entry point. The story of Mozart, of his collaboration with da Ponte, of the Beaumarchais play, *The Marriage of Figaro,* which becomes the opera, etc. Or we can use the story of Darwin, Darwin's voyage on the Beagle, the story of Hitler or Anne Frank or the rise of the Nazis. There are many stories you can tell.

2. THROUGH NUMBERS

The second entry point is numbers. Many people love numbers, quantities, comparisons, proportions, how many finches, what kind, what populations, who died, who lived? Look at the score. What kind of notes? What rhythms? What ratios, etc.?

3. THROUGH LOGIC

All of the topics that I describe, and probably most of the topics that you would teach, have a logic to them. Some people—my wife is like this—need everything boiled down to logic. And boy, if you say something that's not logical, you get torpedoed, even if it's over breakfast in the morning. You say, "I read this interesting article." Well, you'd better have a logical reason for calling it "interesting."

4. THROUGH EXISTENTIALISM

Some people love big questions. My three topics are, in a sense, answers to three very big questions: (1) Where do we come from? Evolution is the only scientific answer. There are faith-based answers, but evolution is the only scientific answer. (2) What are some of the wonderful things human beings are capable of? Classical music is certainly one. (3) What are some of the terrible things human beings are capable of? Genocide is certainly one.

5. THROUGH AESTHETICS

The fifth point of entry into the student's mind is through aesthetics, works of art. Some people like to make and learn from works of art. Who would have thought the three major movies of the last decade would have been based on the Holocaust: *Schindler's List*, *Sophie's Choice*, and *Life Is Beautiful*. Very different approaches to understanding the Holocaust.

6. THROUGH EXPERIENCE

Hands on. Doing things yourself. Many people, especially young people, want to learn things in a very hands-on way. They don't want to listen to *The Marriage of Figaro*, they want to act it out. They don't want to read about evolution: they want to breed fruit flies and see how their traits change from one generation to the other. Even in the case of the Holocaust, there are children's museums about the Holocaust. When you go to the museum, you get a photograph of a child and then when you leave, you hear what happened to that child. That's a very powerful way of learning about the Holocaust.

Some people, people in this room, like to learn through groups, collaboration, role play, debate, interchange, dialogue, dramatization. *I am not saying everything should be taught in seven or eight ways, that would be silly. What I'm saying is that everything can and perhaps should be taught in more than one way.* If you teach more than one way, two important things happen. First of all, you reach more kids because kids don't all have this law professor mind. Second, you show what it's like to really understand something, to be an expert. Because an expert is a person who can think about something in more than one way. When you as a teacher—when I as a teacher explain something and the student says, "I don't understand it. Can you explain it another way? Can you show it to me? Can you draw it for me? Can you act it out?" If the answer is no, no, no, then my own understanding is tenuous. In fact, I'm preparing for class on Monday, and I know my understanding is very tenuous because I can only explain this stuff one way. And so between now and Monday, I'm going to try to think about other ways to explain it. That's the way in which multiple intelligences has affected my own teaching.

WHAT DISCIPLINARY UNDERSTANDING IS NOT— AND WHY NOT

I'm going to use here an example from precollegiate education, but I think it will be true for all of us. This is what understanding is not: it's not *cultural literacy.* This is an idea developed by E.D. Hirsch, a literary critic, the second literary critic of today's talk (Stanley Fish being the first). What Hirsch and his colleagues do, as the subtitle says, is list essential names, phrases, dates and concepts.

I've got nothing against cultural literacy. I love people who are culturally literate, but it's not the same as understanding. You could know five million names, dates, phrases and concepts and, as I said earlier, those facts, those propositions, will not bring you any closer to understanding. The problem is that not only Hirsch but most people, including most policy makers, basically have a view of the mind which I call the "empiricist barn." They think of the mind as a barn. Initially, the barn is empty, the famous *tabula rasa.* There is nothing there. Then the mind begins to fill with facts. They are not particularly related: they're just little "F's" floating around. And more facts enter and finally, your mind is crammed with facts. You've got those 5,000 or 5 million little nuggets and those supposedly constitute your cultural literacy. And you know, if you talk to a lot of policy makers, that's really what they will tell you. They think the person who's got the most facts at the end of the day, the person who has eaten the *Encyclopedia Britannica* and spat it out, is the one who is educated.

THE CONSTRUCTIVIST BARN

I am a proponent of a less popular but I think more persuasive barn, the "constructivist barn." The unschooled mind early in life develops very powerful theories. Even though kids are not taught those theories, they develop them on their own because, presumably, they are equipped to think about the world in that kind of way—the heavier thing falls faster than the lighter, the world is flat. If it's alive it moves, that sort of stuff. It's the common sense and common nonsense point of view.

Kids pick up facts. They are great fact picker-uppers. But my argument is that these early theories have to be razed, R-A-Z-E-D. Kids have to be shown why they don't work. You can't say, "Well, you know, here's a photograph of the earth: it's round. Don't say it's flat any more." You don't get rid of the misconceptions with one quick parry back and forth. Anybody who has a misconception has, over and over again, to see that it doesn't work. Such persons have to construct a new interpretation of the world, an interpretation that's more in keeping with the one that has resulted from careful experimentation and observation. It's only then that children slowly begin to lose their earlier misconception. Then you have a situation where the early theories have been impoverished, and you have a lot of free floating facts around, because again we're good fact collectors. We're like flypaper, facts stick easily. As you get older, they get harder to stick. I can give personal testimony on that.

GOING DEEPLY INTO TOPICS

But then here's what school is really all about: it's trying to build disciplinary structures. My strong argument today is that *the best way to build disciplinary structures and perhaps the only way (but certainly the best way) is to go deeply into topics, approach them in many ways, get a very rich representation of them.* We learn in the process how people who do that for a living—whether they are historians, scientists, artists, or mathematicians—how they think about things.

So when you discover something new, you can say well, "Here's how I went about thinking about something that I understood. How should I go about thinking about something that I don't understand so well?" That's what a discipline is. I'm basically a psychologist. The discipline we learn is to conduct experiments. So the habit of mine that I have as a psychologist is any time I read any science in the newspaper or hear about something, I right away say, "What was the control group? Were there placebo effects? What were the variables?" These are no-brainers for me as a psychologist, but it took me ten years to learn how to think that way. You know, the *National Enquirer* makes a sizable profit based on people who never ask those questions.

INTERDISCIPLINARY WORK

Anyway, disciplinary structures consolidate after a while with good teaching, and then <u>inter</u>disciplinary work becomes possible. I'm now studying interdisciplinary work. Let me simply say that I don't think you can do genuine interdisciplinary work unless you have mastered more than one discipline. If somebody said they were bilingual, you would be skeptical if they didn't have more than one language, right?

So the bottom line about barns and perhaps about brains is that you cannot get to discipline simply by having facts. *You have to construct the disciplines by deconstructing the inadequate ways of thinking and constructing more adequate ones.* As far as I know, it is only when you go deeply into things that you learn how to do that. A good litmus test is to ask people what they remember from high school. Probably, it will be those projects that took weeks or months. Not a lesson in which they had a test and went on to something else. That is because in a project, you really are busy constructing things. You aren't simply memorizing them.

Why all this talk about disciplines? Are they really the most important inventions? Well, that of course was a rhetorical claim, but consider the problems of the world. Globalization, is it good or bad? Stem cell research, pro and con. State of the environment, power of telecommunications, immigration, multiculturalism, racism, September 11th—alas—what you think about in the shower, argue about at the dinner table. These are real things; this is what life today and tomorrow is about.

OUT-OF-THE-BOX THINKING

You can either use common sense about this—good guy/bad guy, flat-earth kinds of views. Or you can try to use your disciplines. Newly at a premium in this century (and this is something which those of us in education have to worry about a lot more than people did fifty years ago) is out-of-the-box thinking, because all the in-the-box thinking is done by computers, almost by definition. So it's the out-of-the-box thinking we have to worry about. We must be able to be flexibile. We must be able to handle just-in-time responses. We must be able to go beyond the disciplines because so much work now is problem based, and you have to bring more one discipline to bear. We must be able to form teams that can do this kind of work.

Hollywood-style projects and productions mean that people don't work for a company forever. They don't work on a project forever. They work on one thing, and then they're hired to work on something else—the way we used to associate with movies. Then of course, there are forms of non-linear thinking, non-linear dynamics, chaos, complexity and so on. Teaching now is not the same as teaching fifty years ago. We've got a whole set of problems, September 11th simply being the most vivid. We have a whole set of needs which are much less true in a factory kind of society where people were trained for a slot, and they stayed in that

slot till they got their gold watch. So if you want to deal with these problems but you think disciplinary understanding is expensive, try ignorance of the disciplines. The poignant thing about the disciplines is that they are available to everybody including our enemies.

TESTS, TESTS AND MORE TESTS

So how do you find out if people have acquired the facts and skills the educators think are important? Give the students tests. If they don't do well, you know what you do? Give them more tests. It's like, if a patient is sick, taking the temperature repeatedly with the thought that *that* would make it better. It doesn't happen that way. A better view, I believe, is keeping in mind that the purpose of school is the acquisition of understanding. If you want to see if people are performing according to a certain understanding, you give them something new and see how they think about it, whether they can use those disciplinary muscles that they have developed.

FINAL THOUGHTS AND REFLECTIONS

Two haunting thoughts for somebody who has spent many years now thinking about the disciplines: One is that "the disciplines are what separate us from the barbarians." Barbarians only have one discipline—wiping you out. I don't want to get too political here, but the irony of what Al Qaeda is doing is, of course, using disciplines which it didn't develop: it's borrowing them, mastering their application, and using them against us. It is using the properties of our own society—its openness and its flexibility and its multi-ism. This is an easy way in. If the society was very closed, the kind of society they want, you couldn't get into them. One other thing you can do is burn the books: that the first thing that any tyrant does. And then substitute *Mein Kampf* or *The Statements of Chairman Mao* or whatever the current iteration is.

Then, a second thought: "What will our species be like in the future?" Evolution hasn't stopped, but for the first time in human history we can affect evolution. We can change our genes. Not only can it be done, it will be done. Some people find it exciting: I find it frightening. But once we begin intentionally to change our genes, then what life will be like, what our disciplines will be like, is anybody's guess. The preparation of teachers at that time will be a very different kind of enterprise.

QUESTIONS FROM THE FLOOR

Conference Participant: I teach the English language in all the arts, the dance, the drama. My question is this: I'm a constructivist at heart, and I want to know whether or not you think it's important to build upon the children's prior knowledge or impressions of any one of these disciplines?

Gardner: Well, I'm glad you asked the question about the misconceptions because some people think that you should ignore them or try to get rid of them, but that's not actually the best answer. The best answer is you have to recognize their existence because they are the way that the kids naturally think. Indeed, I think that the best thing is to bring them out on the table, let the kids actually play with them, explore them, ponder them and see where they don't work.

Every misconception has a reason for existing. I'm not a physicist, but if you think that heavier objects accelerate more rapidly than lighter ones, it is because of the air resistance. So it's the confounding of arguments that makes people have the misconception. On their own, almost no kids will come up with the right explanation. After all, it took until Galileo and Newton to figure out the basic laws of motion. But we need to reach the point where the kids see the inadequacies of the misconceptions. They are ready to try to think about another way, and that's where more directed pedagogy will come in. I think that it's important to find out about the misconceptions diagnostically, meaning you need to know what they are. But a lot of them will come out readily without the need for formal testing.

I'm very much a fan of assessment, but I make a distinction between assessment and testing. It's a semantic distinction but it's an important one. When I use the word "testing," I tend to focus on short answer instruments with right or wrong answers, which don't necessarily give you insight into how the child is thinking. When I talk about assessment, it's always giving the child something new and saying make sense of this. Because when the child has to make sense of it, the child shows you what he understands and what he doesn't understand.

A person takes a college board *test* and gets a score back. Such people are really no better off than they were before they took the test, but now they have a number. But you know, if you give them an *assessment* where they actually have to solve some problems and show their thinking or explain some situations, and you get the results back, there is a chance you might understand better where they're off base.

Conference Participant: Could you talk a bit more about how you would deconstruct some common sense idea?

Gardner: Right. If I can paraphrase your question, nowhere in our lives are unschooled ideas more powerful than in the education world. So it's up to us to find out what those ideas are and then correct them. The way we find out what they are is by testing. If the students don't do well, test again. I mean, I used to laugh at the Bush-Gore debates because, Bush would say, "I'd test them once a year"; Gore would say, "I'll test them twice a year." Bush would say, "I'll

test the principals." Gore would say, "I'll test the custodians." It's the unschooled mind at work.

One thing I've learned which I should have known from the start, is that you can never get rid of something by criticizing it. The only way you can only get rid of something is by creating something that's new and better. The reason that standardized testing exists is not because it's very good, but because people have been reluctant to use other forms of assessment.

THE COALITION OF ESSENTIAL SCHOOLS

Working alone, it's pretty tough, especially if you're in the public schools or in a public university. Working with other people, it becomes less difficult. The best example here is something called the *Coalition of Essential Schools*, which is a network of high schools. There are about 1,000 Essential Schools in the country, and they adopt many of the ideas that I'm sympathetic to. One of these ideas is that, "Less is more." It's better to go deeply into topics rather than try to skim a lot of stuff very superficially.

When you graduate from a coalition school, you don't take a bunch of tests. You have to make 14 exhibitions. These are evaluated not only by teachers but by outsiders. When these schools are well done—and there are not that many because it's hard—their graduates are very attractive to colleges. Many of you will know Debbie Meier, who for many years was the principal of Central Park East Schools in East Harlem and who now is a principal of the Mission Hill School in Boston.

Students from the Central Park East Secondary School in East Harlem did very well in getting into college and in graduating from four-year colleges, even though they weren't particularly standardized test types. That is because there was a curriculum there focused on understanding. The school was very committed to it, and Deborah Meier was a very tough customer who the city fought at its peril. She was a great believer that it's better to ask for forgiveness than permission.

So at the secondary level, if you want to fight the establishment, it's hard. You have to be courageous, and you have to be prepared to lose and then fight again. At the tertiary level, it is easier especially in private universities because nobody tells you what to do. But I think the heat is on, especially for public universities. There will be more accountability, and the issue is not the accountability which I am in favor of, it is—to put it in a kind of a sophomoric way—are the assessments going to be stupid ones or smart ones.

There are people who are working on creating smart assessments. You know, the University of Phoenix was mentioned before. There is probably a lot to be learned from the University of Phoenix. I personally wish it didn't have to exist, and in my book, *The Disciplined Mind*, I have a section that's rather critical of the University of Phoenix. But they are demons on assessments, and their assessments focus on the things which their students want and which their employers want. Of course, what they don't have is liberal arts. They don't have a library—things which to me are the center of the university. They are parasitic in a sense on the rest of the world to do scholarship and so on. Nonetheless, I think they're very serious about assessment, and there are things to be learned from them.

Conference Participant: How can you emphasize or portray even at the younger ages the role of participating students in such a complex system? That not so well put, I…

Gardner: That's a good question and it's a just and implicit criticism of my presentation. I guess if I were talking to students, I hope I wouldn't have given exactly the same talk. First of all, these ideas about intelligence are actually very freeing for young people because they realize that it is too simplistic to think about just one kind of smart. But I think the more important thing is this: kids must come to understand that basically they're responsible for their own learning, that is the most important step. But it takes often decades for that to be achieved. Constructivist progressive approaches are much better on that score. They leave a lot more to the learner's invention. If you have a teacher who tries to control everything, of course, that's going to create a feeling of inefficacy or of patienthood rather than agenthood on the part of youngsters.

But the biggest problem is really motivation. Multiple Intelligences and understanding would be much, much simpler to implement if most kids were interested in school and what goes on in school. And they're not. And the question is: Why not? Probably, the fault is multiple. There are a lot of interesting things outside of school. In a sense, we're competing with things which didn't have to be competed with fifty or one-hundred years ago. But also, the lot of teachers is harder because we feel there is more to teach and there are more people spying on us about what we're doing, so there is less flexibility to adapt things to students.

I've been very much influenced, as you may know, by the work of Mihaly Csikszentmihalyi on flow. Csikszentmihalyi argues that you are motivated to do something when you're in a state of flow. A state of flow is one where you are so interested in what you're doing you lose track of everything else. Flow occurs in the zone—not a term I always use—between boredom and anxiety. If you are too skilled, you get bored. If the challenges are too great, you get anxious. So what you want as an educator is to create a space for kids where the challenges and their skills mesh with one another. Plato said the purpose of education is to make you want to do what you have to do. We cross a Rubicon when the child realizes he or she is responsible for the learning and nobody else can do it—not the parents, not the tutor, not the teachers. By the same token, once a child gets interested in learning and wants to learn, then you can stop paying tuition.

I'm lucky enough to teach at Harvard and especially at Harvard College. We could get rid of the faculty, and the students would instruct themselves. That's not the problem in most places. The problem in most places is that students are saying, "Why am I in school?" If we don't have good answers to those questions, then it's very tough.

Conference Participant: (Inaudible question)

Gardner: I'm told this is the last question so I'm going to use it to answer it as best I can, and then to give an answer in a more general comment. An honest answer to your question is that until September 11th, my conception of education was further from being realized in our country than it had been 10 years ago. The reason is one for which people like me should take some blame. In the early 1990's, there was an excitement about performance-based assessments, and a number of states, Vermont chief among them, embraced these perhaps somewhat prematurely and uncritically. Then they had trouble getting reliability, which means getting people to agree on the scoring. So as often happens in America, there was an overreaction, and people kind of condemned the whole method rather than its initial implementation.

There are some states such as Massachusetts that I would give not a bad grade to. There are others, I think Maryland and Connecticut are examples, where the assessments have a significant performance-based component. I think you probably all know the one where it's the least. That is Texas. You have this situation in Texas where the kids get steadily better at the task, but when other instruments are used, the kids aren't better at all. So this is a typical example of teaching to the test rather than developing more generalist skills.

One last comment. The new work I'm doing is called *Good Work*. The subtitle of the book that just came out is *When Excellence and Ethics Meet*. It is a book about what it means to be a professional. Even though the examples are drawn principally from medicine, science and journalism, they apply to every area. What does this have to do with teaching? Well, and I'm trying to be objective here without being invidious, teaching at the college level in America is basically a profession. Teaching at the precollegiate level especially in public schools is aspiring to be a profession. It's not a profession yet. When I say that, what I mean is that a profession is an agreement between (1) the laity, the general public, and (2) a group of people who are called professionals. In return for certain services to the society, the professionals are given a certain status and a certain amount of autonomy.

This has not happened in America with pre-collegiate education yet. It doesn't have the respect that it needs and doesn't have the autonomy that it needs. *However, and here is the deep dark secret: Professionalism cannot be given; it has to be seized.* Nobody made doctors professionals, they made themselves professionals. So to with other areas.

In England in the late 1980's, a very demanding test was imposed on all the teachers to give to the students. The teachers said "We won't do this," and the government backed down. I'm not recommending civil disobedience, that's your decision not mine, but I am saying that if doctors are told, "You can't see a patient for more than five minutes because you're in an HMO," the doctor should say, "I have a Hippocratic oath. I've got to see the patient as long as necessary."

It's very hard to be a teacher in pre-collegiate America today, but unless the teachers have a sense of the lines that they won't cross even though they're told to, teaching will never be a profession. So lurking in this question about examinations is the proposition that you may have to give the exam that the state mandates, but if you believe other kinds of exams are better, you've got to give those, too. And the more that you can show people that those are getting at things which are really important, the quicker teaching will become a profession.

*N*ow that we know about the enormous differences in how people acquire and represent knowledge, can we make these differences central to teaching and learning? Or will we instead continue to treat everyone in a uniform way? If we ignore these differences, we are destined to perpetuate a system that caters to an elite—typically those who learn best in a certain, usually linguistic or logical-mathematical manner. On the other hand, if we take these differences seriously, each person may be able to develop his or her intellectual and social potential much more fully.

Howard Gardner, *Intelligence Reframed*

MUSIC, IMAGERY AND PERFORMANCE IN FIRST YEAR WRITING

CHRISTINE LILIAN TURCZYN

I. "THE SUN STEPPING DOWN THE LADDER OF THE SKY"

A construction worker who loves the outdoors comes into my first-year writing classroom. He brings along with him notification that states that I should be aware of the fact that he has a learning disability. I am told that the use of imagery might help. I ask him if he'd like to sit down and talk about the material that he's brought with him. "No," he adamantly replies, and I believe he's had this conversation one too many times, not to his liking, as it draws attention to a part of him that does not represent his entire self, and is, after all, an unusual form of introduction. "All right then, I'll stand up," I offer.

On the second or third day of class, I remind students of the dryness and imprecision of clichés, and the fact that their vagueness is often misleading, as in the phrase *"theater of war."* "Could you," I ask, "think of an anti-cliché, one that uses a fresh image to describe a worn, oft-used word?" "Let's try *sunset,"* I suggest. The above student answers: "the sun stepping down the ladder of the sky" and his subsequent essays are complex, writerly, richly poetic—I wonder if he is meeting me halfway.

During in-class writing another student, in preparing a position statement for a persuasive essay, raps his claim. A future accountant, he is a nineteen-year-old father, a poet, and a member of the EOF Band. The letters **EOF**, painted on his knapsack, signal community and pride. In his piece, he offers advice to younger students, and they are gripped—nodding as a sign of affirmation, they are readily convinced. My class, he later tells me, allows him a great deal of expression, more than he has experienced in most other classes at our university. I am overjoyed, though not surprised, at the directness that his subsequent essays offer, steeped as they are in music, in the awareness of a reader, of a real audience, of a lasting effect. He has won a university-wide poetry competition, but more importantly, he has influenced his peers with what he hopes is a positive message "for young people." It is surprising that a young man should feel so old.

II. ACKNOWLEDGMENTS

I compose this paper as a tribute to my students— brilliant writers, dramatists, poets, and musicians with an experiential wisdom that cannot easily be measured, for who can map the diverse geographies of lives without understanding the languages of survival and compassion, particularity and song? Many of the students I was privileged to teach were survivors of economic hardship, of academic degradation, of teachers who had told them that "they could not write," of relatives who had abandoned them, of lovers who had abused them, of parents who had died too young. Yet they were also members of strong communities, multicultural and multilingual translators of joy, practitioners of artistic excellence, weavers of tongues. Throughout my life, I'd heard disparaging remarks about "the inner city," vague and highly disturbing comments that bore the defaced stamp of generalization, as there are *many* inner cities, and where, after all, is *the* inner city? Having lived half my life in Passaic, New Jersey, I wonder if the term refers to the tremendous innovation and sense of community I have encountered in urban poetry centers, or if it refers to something else, a reductive assertion of "otherness" a not-place, if you will. In this presentation, I give tribute to urban arts wherever they arise.

THE INTELLIGENCE OF A SURVIVOR

I honor the multiple forms of intelligence that help artists to survive, and wonder what the intelligence of a survivor is. It stands to reason that the intelligence of a survivor must be extreme and multifaceted, that in order to survive a concentration camp one must employ languages of knowledge that translate from one changing context to the next, from one millisecond of decision to a life-altering moment of courage, from silence into words. I praise life-saving art that endures past all destructions and holocausts, and artists in the academy, whose insights are often over-looked, even silenced. As a result of my experience and my own art, I strongly believe that multiple intelligences should be acknowledged at the post-secondary level so that students' diverse potentials will be affirmed in ways that contribute to their academic development and enrich multicultural interaction. This goal can be achieved in first-year classes, where students develop, early on, a sense of academic community and an increased awareness of diversity that will help them meet the challenges of a multicultural workplace. The affirmation of multiple intelligences at the post-secondary level is also an affirmation of diversity. Furthermore, the acknowledgment and cultivation of musical, visual, and dramatic potential at the level of first-year writing contributes to audience awareness, to the cultivation of academic community, and to the creation of engaging, sophisticated texts.

What are the advantages of acknowledging multiple intelligences—in this case, specifically those that relate to musical, dramatic, and visual capacities? I root my work partly in Freirian theory, in Paolo Freire's basic assumptions (1) that there is no true humanity without praxis; (2) that students are not, as per the banking concept of education, "receptacles" that should be "filled by the teacher," but rather individuals with histories and socioeconomic contexts, who, if provided with an educational environment that encourages inquiry, might become "transformers of the world" (*Pedagogy of the Oppressed* 72-73).

In this landmark text, Freire asserts: "Implicit in the banking concept is the assumption of a dichotomy between human beings and the world: a person is merely in the world, not with the world or with others; the individual is a spectator, not re-creator"(75). Clearly, if instructors at the level of first-year writing provide a forum for the expression of their students' diverse musical, visual, and dramatic potentials, students are recognized in artistic areas that might already be extremely developed before they enter college. Such recognition takes into account experiential knowledge, a knowledge of the world and its questions, as any form of art that aspires to transformation must tend toward a community consciousness as well as personal inquiry. Who knows more about community than a member of an orchestra or a rap poet who speaks of her neighborhood, the friends she grew up with, and the triumphs that a community experiences? Insofar as language is rooted in history, who, better than a rapper, relays the currency, the pulse of language as it changes, theorizes, asks?

In *Teaching to Transgress*, Bell Hooks notes: "Accepting the decentering of the West globally, embracing multiculturalism, compels educators to focus attention on the issue of voice. Who speaks? Who listens? And why?" (40). These critical questions can be related to the application of Multiple Intelligences Theory to the post-secondary setting. Encouraging students to root their writing in artistic capacities that lend them confidence (and, in many cases, the expression of cultural authority) contributes to the development of voice. Working with a section of music majors in first-year writing, I often ask students to bring in a CD of their choice that we, as class participants, might listen to and write about. I have found that students feel comfortable risking music that *they* define as essential to their cultural backgrounds. This way—rather than presenting a paper about music that they personally enjoy—they choose music they deem crucial to their lives. Voice enters the class community as a palpable presence, as a spoken or sung assertion of identity that writing follows.

DIALOGUES WITH A YOUNGER SELF

In *Intelligence Refrained: Multiple Intelligences for the 21st Century*, Howard Gardner defines intelligence as a "biopsychological potential to process information that can be activated in a *cultural setting* [emphasis mine] to solve problems or create products that are of value in a culture" (33-34). In tapping Multiple Intelligences, I keep my assignments open to as many potentials as possible, and in so doing, am keenly aware of cultural differences in terms of values placed on different forms of expression such as the *oral tradition versus the written one*. In preparing students for a narrative essay through in-class writing, I might ask students to compose a dialogue between their current and their younger selves. Students can, for example, sit their childhood personae on a "Borgesian" bench and discuss from their current standpoints, pivotal moments, or central assumptions that they have held that changed through the course of time. I might take my class to the art gallery, have each student select a painting, and, in writing, make it speak.

IDEAS BREAKING LIKE GLASS

In tapping imagery, I call attention to the concreteness of language, to its gritty physicality, historical layers. Indebted to Wendy Bishop for the use of a successful assignment titled "Images of Writing" (found in *Released into Language*) that I have adapted for first-year writers, I ask students to complete the prompt "Writing is like…" with an image (77). Amazingly, students construct quite memorable images for their writing difficulties or successes. Is it possible that images creatively subvert the causal linkages of standard English grammar that some students have had trouble mastering? Or do images, lodged as they are in the subconscious, emerge readily from a place of deep feeling only later to be accessed by words? A first-year writer who stated (and had been told) that her writing was "worthless," composed a passage in class that has indelibly marked my views of standard assessments of writing. Asked to provide an image for writing, she jotted down:

> *Writing is like trying to talk when you are mute. It's very difficult for me to write as freely as I speak. When I begin to write, I have many prominent ideas in my mind, but something happens to those ideas when they fall out of my head onto the paper. I can only imagine my ideas being like pieces of glass that seem so perfect in my head but the trip that they take from my head to the paper is too rough and they break when they land…*
>
> (Maritsa Montalvo)

When I teach, I strive to counter marginalization, lead students toward their own voices, and summon imagery, art, as spaces where persons of many cultures and economic backgrounds can meet without subscribing to a universal elision of differences. I attempt, insofar as possible, to validate multiperspectival approaches to written language and to incorporate the narrative intricacies of oral traditions. Having belatedly come upon Howard Gardner's theories, I find that Dr. Gardner's discussions of pedagogical "entry points" coincide with techniques I have been using for years. Various forms of in-class writing that elicit multiple intelligences could be viewed as "entry points," segues, as it were, into complex essays.

III. MUSIC

VOICE

For Andrea Bocelli

If you could walk
through the streets
of the body
without seeing stars
it would sound
like this.

Christine L. Turczyn

At William Paterson University, where I was employed most recently, I taught first-year writing classes attended by students who were interested in writing and composing music, as well as visual artists actively involved with their arts. I cannot really explain why this was the case: perhaps the students had heard that I was, in all of my writing classes, receptive to the other arts. Arguably, the composition of students had something to do with the fact the William

Paterson University hosts a premiere jazz program with a national reputation. Whatever the cause, I found myself quite pleasantly situated in a community of artists, primarily musicians; some had little formal training, while others had appeared on stage with Al Grey and Paquito D'Rivera. The Freirian perspective became central as I considered how I might learn from my students (from their multifaceted artistic forms of knowledge) and incorporate the musicality of language and the arts into my first-year writing class rather than bypass the first year writers' potentials in favor of my own pedagogical preferences.

SYMBOLS AND RHYTHM

A situation that comes to mind from a section that was almost entirely filled with musicians is the following: A classical musician would, from time to time, ask me for synonyms for key words included in his essays. At first, it occurred to me that his request could fall into the category of challenges that a speaker of English as a second language such as I am faces at the beginning of a first-year writing course. Yet this student's motives seemed sincere. One day, he explained to me that he composed his essays according to musical rhythms; if a word did not have the requisite number of syllables, the rhythm of the line would be destroyed. For me, this amounted to a moment of pedagogical enlightenment. Although my poetry relies heavily upon internal rhythm, albeit one that does not necessarily coincide with iambic pentameter, it had never occurred to me that an individual's way of apprehending language could be entirely allied with music, that his commitment to music could so intimately be connected with words. I did not discourage him from this fundamental way of approaching nonfiction, as it was an affirmation of his personhood, perception, and values.

I decided at that point that it would be productive and enjoyable to cultivate all of the musicians' capacities by creating assignments that encouraged musical expression. Rather than inviting students to the art gallery for the purpose of descriptive writing, I invited a saxophonist, a participant in my first-year writing class, to improvise a piece that we could write about. In order to lend structure to the in-class writing, I asked students to first record, as they were listening, images that occurred to them as the student composed, and then to write about feelings associated with the music. Far from being a B-grade attempt at the *Dead Poets' Society,* my assignment called attention to the fact that quality essays of description provide more than a surface of glittering imagery, that images, like notes, are distillations of time—dreams at the surface of one's skin that only point to substrata of emotion.

BEYOND THE CONFINES OF A TEXT

My most radical assignments occurred at the level of in-class writing, a non-graded form of composition that allowed the students to gather material for essays gradually, and gave them a feild for linguistic and intellectual exploration. In all of my writing classes, I encouraged students to keep journals of images, defined, within the context of that course, as visual moments that struck them when they were not in class, such as an unusual billboard photo, a work of graffiti, or a cirrus spine of cloud stretching across a winter sky. As an instructor, I maintain a philosophy of adaptability, and journal writing, due to its malleable nature, sensitizes a writer's awareness to the landscapes of writing that stretch beyond the confines of a text. I should also add that any reading of in-class writing was purely voluntary, so that students did not feel that they needed to share their pieces prematurely, or to expose to the listener feelings that they were not prepared to share. In *Intelligence Reframed*, Gardner writes, "A master of change readily acquires new information, solves problems, forms 'weak ties' with mobile and highly dispersed people, and adjusts easily to changing circumstances" (2). In the sense that in-class writing is of its nature improvisational, its ongoing process both prepares students for change and reminds them of the fact that writing takes a variety of forms along a continuum of contexts. Students were encouraged to use their in-class writing toward their essays. To borrow Gardner's phrase, in-class writing provides a marvelous "entry point" for the composition of essays, one, within the community of my class, that is non-threatening. A music major who'd at first confessed to me privately that he'd felt alienated by the backgrounds and perspectives of some of the more privileged students eventually wrote a persuasive essay ("Dear Senators") that argued, before his fellow listeners, the necessity of establishing music programs for children in Passaic. It is my belief that in-class writing urged this writer to move away from the socially inscribed "I can't write" assumption that hindered his pre-college work. His essay was one of the most eloquent I'd read in the course of that year, and, with the help of an alumnus, he hoped eventually to establish a music school in my hometown.

IV. IMAGERY

Imagery is useful in providing reticent students with spaces in which their expression can find room for development without the risk of undue personal exposure. If an instructor takes a first-year writing class to an art gallery and encourages the students to allow a particular painting to "speak," students can assume, in this form of in-class writing, a persona through which their feelings may find expression. In my experience, images have also been very useful toward illustrating concepts such as "objectification" that may initially puzzle students when we discuss a feminist text submitted to class opinion and analysis. John Berger's comprehensive and accessible film *Ways of Seeing* includes an analysis of women as objects of painting that engenders lively class discussion regarding the power differential between the viewer and the viewed.

FIELDS OF PATTERNED TEXTURE

It has also been my experience that the use of poems with vivid images enhancing characterization, such as Luis Rodriguez' "Tia Chucha," contribute to the crafting of lively characterizations in student writing. In describing a free-spirited aunt who periodically distances herself from her family, Rodriguez, in *The Concrete River*, creates a visible, beautifully imperfect, wonderfully assured, thought-provoking, and outspoken relative whose characteristics are photographed in striking images such as, "She was a despot of desire/uncontainable/as a splash of water/on a varnished table" *(49-53)*. Adrienne Rich's "North American Time" highlights, also, an image of women braiding each other's hair that I have integrated into discussions of how cultural appropriation can be avoided. Thus, imagery enriches the first-year writing class through a concretization of abstract ideas, giving fields of patterned texture to thought, as it were.

V. PERFORMANCE

Throughout the years, I have discovered that on a day when I am exhausted and encourage the class to improvise, students have stunned me with their energetic, multivalent, and complex impromptu renditions of integral issues. These have ranged from the humorous, in which a student volunteered to perform Christian Morgenstern's concrete poem "Fish's Nightsong" (incorporated into a discussion of Modernism and the concrete and visual possibilities of language) to vital student concerns regarding racial profiling. In creative writing classes, I taught the monologue and found that some of the most powerful and direct student writing emerged from this form, perhaps because of its reliance upon speech and its creation of a forum for voice.

THE WRITER AND THE AUDIENCE

In addition, performance urges students to become "re-creators," not "spectators." At the end of every semester, I request that students read their essays as part of a "literary reading" that remakes the title of the course into a headline: "Writing-Effective Pros." Orally delivering an essay encourages accountability, as the writer must face his or her audience. The act of bringing one's words to life through the body cultivates an awareness of voice and of writerly conviction, as students can much more easily slip an essay to a professor (audience of one) than to a group of influential peers. Performance elicits immediate responses—thus, a sense of revision becomes a dialogue that the writer can internalize at will. And who, more than a writer and his/her community, defines standards, establishes ideological norms or deconstructs them, knows of trends, coins new words? In dialogue with other class participants, students write about topics that are meaningful and current, become excited about the reality of writing as it stems from the material of their days. In "performing" their essays, students speak assertively and emerge from the "culture of silence" (*Pedagogy of the Oppressed*, Freire qtd. by Richard Shaull) that Freire believes surrounds economically oppressed people. Furthermore, in *Teaching to Transgress*, Bell Hooks writes: "One of the central tenets of feminist critical pedagogy has been the insistence on not engaging the mind/body split. This is one of the underlying beliefs that has made Women's Studies a subversive location in the academy"(193).

VI. Choreography

I do not believe that the mind and the body, the body and the word, narrative writing and research are mutually exclusive; current examples include the richly poetic, bilingual, and extensively researched writing of Gloria Anzaldua. It has been an enduring wish of mine to implement a cluster course consisting of a fine arts course, a course in music, and a course in the crafting of fiction or poetry that could be taught at the level of first-year writing. Thus, artists within the academy could form communities very early in their university careers. Howard Gardner and Paolo Freire both emphasize problem solving and community; courses such as this one would cultivate pragmatic approaches to learning. In my classes, I emphasize community as well as continuity; in constructing syllabi, I draw upon texts from diverse cultures (including the diverse cultures of disability) and create bridges between assignments that build upon earlier ones. A descriptive essay cannot merely describe, it must mine ideas and draw conclusions. A line from a first-year, in-class poem written by Jill Scalice titled "Daddy," asks: "Nineteen years old, yet I cannot understand/Does deserting your family make you more of a man?" This question might form the matrix of a research essay about the psychological effects of divorce. "Is there a driving question that has followed you all your lives," I ask students in advance of preparing them for research.

Complex Linguistic Intelligences

I believe that the acknowledgment of Multiple Intelligences encourages the development of multicultural awareness and a sustained, inquisitive critical thinking that helps individuals to become resilient and open-minded without having to sacrifice what is essential to them. Furthermore, the cultivation of musical, visual, and dramatic potentials in first-year writing does not obviate issues of research and Modern Language Association (MLA) style. I find that it is most beneficial to introduce issues of such style midway into the semester at about the time when students begin to study the effective elements of persuasion and need to incorporate research that will lend credibility to their arguments. In this manner, students with writing difficulties find that writing is more than *not-writing*—*that* hidden but elusive prototype of commas, a poetic meter without the synergy of wisdom. In acknowledging the complex linguistic intelligences and diverse backgrounds of students whose cultures might greatly value storytelling, I, among others, encourage writing that evolves and takes many forms. Rather than discouraging all future writing by merely insisting on one form, I vary composition through opening up creativity to its musical, dramatic, artistic, and cultural influences.

Conclusion

All too often, a uniform approach to the teaching of writing results in a leveling of differences that are both personal and cultural, individual and historical. A respect for individual differences, however, delineates the boundaries between cultural approach and appropriation, between writing that encourages an imaginative approach of another's experience, and writing that appropriates that experience through a limited, controlling and, at best, clichéd understanding.

Through integrating music, imagery, and performance into the first-year writing curriculum, instructors address their students' multifaceted, artistic forms of knowledge. As a result, writers become determiners of their own complex identities, strengthen their voices, and acquire authorial confidence. Without having to sacrifice what is essential to their fundamental perceptions, students engage in a lively dialogue within the context of a multicultural community. This dialogue stimulates intellectual inquiry and results in texts that address a wider audience, as concepts of intelligence vary with cultural perspectives.

REFERENCES

Achebe, C. (1989). *Hopes and Impediments: Selected Essays*. New York: Doubleday.

Behar, R. (1994). "Dare We Say 'I'? (Bringing the Personal Into Scholarship)" in *The Chronicle of Higher Education*. 29 June: B 1-3.

Berger, J. (1972). *Ways of Seeing*. London: British Broadcasting Corporation.

Bishop, W. (1990). *Released into Language*. Urbana: National Council of Teachers of English.

Borges, J. L. (1964) "Borges and I." in *Labyrinths: Selected Stories & Other Writings*. Eds. Donald A. Yates and James E. Irby. New York: New Directions.

Clifton, L. (1991) *Quilting*. Brockport: BOA Editions, Ltd.

Diaz-Lefebvre, R. and Finnegan P. (1997). "Coloring Outside the Lines: Applying the Theory of Multiple Intelligences to the Community College Setting." in *Community College Journal* Oct/Nov: 28-31.

Freire, P. (2001). *Pedagogy of the Oppressed* (30th Anniversary Edition). Trans. Bergman Ramos. New York: Continuum.

—. (1998). *Teachers as Cultural Workers: Letters to Those Who Dare Teach*. Trans. Donaldo Macedo, Dale Koike, and Alexandre Oliveira. Boulder: Westview Press.

Gardner, H. (1993). *Creating Minds*. New York: Basic Books.

—. *Frames of Mind*. (1983). New York: Basic Books.

—. (1999). *Intelligence Reframed: Multiple Intelligences for the 21st Century*. New York: Basic Books.

—. (1995) *Leading Minds*. Howard Gardner in collaboration with Emma Laskin. New York: Basic Books.

Hooks, B. (2000). *Where We Stand: Class Matters*. New York: Routledge.

—. (1994). *Teaching to Transgress: Education as the Practice of Freedom*. New York: Routledge.

MI: Intelligence. Understanding and the Mind. (1996). Producer Robert DiNozzi. Los Angeles, CA: Into the Classroom Media. One-hour presentation with Question and Answer.

Rich, A. (1986). *Your Native Land, Your Life*. New York: Norton.

Rodriguez, L. (1991). *The Concrete River*. Willimantic: Curbstone Press.

Sanoff, A. P. (1984) "Human Intelligence Isn't What We Think It Is" (A Conversation with Howard Gardner). *U.S. News & World Report* 19 March: 75.

Most academics have heard the claim that the average person uses approximately 10-15% of his/her intelligence 99.9% of the time. When pressed for the source of this claim, some may know that it is attributed to either William James or Albert Einstein. Few may be aware that in fact both of these great thinkers of the twentieth century came to this same conclusion independently, as far as I can determine. In other words, it is as if our minds are like automobile engines with ten cylinders and only one is operating. The reason we don't know it is because that is the way virtually everyone's mind is operating. The only exception is the rare "genius" who has two cylinders working. Thus, if the IQ scale were a true ratio scale (with an absolute zero making ratios possible), which it isn't, then the average person has an IQ of 100, geniuses have IQs somewhere around 200, and all of us have the potential for 1000! If that's true, then every student who is sitting in a classroom, every child, is a potential genius.

EVIDENCE

What is the evidence for this incredible contention? I believe the most impressive comes from two sources: the effects of hypnosis and the new research on DID (dissociative identity disorder, formerly known as multiple personality disorder). First, DID. It has recently been defined as a dissociative disorder in which patients hypnotize themselves into an altered state to cope with overwhelming trauma. Former *New York Times* science writer Daniel Goleman has chronicled how the new research on "multiples" (as they are called) has been causing a revolution in the field of psychiatry and shaking up our notions of the power of the mind to affect the body. For example, multiples exhibit some remarkable biological and psychological changes as they switch from one to another personality. These include such phenomena as differential responses to the same drug, the presence or absence of such conditions as color blindness, epilepsy, diabetes, allergies, differences in handwriting, blood pressure, visual acuity, speech patterns, brainwave patterns, and even the presence of scars and other tissue wounds (Goleman, 1988, 111). Is it any wonder, therefore, that Nancy Napier, a New York therapist who works with multiples, has been quoted as saying, "I don't think we have the remotest notion about where all this is taking us (Roberts, 1992, 25)."

THE CASE OF THE ELEPHANT MAN

If all this sounds like what *Time* magazine called "the UFO of psychiatry," then let me share a documented case of the effect of hypnosis on self-healing. In a video produced by the BBC in 1982, titled "Hypnosis: Can Your Mind Control Your Body?" there is presented a 16 year-old male who was diagnosed with having a congenital disease of the skin that rendered him like the "elephant man" as depicted in the popular movie of the 80s with the same title. In other words, the youth was born with a skin in which there were no sebaceous glands, and as a result, instead of flaking off

CARITAS IN THE CLASSROOM: STRATEGIES FOR UNEARTHING THE GENIUS IN OUR STUDENTS

JOHN D. LAWRY

normally, it built up into a grotesque epidermis resembling the skin of an elephant.

Dr. A. A. Mason (M.D.) described how he came upon the case after there had been an unsuccessful attempt to graft on good skin through a surgical procedure. Misdiagnosing the case as warts, Dr. Mason suggested to the surgeon that he try hypnosis. In a moment of pique, the surgeon invited Dr. Mason to take over the case if he thought he could do better. Unwittingly, Dr. Mason tried hypnosis and gave the boy the suggestion that one of his arms become completely normal within a week. The following week the boy arrived at the hospital and indeed the arm was completely normal. Immediately, Dr. Mason showed the boy to the surgeon and only then did the surgeon reveal the true diagnosis and suggested to Dr. Mason that he better come with an explanation since he would be asked to present the case to the British Medical Society. Through further suggestions, the boy's entire body was eventually healed with only a few residual marks from the condition. It was the first case of virtually complete healing of such a congenital condition in the history of modern medicine. As Dr. Mason remarks at the end of a very dramatic presentation of the case, the healing was no less remarkable than if the patient had been healed of a clubfoot. Indeed, if this were to have happened a hundred years ago, it would have been characterized as a miracle.

STRATEGIES FOR REVEALING GENIUS

After reading about the effects of DID and seeing or even hearing about this video presentation, I do not think there is anyone who can question at least the possibility of what I call the "James-Einstein hypothesis." If the mind can do that, albeit under the influence of suggestion, whether trauma-induced or clinically induced, then what is the limit? The challenge of the implications of these phenomena, it seems to me, is how to tap the obvious potential of the mind using less extreme means than trauma or hypnosis.

1. SELF-FULFILLING PROPHECY

The remainder of this paper will present five strategies for "unearthing the genius" in students, which I have developed and used in my courses over the years. The first is what Robert Rosenthal and Lenore Jackson at Harvard University in the 60s termed "the Pygmalion Effect," and what others have called self-fulfilling prophecy. Rosenthal arranged in his experiment, children who were reported to their teachers as showing unusual potential for intellectual growth.[1] In fact, the children were matched on IQ and randomly assigned to the various classes, but the teachers were given false information. Some teachers were told that they had the top 20% of the class ("magic" children) whereas other teachers were told they had the bottom 80% of the class. Most readers probably know that the "magic" children scored higher at the end of the year, and thus Rosenthal concluded that it was primarily because of perceived differences in the relative abilities of the two groups.

Rosenthal and Jackson conclude by suggesting a very prescient application of their findings for its time (1966), one that unfortunately has not been heeded:

> As teacher-training institutions begin to teach the possibility that teachers' expectations of their pupils performance may serve self-fulfilling prophecies, there may be a new expectancy created. The new expectancy may be that children can learn more than had been believed possible, an expectation held by many educational theorists, though for quite different reasons (for example, Bruner). The new expectancy, at the very least, will make it more difficult when they encounter the educationally disadvantaged for teachers to think, "Well, after all, what can you expect?" The man on the street may be permitted his opinions and prophecies of the unkempt children loitering in a dreary schoolyard. The teacher in the schoolroom may need to learn that those same prophecies within her may be fulfilled; she is no casual passer-by. Perhaps Pygmalion in the classroom is more her role (181-182).

So if you "know" that the students sitting in your classroom are potential geniuses and it is just a matter of unearthing that genius, is not that very fact going to make a difference in the outcome? The growing research on self-fulfilling prophecy would argue that it will, and I can speak from personal experience that it does. There is a lot of speculation about *why* it works, but there is no question in my mind that it works. In fact, I go one step further than the implications of the Rosenthal study. I *tell* my students they have the capacity for genius and guess what? Some of them begin to believe it and begin to perform as if it were true! They begin to think of themselves as "smart," "bright," "intelligent," whatever word they feel comfortable with and which enhances their mental functioning.

2. SELF-HYPNOSIS AND POSITIVE THINKING

This brings me to the second and related strategy, teaching students the use of self-hypnosis and positive thinking. Several years ago, I taught a graduate course on developmental psychology for teachers. One of my students was doing much better than all of the other students on the objective tests I was administering at the time. When I queried him about his "secret," he informed me that he was a hypnotist by avocation and that he would study the text by putting himself in a light trance and giving himself a suggestion such as: "The material I am about to study will become fully assimilated in my storehouse of memories. When I am studying, my mind works clearly and sharply, and I retain everything I learn." He assured me that he only needed to read the text once and he retained virtually 100% of the material, at least for the exam.

I now teach self-hypnosis in virtually all of my classes and give them a sheet of suggestions for "Increasing Creativity and Developing Dormant Talents, Improving Memory, and Improving the Learning Process and Performance on Examinations." This is what a student by the name of Claire wrote about this part of a first-year college survival course that was called *University 101*:

> In class, the session that really impressed me was "Positive Thinking." I realized that I always degraded myself about things before I even attempted them. It wasn't so much that my mother told me that I couldn't do things, because she never discouraged me in anything I wanted to do. It was just having to see her life the way that she did; never becoming the accountant or nurse or entrepreneur like her other siblings. It made me think that I would be exactly like her, not because of a lack of intelligence but ambition. I was able to quit that negative thinking and begin to think positive thoughts with your "Positive Thinking" technique. Before

---

[1] This experiment was conducted at Oak School in San Francisco with grades 1-6 in 1966.

each class and every test I would clear my mind of all thoughts and begin by telling myself that "I will retain all things I learned in class," or "I will retain all things I studied." Because of these techniques I have improved from a C- to a B in Microeconomics *and have been getting all A's on my mathematics exams!*

3. CHANTING, CLEARING THE MIND AND "JAI BHAGWAN"

The reference to "clearing the mind" brings me to the third strategy. I believe that the beginning of class is a critical moment, i.e., the manner in which the class is begun influences the experience of everyone, thus the efficacy of rites and ritual for beginnings. Ever since we discontinued beginning class with a prayer to the Holy Spirit at Marymount College in the 1960s, I have struggled and searched for some kind of meaningful replacement. When I visited the yoga ashram, Kripalu, in Lenox, Massachusetts several years ago, I found the answer. I now begin class with chanting "OM" followed by the Sanskrit greeting, "Jai Bhagwan," which translates loosely into "I honor the divine within you." Why "OM"? Well, to quote briefly from Swami Sivananda, "OM is everything…The repetition of OM has a tremendous influence on the mind…OM is the inner music of the soul. It is the music of Silence, the voice of God."

This is how Dr. Deepak Chopra, author of *Quantum Healing* and other best-selling books, described it more scientifically in a lecture he gave in 1992 at Kripalu:

> *If you make that sound OM in front of a drop of oil, for example, then you will see that it manifests into a very specific visual form (under a microscope). If you examine that visual form, you will find that it's a "mandala," which is a very symmetric pattern that comes out of that vibration and every bit of it contains all of it. In other words, it is a hologram. It's a hologram of information and energy coming from the original information and energy field that contains every single thing in creation.*

More importantly, what is the student reaction to such an unusual class beginning? Well, for one thing, they become so habituated that they remind me when I forget. When we all forget, the class does not seem to go as well. But the experience is much deeper than that. This is what Nahoko, a Japanese-American student, wrote about her experience of chanting OM:

> *One of the most attractive qualities that made me and all the students comfortable was the famous OM at the beginning of the class. This simple sound of OM not only was a pleasing start, but it was also the strong, magical word that brought the entire class into a unity. For me, in addition to the harmonious quality, it was a moment of experiencing a spiritual atmosphere, where I was always reminded to think about or say a prayer for someone in my mind by*

creating a bridge from my heart to the loving God. Through the repetitive, ritual OM at the beginning of each class, the whole class was melted from a solid sugar into a blended, sweet liquid solvent, in which everyone could be open and interact with one another by sharing one's own experiences as well as her opinions.

I could not have said it better myself!

4. THE JOURNAL

The fourth strategy is one I have been using ever since I started teaching a *Senior Seminar* for psychology majors more than 20 years ago. Requiring students to keep a journal for the duration of a course is a very powerful technique, not only for facilitating student reflection of course content but also for getting to know the students. To help the students in this regard, I provide an edited handout on journal keeping from McCarroll's book,

Exploring the Inner World, which unfortunately is out of print but is available in an anthology I edited (Lawry, 1999). To quote from my introduction for this reading:

> *For the majority of my students in* University 101, *nothing in the course requirements causes more initial resistance than the requirement of keeping a journal. "I hate writing." "How can I be personal if you are going to read it?" "I don't have time to keep a journal." Etc. And yet, nothing seems to match the journal in its power to teach self-exploration. As McCarroll says: "It is through my journal that I begin to hear my own story and to search for my part in the story of life." Most of my students acknowledge this at the end of the course and can't wait for me to read their journals (p. 1).*

Rather than my telling you how the students responded to the keeping of a journal, let me quote from Christine's final self-evaluation:

> *My journal reintroduced me to myself, a part of me that was lost in lectures, studying, and writing papers. I've learned that it is important to take the time to be by myself. A time to be free, a time to dream and a time to write. I've always tried to keep a journal, but with my busy schedule I forget to write for weeks at a time. I want to start over again with a new journal and my new attitude. I feel happier about relationships and myself as a result of my taking time to write my thoughts out. I've learned a great deal from this class, but most importantly,* I've learned a lot about myself *[emphasis added].*

5. LOVING OUR STUDENTS

The fifth and final strategy is "loving our students." It was Goethe who said that it was not the most brilliant teachers who had the greatest impact on his life; it was those who loved him. Would not that be a fair statement for most of us? It is interesting to me that the importance of love is becoming recognized in other professions as well. For example, Dr. Deepak Chopra, author of *Quantum Healing*, in a recent interview said that love was the single most important ingredient in the physician-patient relationship.

The empirical evidence comes from the work of David Asby and Florence Roebuck (1986) who have dedicated practically their entire professional lives to analyzing more than 200,000 hours of classroom instruction and found that what Carl Rogers calls empathy, congruence and positive regard, as measurable characteristics in grade-school teachers, contribute significantly to classroom learning. Not only that but the pattern holds for the entire school when the principal possesses those characteristics; such is the power of love.

How does it work? No one knows for sure, but I believe that love creates an energy and atmosphere for learning as well as for healing. As Yogi Amrit Desai phrased it in a lecture: "The highest form of learning occurs when the teacher loves and accepts the students so fully that they feel safe enough to go within to see themselves and to emerge with new answers about themselves and their lives." Think of the greatest teachers down through the centuries: Buddha, Moses, Jesus, and in the modern period, such educational geniuses as Rousseau, Pestalozzi, Steiner, Krishnamurti, Neill, and Montessori. What did they all have in common? I would argue that all of them had an awareness of the importance of love in teaching, as the following quotes would suggest.

PERSUASIVE AND GENUINE

First, it was the great Swiss educator, J. Heinrich Pestalozzi (1746-1827), "Father of Modern Elementary Education," who said, "Love is the sole and everlasting foundation on which our nature can be trained to humaneness" (164). But, as Noddings and Shore (1984) remind us:

Pestalozzi was not simply an educational theorist; he practiced what he preached. His school at Yverdon stood in dramatic contrast to other schools in early nineteenth-century Europe, where beatings, endless recitation, and harsh teachers were common. At Pestalozzi's school, children were treated with respect and kindness, given tasks equal to their abilities, and above all taught by word and by example that love in its most generous, altruistic form is important. So pervasive and genuine was the emphasis on love as an educating form that when a peasant came to visit the school at Yverdon, he exclaimed, "This is not a school, it is a household." Although Pestalozzi's school fell into decline and eventually closed during his own lifetime, his message to educators to fill their teaching and living with love was not forgotten and remains one of his most important legacies (162-163).

Rudolf Steiner (1861-1925), founder of the Waldorf school system as well as anthroposophy, was, in my opinion, a man ahead of his times. For example, this is what Steiner (1947) wrote about the sensitive soul of the child:

It is not easy, at first, to believe that feelings like reverence and respect have anything to do with cognition. This is due to the fact that we are inclined to set cognition aside as a faculty by itself—one that stands in no relation to what otherwise occurs in the soul. In so thinking we do not bear in mind that it is the soul which exercises the faculty of cognition; and feelings are for the soul what food is for the body… Veneration, homage, devotion are the nutriment making it healthy and strong, especially strong for the activity of cognition. Disrespect, antipathy, underestimation of what deserves recognition, all exert a paralyzing and withering effect on this faculty of cognition…Reverence awakens in the soul a sympathetic power through which we attract qualities in the beings around us, which would otherwise remain concealed (12-14).

CARING FOR ONE ANOTHER—THE HARDEST OF ALL

In her excellent treatise on the Waldorf educational philosophy, *Toward Wholeness: Rudolf Steiner Education in America*, M. C. Richards (1980) sums up the place of caring in this unique school environment where the child has the same teacher for the entire eight years of elementary schooling:

Teaching and the preparation of the teacher is a spiritual practice. But again let us ask what this means. For, as has been suggested, one does not go directly to something termed spirit, but rather one works through physical materials, activities, relationships, perceptions, meditations. In order to affect their mobility of thinking and their individual creativity of will, the teachers practice the various arts of painting and music and eurhythmy, poetry, and whatever else may attract them. To affect their feeling life, they attempt to observe rhythms in their waking and sleeping; to work imaginatively in their class preparation, using stories and colors and sound and movements and play; and to care for one another. This last is the hardest of all, of course. To care for another person more than for oneself, to let the ego of another person live in oneself as vividly as one's own—this we can barely begin to do. The teachers, through their faithful championing of a group of children through continuous years of schooling, have an opportunity to practice this high art, and to try gradually to develop a true sense of "the other" (120).

Krishnamurti (1890-1986), one of the great spokesmen for Eastern thought to the West in the twentieth century, had this to say about loving students:

Only love can bring about the understanding of another.

Where there is love there is instantaneous communion with the other, on the same level and at the same time. It is because we ourselves are so dry, empty and without love that we have allowed governments and systems to take over the education of our children and the direction of our lives… If the teacher is of the right kind, he will not depend on a method, but will study each individual pupil. In our relationship with children and young people, we are not dealing with mechanical devices, that can be quickly repaired, but with living beings who are impressionable, volatile, sensitive, afraid, affectionate; and to deal with them, we have to have great understanding, the strength of patience and love [emphasis added]. (23-24)

SELDOM A CRYING CHILD

A.S. Neill (1883-1973), the founder of Summerhill school in England, wrote the following editorial in the student newspaper at the University of Edinburgh in 1912, chastising his professors for their aloofness: "They stand upon their dignity and their whole attitude which says, 'I don't want any of your familiarity. I am a Professor. . .' If he fails to be a man of charity, of kindliness, of love, the honorary degrees count for nothing; he is unfit to be a professor, for, in teaching, the man is greater than his subject" (Hemmings, 8).

Neill titled one of his early books, *Hearts, Not Heads in the Schools*, and this is what he wrote in *Summerhill: A Radical Approach to Child Rearing*:

Summerhill is possibly the happiest school in the world. We have no truants and seldom a case of homesickness. We rarely have fights—quarrels, of course, but seldom have I seen a stand-up fight like the ones we used to have as boys. I seldom hear a child cry, because children when free have much less hate to express than children who are downtrodden. Hate breeds hate, and love breeds love. Love means approving of children, and that is essential in any school. You can't be on the side of children if you punish them and storm at them. Summerhill is a school in which the child knows that he is approved of (1960, 8).

Robin Pedley in *The Comprehensive School* considered the changing relationship between teacher and child as the most significant area in which Neill's influence was felt:

Neill, more than anyone else, has swung teachers' opinion in this country from its one reliance on authority and the cane to hesitant recognition that a child's first need is love, and with love, respect for the free growth of his personality…The magic of the inspired reformer is there in Neill's books, in his talks to teachers who still (1963) flock to hear him…Today's friendliness between pupil and teacher is probably the greatest difference between the classrooms of

1963 and those of 1923. The change owes much to Neill, and to others in independent co-educational schools who have practised similar principles (1963, 174).

Maria Montessori (1870-1952) called education a "technique of love" and is said to have hugged the street children in those first "Case dei Bambini" she founded in Italy at the turn of the century. She argued strongly for the importance of caring and nurturance on the part of the teacher, something that was unfortunately lost in the American translation of the Montesorri method if my daughter's school was typical. Listen to what Montessori says in the chapter "The Love Teachers," in *The Child in the Family*: "And who are these instructors who would teach the child to love? Those who judge as misbehavior all the child's activities and who deal with them punitively? No adult can become a teacher of love without a special effort, without opening the eyes of his consciousness in order to see a world more vast than his own" (1970, 40).

So what happens when the teacher is able to bring love as well as all of the other things we know are important to the learning process? This is what the famous lecturer, Jean Houston, wrote about a visiting young Swiss professor of religion, Dr. Jacob Taubes, at Columbia University who saved her life when she was in the midst of a personal crisis in her junior year:

Dr. Taubes continued to walk me to the bus throughout the term, always challenging me with intellectually vigorous questions. He attended to me. I existed for him in the "realest" of senses, and because I existed for him I began to exist for myself. Within several weeks, my eyesight came back, my spirit bloomed, and I became a fairly serious student, whereas before I had been, at best, a bright show-off.

What I acquired from this whole experience was a tragic sense of life, which balanced my previous enthusiasms. I remain deeply grateful for the attention shown me by Dr. Taubes. He acknowledged me when I most needed it. I was empowered in the midst of personal erosion, and my life has been very different for it. I swore to myself then that whenever I came across someone "going under" or in the throes of disacknowledgement, I would try to reach and acknowledge that person as I had been acknowledged (1982, 122-123).

KNOWING IS LOVING

I believe this first example contains what Parker Palmer (1983) is talking about in his seminal book, *To Know As We Are Known: A Spirituality of Education*. In the first chapter, "Knowing Is Loving," Palmer writes: "Education… means more than teaching the facts and learning the reasons so we can manipulate life toward our ends. It means being drawn into personal responsiveness and accountability to each other and the world of which we are a part" (Palmer, 14-15). Dr. Taubes had the courage to become a person to a troubled student and look what happened!

My second example is closer to home in that it is a quote from a final self-evaluation paper of a student of mine whose name is Alyssa for a psychology course I taught several years ago called *Perennial Quest*:

> *Reading over my journal in its entirety forces me to acknowledge the incredible growth I have experienced this semester as a result of "Perennial Quest." As the journal indicates, and as my memory confirms, I began the course reluctant, or more appropriately, unable to share openly in the class discussions, or even to honestly express myself in the journal. This closed-ness made itself more apparent to me through the psychosomatic pain I experienced for the first half of the course. However, I decided at the beginning to take a risk and to allow myself to speak and write freely, as well as to listen and read closely. My journey of the semester presented itself in the journal. The end result is that right now I feel a tremendous sense of peace. In fact, the stomach pain, which has tormented me for years, has not been active in these last few weeks. I see this in itself as a clear sign of my personal growth.*

For modesty's sake, I hesitate to go on but I feel I must because it makes the point:

> *I want to thank you for inviting me to make this journey and for these many gifts. I am so grateful that I could partake in this growth process and attain this delicious sense of peace. Thank you most especially for your openness, your nonjudgmental approach to your students, and for your love. Not only will I carry with me the lessons I have been granted during this semester, but I will also always remember you as a role model of healthy living, sincere interest in your work and your students, and the expression of genuine caring. Your living out of the words you impart to others, "Jai Bhagwan," has inspired me to embrace the radical transformation that has begun within me in order to be able to, as I see you do, breathe the divine with such peace and such profound joy.*

REFERENCES

Asby, D. (1986). *This Is School! Sit Down and Listen!* Amherst, MA: Human Resource Development Press.

Goleman, D. (1988). "Probing the Enigma of Multiple Personality" in *New York Times*, 28 June.

Houston, J. (1982). *The Possible Human.* Los Angeles, CA: Tarcher.

Krishnamurti, J. (1953). *Education and the Significance of Life.* New York: Harper.

Lawry, J. D. (1999). *College 101: A First-Year Reader.* New York: McGraw-Hill College, 2nd ed.

Montessori, M. (1970). *The Child in the Family.* New York: Avon.

Napier, N. (1992). Quoted in Susan Roberts, "Multiple Realities" in *Common Boundary*, May/June.

Neill, A.S. (1960). *Summerhill: A Radical Approach to Child Rearing.* New York: Hart.

——. (1973). Quoted in Ray Hemmings, *Children's Freedom: A. S. Neill and the Evolution of the Summerhill Idea.* New York: Schocken Books.

Noddings, N. and Shore, P. (1984) *Awakening the Inner Eye: Intuition in Education.* New York: Teachers College Press.

Palmer, P. (1983). *To Know As We Are Known: A Spirituality of Education.* New York: Harper & Row.

Pedley, R. (1963). *The Comprehensive School.* New York: Penguin.

Pestalozzi, J. H. (1970). Quoted in Ashley Montagu, *The Direction of Human Development.* New York: Hawthorn Books, rev. ed.

Richards, M. C. (1980). *Toward Wholeness: Rudolf Steiner Education in America.* Middletown, CT: Wesleyan University Press.

Rosenthal, R & Jackson, L. (1966). *Pygmalion in the Classroom: Expectation and Pupils' Intellectual Development.* New York: Holt, Rinehart & Winston.

Sivananda, S. "The Meaning of OM" in *Japa Yoga.*

Steiner, R. (1947). *Knowledge of the Higher Worlds and Its Attainments.* New York: Anthroposophic Press, 3rd ed.

VIDEOS

Hypnosis: Can Your Mind Control Your Body. (1982). Video produced by the British Broadcasting System.

M ention the word statistics as part of a required undergraduate curriculum in any major and listen to students groan. It often creates anxiety for even the best students enrolled in our institutions of higher education. Statistics often has a bad reputation as the "horrible course" of the required curriculum. It is usually because students from previous semesters testify to that campus legend of a difficult course. Other times, it is because of the anxiety associated with a fear of the math involved in the course. In either case, the myth of the horrible course needs to be dispelled.

If taught using imaginative methodology not limited to the traditional lecture and test format, statistics can be an opportunity for students to learn a great deal about math and even more about themselves. This author has worked with non-traditional and at-risk college students in two-year and four-year institutions for over sixteen years. She has taught statistics from the traditional lecture format and from a perspective grounded in Multiple Intelligence (MI) theory espoused by Howard Gardner (1993a, 1993b, 1999). Her students have consistently achieved higher grades when the instructor used alternative methods.

HOW AND WHY OF MI

The question under consideration in this paper is why and how should we incorporate MI Theory in higher education? Methodology courses in Kindergarten through grade twelve (K-12) often advocate the use of MI as a means of differentiating instruction for students. It is also used to enable students to learn something new through their stronger forms of intelligence and to enhance their weaker forms of intelligence. In higher education, MI can be used to do the following:

- Accommodate different populations present in the same classroom,
- Encourage collaboration and teamwork among students,
- Use a project-based focus to help reduce competition between students,
- Help to reduce anxiety,
- Enable students to demonstrate mastery in different ways, and
- Develop confidence in math through the use of one's stronger multiple intelligences.

This technique was used in an *Introduction to Statistics* course at a small college. At the completion of this course in basic statistics students were able to apply, interpret, calculate or use:

- Elementary descriptive and inferential statistics,
- Fundamental probability concepts,
- Measures of central tendency and dispersion,
- Confidence intervals,
- Hypothesis testing about a population from a sample, and
- Basic concepts of correlation and regression analysis.

Since these course objectives were broad in nature, it was easier for the author to take an innovative approach to the course.

STATISTICS, GROANS AND MULTIPLE INTELLIGENCES

SUSAN M. PERLIS

The primary instructional activities were adapted from K-12 pedagogy. Lectures were not eliminated from the course but minimized. The instructor provided mini-lectures that then enabled students to move to group centered activities to explore concepts. Instructional focus became much more learner-centered and constructivist in nature. One of the primary group activities used was simple problem solving. Usually done in pairs, students would work on a problem similar to the one presented by the instructor. This significantly reduced the stress in students who were anxious about math. Knowing that they did not have to work alone enabled them to relax and concentrate on understanding how the problem was solved and the correct answer arrived at. The old saying "two heads are better than one" clearly enabled most students to gain confidence.

PREPARING FOR GROUP ACTIVITIES

In order to prepare students for working in pairs and in groups, the instructor adapted techniques from Kagan & Kagan (1998, 2000), leaders in the development of cooperative group and multiple intelligences pedagogy for K-12 teachers. The first activity students completed to prepare them for group work throughout the semester was done on the first day of class. The instructor adapted a Kagan & Kagan (1998) exercise called "A Little About Me." Students were divided into small groups where they completed a short handout about themselves: Name, major, activities on campus, activities off campus, something they would like us to know about them, fears and concerns about this class, what they would like in terms of support from their classmates in this course, and what they would like in terms of support from their instructor. They shared these with each other and talked about their goals for the course. The instructor then used this information to create permanent groups of students and sub-pairs of students.

NUMBERED HEADS TOGETHER

Two group activities that worked particularly well were "Numbered Heads Together" and "Rally Coach" (both Kagan & Kagan, 2000). In Numbered Heads Together, the instructor asks the class a question or poses a problem. Working in their assigned groups, students consult to make sure everyone knows the answer. Then one student from the group is called upon to give it. This technique is particularly well suited to higher education because it teaches students how to work in teams. It reduces competition because members are responsible for each other's learning. This is a valuable skill that transfers to the world of work for students upon graduation.

THE RALLY COACH TECHNIQUE

In "Rally Coach," students once again work in their assigned groups on solving a particular problem. One person in the group attempts to solve the problem while others in the group coach, that is offer advise and encouragement. Group members take turns solving and coaching until all members can solve the problem. This technique is particularly well-suited in mixed ability groups. In other group activities the stronger students often take the lead and do all of the work for the other students, while the other students who did not have to do the actual work may never learn the skill. In the Rally Coach technique, however all students need to learn to solve the problem and all benefit from the (1) coaching of their peers and (2) increasing the ability to coach their peers through the process. This author feels that group work is an essential part of the learning process because it teaches skills related to team building and interpersonal relationships between students—two essential skills for survival in the world of work, but often never addressed in a traditional lecture environment in higher education.

SPECIFIC MI STRATEGIES

The following strategies were used by this author in teaching an introductory course in statistics. The levels of students varied in each course section, depending on their majors and their year in school. Classes typically contained students from all majors requiring statistics as part of their undergraduate major and from all levels—first-year through seniors. The techniques worked well with all students and were also used in another math course that the author taught in mathematical reasoning.

1. VERBAL/LINGUISTIC STRATEGIES

Students are very comfortable with Verbal/Linguistic

strategies. These are traditional lectures, class discussion and a commonly used strategy called "Exit Pass." The latter is simply an index card that students complete on their way out of class (saving the last one or two minutes of class for this activity) that tells the instructor what they learned that day. After class, instructors can immediately assess if the students learned what they were supposed to.

2. LOGICAL/MATHEMATICAL STRATEGIES

There are four primary strategies that this author used involving Logical/Mathematical Intelligences. Traditional question and answer techniques are the easiest ways to determine if students have mastered a concept or to pose a question for students to work on together or in pairs. "What-If Case Analysis" gives students the opportunity to work with data and analyze it according to predetermined questions posed by the instructor. Numbered Heads Together—described above—allows students to process the problem together, ensuring that all students know and can explain the answer. Rally Coach enables students to work on a problem independently, but having the benefit of peer coaching to help them move past stumbling blocks that would have prevented them from completing the problem on their own.

3. VISUAL/SPATIAL STRATEGIES

The instructor regularly provided chapter outlines and/or concept maps at the beginning of each new chapter or topic under study. This helped to organize the student's thoughts about the sequence and focus of materials. Graphs and charts were used almost on a daily basis. These can be done by hand on the blackboard, flip chart paper, overheads or computer. While computers can make easy work of sophisticated graphical representation of statistical data, the other methods can produce excellent examples to help students picture the concepts under study. Visual supports preferred by this instructor were the blackboard, overhead projector, newsprint, markers and cartoons. By not relying solely on the computer or graphing calculators, students learned more about the actual process of doing math.

4. MUSICAL/RHYTHMIC STRATEGIES

The author readily admits that Musical Intelligence is not one of her strengths; however, background music was often used in the class to help foster a climate conducive to group activities and to reduce anxiety. Students were surprised at first at the use of music in the math classroom, but quickly became accustomed to it. Students often included music in their group projects at the end of the semester.

5. BODILY/KINESTHETIC STRATEGIES

Experiential learning was the primary Bodily/Kinesthetic strategy used by the instructor. Decks of cards were used to help the students understand the basic tenets of probability. Students also had the opportunity to conduct simulations in the forms of taste tests and surveys to gather data sets which were then manipulated and analyzed.

6. NATURALIST STRATEGIES

The main naturalist strategy employed in this class was observation. Students constructed data sets by observing data in the field. They then had the opportunity to compare data sets.

7. INTERPERSONAL STRATEGIES

The group activities of Numbered Heads Together and Rally Coach were used on a regular basis. Students also did Paired Problem Solving, where they worked in sub-teams of two to solve longer problems or to do homework activities. Group projects and a group presentation were another facet of interpersonal strategies used in this course.

8. INTRAPERSONAL STRATEGIES

A statistics journal was occasionally used to promote Intrapersonal Intelligence. It varied by the class group from semester to semester. When students did keep a journal, it was a great help to stress reduction. The instructor periodically collected journals from students who wanted feedback, although it was not a class requirement to do so.

EVALUATION ACTIVITIES

Most students think of evaluation in a math course as taking tests, usually in a one-hour time frame, which may actually create a great deal of the anxiety. The instructor asked students about their fears and concerns about taking a math course on the first day of every class, and most often the fear of taking tests was at the top of their lists. After using class-based tests for several years, the instructor decided to break from them. She had already permitted students to use their notes, textbook, and a calculator during in-class examinations. The only constraint upon students was time. This was dropped and students were permitted to keep their examinations for forty-eight hours. Students did sign a statement of academic integrity before leaving with the examination indicating that they were to speak to no one about the examination, and that any case of suspected cheating would rest with the instructor and would result in a failing grade. In a two-year period, only one student was confronted and admitted to cheating.

In-class evaluation activities included problem solving, mini-lectures with discussion, practice group interpretation projects, and general class participation. Out-of-class evaluation activities included individual take-home tests, an individual Reading/Writing assignment, a group interpretation assignment, and a group semester project. For the individual Reading/Writing assignment, students were to select a quantitative refereed journal article from their major field of study and analyze the article with particular empha-

sis on statistics. This helped students to begin to review literature in their field, to become familiar with refereed journals in their field, and to spend time on the statistics reported. Group interpretation projects varied each semester and were provided by the instructor. At least one of them each semester addressed issues of diversity including issues of race, gender, and social class discrimination in the United States. Students read the material and then answered questions posed by the instructor which supported their analysis of the materials provided. Thus, diversity issues were incorporated into the math curriculum.

THE GROUP SEMESTER PROJECTS

The group semester project enabled students to select a project that they worked on throughout the semester. A list of potential projects was provided by the instructor, but students were encouraged to develop their own. All of the projects had to demonstrate how statistics were used in the "real world." Students were very creative in the choice and development of their projects, which included the calculation and reporting of basketball statistics, gambling in professional sports, and average tipping in a variety of restaurants where students worked in the area.

The following grade breakdown was used in this statistics course:

Test 1—20%, Test 2—20%, Test 3—20%, Reading/Writing Assignment—15%, Interpretation Assignments—10%, Group Project—10%, and Class Participation—5%. However, in future classes, this instructor would change this grade breakdown to put greater emphasis on the projects that related to the daily class work. The following breakdown is recommended: Test 1—15%, Test 2—15%, Test 3—15%, Reading/Writing Assignment—15%, Interpretation Assignments—15%, Group Project—20%, and Class Participation—5%.

CONCLUSION

The use of Multiple Intelligences in higher education holds promise as a means of equalizing the playing field for all students. As we look at the changing demographics of our campuses, with more non-traditional students attending, and increasing students from diverse backgrounds, it is our responsibility as college and university professors to adapt our teaching strategies to incorporate the different ways of knowing and learning of our students. This course in statistics evolved over the four years that this author taught it. Just when it was maturing, the author left to take a position at another university teaching graduate education students. However, this author remains committed to what she learned in this pedagogical process and uses the same techniques for her master's and doctoral students.

REFERENCES

Gardner, H. (1993a). *Frames of Mind: The Theory of Multiple Intelligences* (10th Anniversary ed.). New York: Basic Books.

—. (1993b). *Multiple Intelligences: The Theory in Practice.* New York: Basic Books.

—. (1999). *Intelligence Reframed: Multiple Intelligences for the 21st Century.* New York: Basic Books.

Kagan, S. & Kagan, M. (1998). *Multiple Intelligences: The Complete MI Book.* San Clemente, CA: Kagan Publishing.

Kagan, L. & Kagan, S. (2000). *Cooperative Learning Course Workbook.* San Clemente, CA: Kagan Publishing.

To truly benefit from the instructional opportunities of the in-service curriculum, educators need to engage affectively as well as cognitively in the learning process (Persi, 1997; Mead, 1992; Lortie, 1975). Jersild (1970) claimed that the crucial test in meaningful education is the personal implication of what we learn and teach. Furthermore, learning needs to fit into the fabric of life in a significant and useable way (Jesild). Interactive bibliotherapy (IB)—the interactive reading of written materials and related artifacts to foster intrapersonal growth—allows teachers to merge their affective and cognitive resources. In so doing, a more productive and satisfying version of in-service education may occur.

READING ALOUD AS INTERACTIVE BIBLIOTHERAPY

IB involves participants and facilitators to examine written materials using such techniques as discussions, journal writing, and reader response (Morawski & Gilbert, 2000). The process of IB can also take place via read-alouds. In fact, reading aloud carefully selected texts to students allows them to make academic and personal connections to the subject matter (Axiotis, 2000), and can foster their personal and intellectual growth (Giorgis & Johnson, 1999; Richardson, 1994). For example, in her graduate course with 20 practicing teachers, Richardson read aloud to them on a regular basis and found that these teachers enjoyed being exposed to new works and made personal connections to them. As a result, these teachers read aloud to their own students more frequently.

In another example, Colvin (1994) read aloud from a children's picture book to encourage new teachers to begin articulating a formal teaching philosophy. The children's text, which featured a boy's discovery of an inspirational adult in his life, helped the novice teachers identify and reflect on the individuals who influenced their own learning. Colvin found that the read-aloud activity prompted the teachers to consider the different influences that affected their own classroom practices. Finally, Daisey (1993) employed reading aloud with pre-service teachers to allow them to experience content area literacy while they made intrapersonal connections to a variety of subjects. More specifically, teacher candidates selected content specific passages, such as a speech delivered by Einstein or a letter written by Picasso, to read to their classmates during class time. Daisey claimed that "the read-aloud activity encouraged students to discover and turn to literacy as a resource for social, intellectual, and emotional growth" (p. 439). Recently a study on IB read-alouds was conducted with teacher education graduate students in an effort to foster their affective and cognitive growth. The purpose of this paper is to present the results of that study.

METHODOLOGY

PARTICIPANTS

Forty-one in-service teachers in the Faculty of Education at a Canadian university volunteered to partici-

READING ALOUD: A COMPELLING PATH TO AFFECTIVE AND COGNITIVE GROWTH

CYNTHIA M. MORAWSKI
AND JENELLE N. GILBERT

EDITOR'S NOTE: *Although I lasted only one semester at a Catholic seminary, one of the most memorable of practices was listening to well-chosen books read aloud during part of the mid-day meal. The responsibility of reading changed from student to student every day. I remember that I was as interested in this oral delivery of text as I was in the food—well, almost. Never before or after have I encountered public reading, until I tried it recently in one of my classes. It transformed us. I was almost shocked to find the attention of the class united and focused. I look forward to seeing the place that reading aloud occupies in my class as the semesters pass.*

pate in the current study. The participants were enrolled in either a graduate course on special education (N=24) or integrated language curriculum (N=17) as part of the requirements for a Master's Degree in Education. Traditionally, the majority of the in-service teachers work full-time in the elementary or secondary levels or may work in the schools in another related function (e.g., speech-language pathologist or guidance counselor).

PROCEDURE

To ensure consistency in the read-aloud process, the same instructor taught both courses, each of which consisted of thirteen weekly three-hour sessions. Individual sessions focused on a particular topic such as "creativity" and "Multiple Intelligences" for the special education course, and "reading narratives" and "content literacy" for the language curriculum course. In preparation for each class, teachers read assigned material. To supply opportunities for teachers to engage both cognitively and affectively in the particular class topics, the course instructor used IB in the form of read-alouds. For approximately thirty to forty-five minutes at the beginning of each class, the teachers listened and responded to selections read aloud by the course instructor. Immediately before reading the selection, the instructor provided the teachers with optional guiding questions to encourage their reflection on the work. For example, as the teachers listened to a brief essay about the early school difficulties of a performing artist (Vail, 1987), they referred to the following questions, which were based on McTeague's (1987) approach to reader response:

- What feelings do you experience?
- What's going on in your mind?
- What do you expect to happen?
- What questions occur to you?
- What are you thinking about?
- What images regarding differences and education does this essay present?

When the teachers listened to an Emily Dickinson poem on the mind that Hallowell (1995) recommended for addressing attention deficit hyperactivity disorder (ADHD), they responded simply by generating their own questions on any aspect of the piece (Leggo, 1991). As a way of connecting the teachers to the themes of a picture book on intergenerational literacy (Bunting, 1989), the course instructor first read the initial sentence and then invited the teachers to produce any possible questions or comments (Ash, 1992). For all read-alouds, the teachers then discussed their responses with a partner or in small groups, which the students arranged at the beginning of each class. With a few exceptions, the membership of these groups remained the same throughout the semester. At the end of the smaller-format interaction, the whole class came together to continue the discussion. To collect data in both classes, a trained research assistant administered the following anonymous questionnaire toward the end of the thirteen-week semester.

THE QUESTIONNAIRE

The questionnaire took approximately 15 to 20 minutes to complete. The course instructor was not present at the time of the questionnaire's administration. The questionnaire data were broken into individual meaningful segments of text called meaning units. The second author then analyzed the meaning units and developed a list of emergent themes. After examining the list independently, the authors met to discuss the placement of the meaning units, and the emergent themes. The authors were in complete agreement. A discussion of the emergent themes follows.

THE QUESTIONNAIRE: THE USE OF READ-ALOUDS IN THE COURSE

In order to continue to improve both the content and delivery of the course, your comments on the use of bibliotherapy in the form of read-alouds would be greatly appreciated. Here, bibliotherapy refers to the guided reading of written materials for gaining professional knowledge and self-understanding through critical inquiry.

The following questions have been included to help guide your responses.

1. Gender   F   M

2. Into which division or divisions do your primary teaching responsibilities fall?
   Primary (Grades K-3)   Junior (Grades 4-6)
   Intermediate (Grades 7-10)   Senior (Grades 11-)
   Post-Secondary (Specify)_____
   Other _____.

3. If applicable, indicate your teaching subject major (e.g., special education, History, English, mathematics, etc.). If you include more than one major, specify the one that you consider to be your primary responsibility _____.

4. Please comment on the appropriateness and effectiveness of the readings (at the beginning of each class) for facilitating your own personal and professional development.

RESULTS AND DISCUSSION

In addition to taking one or more courses in the evening, most of the teachers in this study worked full-time. An eight-hour (or longer) day providing educational support for children made it difficult for the teachers to make a psychological transition from their workday to the class. Many of the teachers in this study found that the read-alouds enabled them to make a conscious shift from their daily professional responsibilities to the learning opportunities in the evening class. As noted by one teacher: "The readings were appropriate and effective in that they helped to focus my thoughts on the class ahead rather than the day at work. It was important to have the readings as an official part of each class—this added to the effectiveness."

Another teacher commented that "The anecdotes and readings, which the professor shared with the class, were helpful for me in terms of orienting myself initially for the class." The transition and introduction into the class resulting from the read-alouds was very important because "the personal discovery of meaning does not occur...where the self is regarded as intruder" (Combs, Blume, Newman, and Wass; 1974, p.37).

READ-ALOUDS GROUND THE CLASS

Although most of the teachers interacted with children in some capacity, their type of work varied extensively. The readings at the beginning of class served to unite the teachers as they began to focus their thoughts. One teacher commented that, "These [readings] represented an informal, stimulating way of 'grounding' the class cohesively at the beginning of our work together. I feel that these were a very useful device which offered us a starting point for each evening's session." Another teacher noted that the "Readings are rich in thought and feeling. They provided a grounding experience and tone for the class. I often wanted to hear more." These responses reflect Hebb's (2000) notion of a learning community that stems from collective reading. She acknowledged that "all readers need an environment that is safe, supportive, and encouraging" (p. 22).

CONNECTING TO INDIVIDUAL LIVES

Another major theme that emerged from the data was that the teachers found the readings to be "real" and could relate to them on a practical level. As noted by one teacher, "The readings are very pertinent...Often we get caught up in the textbook-talk and theory-thinking mode. These readings bring us down to reality." Another teacher commented that "I find it much easier to understand concepts-theories if they are made real." According to Barrentine (1996), the purpose of reading aloud has expanded to include instructional purposes such as obtaining content knowledge and strategy information. Barrentine, however, also embraces the concept that read-alouds can connect this learning to individuals' lives.

In one particular case, a teacher found the readings to be engaging, but had some concerns about their use in the class. This teacher stated, "I thought they were—not frivolous, but peripheral to the significant issues of literacy. Because I am more ignorant and inexperienced in literacy teaching issues, I would have liked them to be more 'central', but they were interesting." As a way to deal with this issue, Van Horn (2000) invited her students to select and read aloud their own material to their classmates. Upon reviewing the application of this practice in her classroom, two main results were found. First, the readers and the listeners began to achieve connections between their academic and personal selves; and second, the students were more fully engaged in the read-aloud process. Direct

involvement in the construction of the read-aloud component would apparently benefit the teachers who need extra encouragement as well as those who appear more confident in their learning. Combs et al. (1974) asserted that the self is more likely to change if it is permitted to become an integral part of the learning process.

EXPOSURE TO RESOURCES

Most teachers are constantly searching for new resources to motivate their students to learn. The read-aloud sessions provided the teachers with opportunities to explore new material. As noted by one teacher, "I really liked having the sharing sessions. There are so many good ideas out there that need to be passed on." Another educator commented that she or he found the "exposure to different children's literature interesting." Following many of the read-aloud sessions, the instructor provided a list of additional resources related to the theme of the class. The teachers appreciated this extra support for their learning. One teacher remarked, "I did like the list provided as follow-up on the chalk-board." Even with the additional information, one participant felt that even more resources would be effective and stated, "It would be nice to have a choice of books to read that would apply to different levels (e.g., junior, primary school, adults, etc)."

HELPING LISTENERS INTERACT

Giorgis and Johnson (1999) claimed that what teachers hold in their hands can help listeners interact, laugh, discuss, and live through the power of literature. In an effort to help teachers in this capacity, they have provided an annotated bibliography of children's books that support strategies for sharing literature aloud in powerful and meaningful ways. Teachers can also find additional collections of read-alouds and related strategies in the professional literature. For example, Giorgis (1999) recommends picture books for reading aloud to secondary students while Bloem and Padak (1996) as well as Sharp (1991) advocate children's works for adult education.

Non-fiction, such as true adventure stories, autobiographies, and descriptive pieces, also provide numerous possibilities for learning by way of read-alouds. Doiron (1994) supports this and emphasized that a balanced literacy program should include "the literature of fiction as well as the literature of fact" (p. 623). In fact, as children mature, their reading preferences gravitate toward non-fiction (Carter and Abrahamson, 1991). Finally, Doiron as well as Carter and Abrahamson present a wealth of information on the reading aloud of non-fiction to learners of all ages. The "Read It Aloud" column of *The Journal of Adolescent and Adult Literacy*, which features possibilities for read-alouds that represent a variety of subjects such as second language learning (Richardson & Carleton, 1996), and the understanding of the notion of circumference (Richardson & Gross, 1997), would also be an excellent starting point for locating non-fiction read-aloud material.

CONSTRUCTING PERSONAL AND PROFESSIONAL REALITY

The recognition and integration of self in the learning process requires human nourishment and affirmation through interpersonal communication (Moustakas, 1971). The read-aloud sessions at the beginning of the class facilitated support for this process by first capturing the teachers' interests. For example, one teacher commented that the instructor's readings "were intriguing and thought provoking." The subsequent class discussions then provided a forum in which the teachers could openly explore their responses with the rest of the class. As noted by one teacher, "The class discussions that followed added to what could have been viewed as an unrelated 'filler.' Class members willingly contributed and shared their experiences, personal stories, etc." These discussions, however, can also be viewed as far more important than filler. When teachers explore how the present situation links to their own prior experiences, they are able to engage in reflective learning (Colton & Sparks-Langer, 1993). Perl (1994) asserts that teachers who read and talk together are in a better position to step back critically and construct the personal and professional reality of their lives in the classroom.

A SOURCE OF MOTIVATION

The final category emerging from the data related to motivation. Carter and Abrahamson (1991) underscored the importance of teachers knowing the pleasures, educational benefits and motivational power associated with reading good books. Relevant research, however, finds many teachers disengaged from personal reading (Dillingofski, 1993; Otto, 1992/1993; Williamson, 1991). Some of the comments of the teachers in the current study indicated that the integration of a read-aloud component in their in-service education had the potential to instill a desire to make reading a more regular part of their lives. Several teachers in the current study felt that their interaction with the readings had motivated them. According to one teacher, "There were plenty of opportunities, suggested readings to motivate further reading. Seeing the actual books is a motivation." For at least one teacher, the motivation translated into action. This teacher stated, "I was even inspired to find a couple of these books in the library!" The in-service teachers, in a week-long summer institute on writing, reacted similarly to the teachers in this study when their course instructor read *Missing May* (Rylant, 1992) to them

each morning (Wood, 1994). After having lived and loved the book through the read-aloud process, many of the teachers felt compelled to buy their own copies of the novel.

CONCLUDING COMMENTS

To take full advantage of in-service opportunities, teachers need to approach their learning both intrapersonally and intellectually. When teachers and students enter literature and related texts, they author their coming together, and the classroom becomes a place in which they not only compose and respond to texts, but also themselves (Perl, 1994). The self-knowledge obtained from such an interaction is an essential ingredient in the development of teachers who, according to Moustakas (1967), can make effective use of their own personal and professional potentialities for facilitating significant learning in their students. The preliminary findings of this study, derived from the teachers' responses to their participation in the read-aloud component, underlines the potential of IB for facilitating affective and cognitive growth in in-service teachers. The integration of read-alouds in the in-service curriculum deserves further implementation and investigation.

REFERENCES

Ash, B. (1992). "Student-Made Question: One Way into a Literary Text" in *English Journal*, **81**, 61-64.

Axiotis, V. (2000). "Creating a Community of Readers" in *English Journal*, **89**, 23-25.

Barrentine, S. (1996). "Engaging with Reading through Interactive Read-Alouds" in *The Reading Teacher*, **50**, 36-43.

Bloem, P. & Padak, N. (1996). "Picture Books, Young Adult Books, and Adult Literacy Learners" in *Journal of Adolescent and Adult Literacy*, **40**, 48-53.

Bunting, E. (1989). *The Wednesday Surprise*. New York: Clarion.

Carter, B., & Abrahamson, R. (1991). "Nonfiction in a Read-Aloud Program" in *Journal of Reading*, **34**, 638-642.

Colton, A. & Sparks-Langer, G. (1993). "A Conceptual Framework to Guide the Development of Teacher Reflection and Decision Making" in *Journal of Teacher Education*, **44**, 45-54.

Colvin, C. (1994). "Using Images from Literature to Compose a Philosophy for Teaching" in *Journal of Reading*, **37**, 682-683.

Combs, A., Blume, R., Newman, A. & Wass, H. (1974). *The Professional Education of Teachers: A Humanistic Approach to Teacher Preparation*. Boston: Allyn and Bacon.

Daisey, P. (1993). "Three Ways to Promote the Values and Uses of Literacy at any Age" in *Journal of Reading*, **36**, 436-440.

Dillingofski, M. (1993). "Turning Teachers into Readers: The Teachers as Readers Project" *School Library Journal*, **39**, 31-33.

Doiron, R. (1994). "Using Nonfiction in a Reading-Aloud Program: Letting the Facts Speak for Themselves" in *The Reading Teacher*, **47**, 616-624.

Giorgis, C. (1999). "The Power of Reading Picture Books Aloud to Secondary Students" in *The Clearning House*, **73**, 51-53.

Giorgis, C., & Johnson, N. (1999). "Reading Aloud" in *The Reading Teacher*, **53**, 80-87.

Hallowell, E. & Ratey, J. (1995). *Driven to Distraction*. New York: Simon & Schuster.

Hebb, J. (2000). "Toward a Learning Community of Teachers and Students" in *English Journal*, **89**, 22-23.

Jersild, A. (1970). *When Teachers Face Themselves*. New York: Teachers College Press.

Leggo, C. (1991). "The Reader as Problem-Maker: Responding to a Poem with Questions" in *English Journal*, **80**, 58-60.

Lortie, D. (1975). *Schoolteacher: A Sociological Study*. Chicago: The University of Chicago Press.

McTeague, F. (1987). *Response to Literature*. Toronto, ON: Ontario Ministry of Education.

Mead, J. (1992). "Looking at Old Photographs: Investigating the Teacher Tales that Novice Teachers Bring with Them" (Report No. NCRTL-RR-92). Washington, D.C.: Office of Educational Research and Improvement (ERIC Document Reproduction Service No. ED 346 082)

Morawski, C. & Gilbert, J. N. (2000). "Interactive Bibliotherapy as an Innovative Inservice Practice: A Focus on the Inclusive Setting" in *Reading Horizons*, **41**, 47-64.

Moustakas, C. (1967). *The Authentic Teacher: Sensitivity and Awareness in the Classroom*. Cambridge, MA: Howard Doyle.

—. (1971). *Personal Growth: The Struggle for Identity and Human Values*. Cambridge, MA: Howard A. Doyle.

Otto, W. (1992/1993). "Readers R Us" in *Journal of Reading*, **36**, 318-320.

Perl, S. (1994). "Composing Texts, Composing Lives" in *Harvard Educational Review*, **64**, 427-449.

Persi, J. (1997). "When Emotionally Troubled Teachers Refer Emotionally Troubled Students" in *The School Counselor*, **44**, 344-352.

Richardson, J. (1994). "Great Read-Alouds for Prospective Teachers and Secondary Students" *Journal of Reading*, **38**, 98-103.

Richardson, J. & Carleton, L. (1996). A Read-Aloud for Students of English as a Second Language" in *Journal of Adolescent and Adult Literacy*, **40**, 140-143.

Richardson, J. & Gross, E. (1997). A Read-Aloud for Mathematics" in *Journal of Adolescent and Adult Literacy*, **40**, 492-494.

Rylant, C. (1992). *Missing May*. New York: Bantom

Sharp, P. (1991). "Picture Books in the Adult Literacy Curriculum" in Journal of *Reading*, **35**, 216-219.

Vail, P. (1987). *Smart Kids with School Problems*. New York: E.P. Dutton.

Van Horn, L. (2000). "Sharing Literature, Sharing Selves: Students Reveal Themselves through Read-Alouds" in *Journal of Adolescent and Adult Literacy*, **43**, 752-763.

Williamson, J. (1991). "Teachers as Readers" *Reading,* 30-38.

Wood, K. (1994). "Hearing Voices, Telling Tales: Finding the Power of Reading Aloud" in *Language Arts*, **71**, 346-349.

Discovery consists of seeing what everybody has seen and thinking what nobody has thought.
Attributed to Albert Szent-Gyorgyi
by J. D. Bernal, 1962.

"The best thing for being sad" replied Merlyn, beginning to puff and blow, "is to learn something. That is the only thing that never fails. You may grow old and trembling in your anatomies, you may lie awake at night listening to the disorder of your veins, you may miss your only love, you may see the world about you devastated by evil lunatics, or know your honour trampled in the sewers of baser minds. There is only one thing for it then—to learn."

Merlyn, advising the young Arthur,
from *The Once and Future King* by T.H. White

USING SMALL GROUPS AND RESEARCH PROJECTS TO TEACH SCIENCE

JANICE MARCHUT CONRAD
AND PETER L. CONRAD

EDITOR'S NOTE: *This paper is very much a specific and rich de facto endorsement of Howard Gardner's keynote address, which appears on page 1 of this volume. Dr. Gardner zeroes in on the importance of teaching for understanding and not for the simple fact of having covered a particular body of information.*

INTRODUCTION

Merlyn's advice to young Arthur is affixed to a wall in the lab and each fall the students troupe in, plunk down in a seat clutching their backpacks and seem to dare me to make it happen for them. I tell them that I'm not sure what their previous experience has been, but this experience is likely to be different. We don't do canned labs, labs last for approximately three hours and students are expected to learn by doing. By the end of the fourth week, they have learned to rely on each other to some degree and have designed and executed an experiment. They have also presented their results, group by group, in a poster format seminar to their lab mates, and they now know that are expected to learn by doing.

TEACHING SCIENCE IN AN INTRODUCTORY GENERAL EDUCATION BIOLOGY COURSE

Higher education must not simply be about knowledge-based instruction where students are passive receivers of material. It can never be truer than now, with the advance of electronic information systems, that there is an overabundance of facts. So, the student who comes to us thinking that higher education is about acquiring more information doesn't really understand the campus-based experience that offers many more possibilities for connected learning and understanding. However, students are often not prepared to learn in introductory courses. They come directly from high school where the emphasis is on being taught, as opposed to learning to integrate knowledge and to make it available for problem solving. In short, the students arrive on campus prepared for their role as receivers of information.

In this article we describe in detail a course that is designed to teach students both passive and active knowledge. A statistical study on the performance of students and comments from them add depth to our theories concerning pedagogy. It should be added that the integration of knowledge aimed at is the kind Gardner mentioned in his

keynote address at the conference at New Jersey City University on which this essay is based. It was rewarding to learn of these parallels, which strengthen our conviction that we are on the right track.

THE SHORTSIGHTED FOCUS ON FACTS

In a recent article "Reintroducing the Intro Course," Stokstad states that the only science exposure most college students get is in an introductory course that is usually taken for general education credit. Most leave without any understanding of how science works, and most often their exposure is to the stalest form of pedagogy—the lecture. Often lectures emphasize facts with little time given to developing concepts and understanding of processes. Nowhere is this probably more evident than in a standard introductory biology course that focuses on a plethora of information rather than depth of knowledge and understanding (Stokstad, 2001).

Passing grades may not reflect learning. If exams are properly constructed, you can demonstrate to yourself the difference between what students have been taught, what they know, and what they have learned. For example, if information is given in a graph, students very often cannot see the information in a way that allows them to successfully deal with the question. However, they may have been able to answer another question, that asks for a description or definition, and addresses the essence of the knowledge that they do not recognize or understand in unfamiliar form (Bello *et al*, 2001). After being taught, does the student possess knowledge? We know that they do. Does the student understand what he/she knows? At the beginning, we would say, not often. The most difficult hurdle is convincing the student of biology that memorization of facts, formulas and plugging of numbers into equations is not learning. Seeing the connections between things and knowing what is useful and what is probably not requires an understanding. If they are only taught to know, then they are always looking for the place where information is plugged in.

LEARNING TO LEARN

General Biology I (Bio 101) lecture exams are open notebook (lecture and laboratory) essays and problem solving, and the questions address the student's ability to use information to synthesize answers and apply knowledge. The anger, frustration and hostility this engenders are evident after the first exam. The usual comments are "you never ask us anything that we know" and "the material on the exam was never covered in the book or in lecture." We know that they come to this conclusion because they are accustomed to memorizing and repeating. By the end of the semester, a majority of the students realize that they have learned how to learn and come up with solutions to open-ended problems. However, initially they feel that the exams are unfair. We conclude that they do not understand the distinction between what they know and what they understand. In short, the time and effort of both the students and their teachers is largely wasted. This article will present ways of avoiding this unfortunate situation.

PASSIVE AND ACTIVE KNOWLEDGE

At a recently held State University of New York (SUNY–wide) General Education assessment conference, Nassau Community College faculty gave a presentation (Bello *et al*, 2001) that made us think about the format of our exams. We realized that the first exams should contain a few knowledge-based questions—the type of question that they were probably used to—so that they might feel some measure of accomplishment in being able to answer those questions. Accordingly, a week before the lecture exam, a quiz was given in lab where the first two questions required

that the students demonstrate knowledge and the second two required that they use that knowledge. The knowledge-based questions addressed the graph (Figure 1) that shows the relationship between dye binding to increasing amounts of protein and the correlative absorption of light by the protein-dye complex. In the first part of the quiz, most students could correctly state that portion C of the curve is not useable because there is no correlative increase in light absorption relative to increasing amounts of protein. Yet in the second part of the quiz—when students are asked to use such a curve, and they are given two numerical values, one that falls on the A part of the curve and requires an additional calculation, and one that falls on the C part of the curve and requires no additional operations—the majority of the students chose the C value.

After reviewing the outcome of the lab quiz, where the average grade for all four lab sections was failing, it was determined that for the most part students gave a passing performance on the first two questions, but as a whole were not able to deal with the second two. They were then told that the first two questions were given to test what they knew, the second two were given to test what they understood. They were also informed that lecture exams would have a similar built-in assessment relative to passive knowledge and active understanding. This fall we included questions that addressed what the students knew (knowledge-based) and those that demonstrated what they learned (ability to use and apply). The lecture exam format remained essay and problem solving, and students could use their lecture and laboratory notes during the exam.

The results given (Table 1) clearly indicate that although the class attained a C minus average if the questions were knowledge based, they could not pass the learning based portion of the exam. Their asymmetrical performance in both lab and lecture tells us that they have been taught but have not yet learned. This interpretation at least allowed us to formulate a hypothesis which could account for our general observations.

FIGURE 1: LIGHT ABSORBANCE VERSUS PROTEIN CONCENTRATION

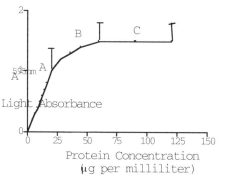

NOTE: *This graph was used in both knowledge-based questions and learning-based questions requiring the <u>use</u> of that knowledge.*

INVOLVEMENT AND LEARNING

It is probably fair to say that the educational community agrees in principle that the best learning takes place when students are involved in the learning experience. Nowhere is this probably more critical than in a freshmen introductory general education course predominantly populated with freshmen. As Tobias (1992) has pointed out, quality instruction in an environment that provides an opportunity for exploration and discovery is of vital importance. Departments should value the importance of introductory courses, and assignment of faculty to these courses should be carefully weighed. Fuentes (2001) emphasizes that introductory courses are often part of an institution's general education program and therefore a bridge to the public of the future. Here students are provided with an opportunity for discovery in a non-traditional lecture course where productive researchers participate in teaching freshmen and sophomores by integrating current research into the course. This allows the students to see that science is a process of inquiry where a hypothesis is rigorously tested and then accepted or rejected. Inviting the young student to participate in reviewing the work within the context of a formal course can be very beneficial to both the student and the instructor. Dennis Jacobs, a chemistry professor at Notre Dame University, got students to collaborate in the classroom by having them use cards to indicate an answer to a question and then to record the outcome. What made his approach welcome was that each student then had to turn to a classmate and defend that answer. The students who got the concept were quite successful in convincing the person sitting next to them of the more appropriate answer. This participatory classroom made the students start to think about concepts and the reason for choosing the answer instead of what the right answer is (Cox, 2001). The approaches of Fuentes and Jacobs are excellent examples of the kind of reform suggested by Stokstad.

THE IMPORTANCE OF COLLABORATIVE WORK

Ten years ago, a paper on active learning stated that students taught by individuals who transmit information are unlikely to rely on that knowledge in the future (Goodwin et al, 1991). They will in fact need to know how to participate in collaborative work and have good problem-solving skills that come from their active participation in the learning process. The authors concluded that biology majors received substantial benefit from the group project approach, which included information gathering and setting up experiments, when compared to freshmen participating in a standard lecture format course.

In 1989, we started conducting project-based experiential labs that made students learn how to teach themselves and each other (Marchut Conrad and Conrad, 1993). We expanded this way of knowing to an introductory general education biology course (*Bio 101*) and to an upper level research course (*Bio 490*). Like most introductory courses, *Bio 101* serves a wide audience. Although geared for majors, it is a general education course open to all students. This course follows a highly integrated lecture/laboratory format, but while most courses emphasize lecture, we emphasize laboratory, where students learn by doing. Collaborative learning, in which students are engaged in a project together, helps the students recognize what they do not understand and to work through the process together. They learn to rely on each other and on their own intelligence. If they listen and can repeat, then they have been *taught*. If they can also solve, design and apply, then they have *learned*.

DIFFERENT APPROACHES TO THINKING ABOUT BIOLOGY

Using the latest techniques and equipment does little

TABLE 1: EXAM CONSTRUCTION. KNOWLEDGE-BASED VS. LEARNING-BASED QUESTIONS

Part A consisted of short answer, descriptive, or simple problem-solving questions.
Part B consisted of questions that students could choose from and that required them to apply knowledge and to synthesize answers.

EXAM	MEAN	STANDARD DEVIATION	TOTAL POSSIBLE POINTS	% CORRECT ANSWERS	N
Knowledge-based Questions					
1	28.2	7.19	40	70	70
2	29.2	5.86	40	73	67
3	20.8	6.77	30	70	66
Learning-based Questions					
1	25.7	8.66	60	43	70
2	37.7	11.61	60	63	67
3	39.2	15.44	70	56	66
Total Exam Questions					
1	53.8	14.50	100	54	70
2	66.91	16.00	100	66	67
3	60.0	22.23	100	60	66

good if it is perceived by the student as having magical rather than scientific qualities. After all, the purpose of science education is to promote an understanding of how the world works and curricula should foster a general awareness of our surroundings and enhance the wonder of how it comes together so well within the constraints of physical laws. Biology students should have wide exposure to other ways of looking at the world that include art, music, theater and literature in order to better appreciate a perspective of knowing that is biological, and to realize that biology is just one way to know the world. We try to address this through reading assignments. In addition to the technical material that students are required to read, this year we assigned two books, *Sacred Depths of Nature* (Goodenough, 1998) and *Climbing Mount Improbable* (Dawkins, 1996) for *Bio 101*. This literature introduces students to biology in a non-fact-oriented way and encourages them to think about "seeing" outside the context of the laboratory protocol.

IN-HOUSE EXERCISES AND EXPERIMENTS

All laboratory exercises and experiments are generated in-house. Prototype experiments with explicit protocols are tested and then provided to the students. The students run the experiment following protocols. They are expected to read assigned material before coming to the laboratory so that they have some sense as to the purpose of the experiment and the fundamental biological concepts being addressed. They run the experiment, and keep a careful record of what they do and results obtained. Then they write a proposal outlining a logical follow-up experiment to test a hypothesis that they formulate based on their reading and the outcome of the prototype experiment.

INTELLECTUAL PREPARATION FOR EXPERIMENTS

A paper in *Annual Review of Plant Physiology and Plant Molecular Biology*, (Harris, 2001) describes the eyespot and phototaxis of *Chlamydomonas reinhardtii*, and light measurement is addressed in *Practical Skills in Biomolecular Sciences* (Reed et al, 1998). An essay on "Awareness" is assigned from *Sacred Depths of Nature* (Goodenough, 1998) and "The Forty Fold Path to Enlightenment" (Dawkins, 1996) is assigned from *Climbing Mount Improbable*. The students are told that these readings should mentally prepare them before coming to laboratory. The majority of students do not do the reading before coming to the first "phototaxis" lab. When their questions are not answered directly and instead we discuss how an answer to the question is presented in the assigned reading, they begin to realize that they are expected to be more than receivers of information.

SMALL GROUPS AND RESEARCH PROJECTS TO TEACH SCIENCE

The first prototype experiment this year investigated the swimming response of a microscopic green alga, *Chlamydomonas reinhardtii,* when it is exposed to light. This directional swimming in response to light (towards the light or away from the light) is called phototaxis and vision in algal eyes is measured by unidirectional mobility in response to light. Vision within our own species, *Homo sapiens,* also relies on light sensing by rhodopsin. And although the *C. reinhardtii* and *H. sapiens* rhodopsin molecules are not entirely the same, they do share significant homology and the point is to get students to think about how much is involved between seeing the light and responding to it.

The students are asked to address parameters involved in the pathway from perception to reaction. This concept (signal transduction) is the basis of the student-designed experiment. They usually design three experiments during the semester and each student-designed experiment is followed by a group oral poster presentation. They begin the prototype experiment using a phototactic mutant, CC806, and do not know that it is a "seeing" mutant at the time of the initial experiment. They clearly determined that CC806 exhibited negative phototaxis, swimming away from the light source, regardless of light intensity whereas some of the other strains gave mixed results. Mixed results are often due to some cells not having flagella (they are dividing) or some respond by swimming toward and others away from the light because of uneven light intensities hitting the dish. More than one student concluded that CC806 must be a mutant because a photosynthetic cell exhibiting aversion to light could not live in the natural world. After an initial characterization of their cells, they have an in-place assay system. Then they outline a proposal designing an experiment that they will run during the next lab. Because this is also a writing assignment, each student turns in an individual proposal, but the proposals must outline the same experiment. This means that they must get together outside of class to discuss the results, review the reading and decide what to propose for a group experiment.

SOME QUESTIONS GIVEN FOR CONSIDERATION

Is aerobic respiration involved in phototaxis? Does the color of light that the cells see affect the response? Because calcium is involved in the phototactic response, can you affect external/internal calcium concentration and subsequently alter the characterized response to light? The students addressed their own experiment in one of two ways. *They looked at **perception** of the signal or **processing** of the signal.*

For example, they came up with the hypothesis that

not all colors of the visible spectrum will be perceived the same to give a swimming response and tested green, light red, dark red and blue filters. They found that cells subjected to blue and green filters responded similarly to control. This is because these filters let through colors, in the 460-560nm range, that are absorbed by rhodopsin, the sensing molecule. The red filters let very little of the correct light through so the cells did not respond to the stimulus. Because they knew that energy is required for flagella beating, they asked if inhibition of aerobic respiration (defined as making adenosine triphosphate (ATP) in the mitochondria) would prevent the swimming response. Also, *Chlamydomonas* swim using a breaststroke motion. Calcium fluxes are altered as light stimulus changes the conformation of the sensing molecule rhodopsin. Each flagellum responds to a different concentration of calcium by changing the beat, and this determines if the organism moves towards or away from continuous light. Students found that aerobic respiration was involved in processing the stimulus, and they altered available calcium by blocking calcium channels with lanthanum chloride, chelating calcium with ethylene glycol-bis (2-amino ethyl ether)—N,N,N',N'—tetra acetic acid (EGTA) and closing calcium channels with nifedipine. Their results proved that calcium is required for the processing of the light signal.

DISCUSSION

Through their own experiments, *Bio 101* students started to understand the basic principles that a stimulus is tied to the response, and that *Chlamydomonas* is a useful model to understand vision. In *Sacred Depths of Nature*, Goodenough (1998) states "a locus of human pride is our sense that we possess the capacity for a special kind of awareness, often called consciousness or self-awareness, that distinguishes us from the 'dumb creatures' over which we have been assured we 'have dominion'." As she so eloquently points out, awareness is regulated by receptors. The processing of a stimulus involves a series of biochemical events where smelling and tasting involve processing of molecular shapes; while hearing, touch and vision involve processing of energy absorption. Based on that definition of awareness, students are asked if *Chlamydomonas* is aware. If it is not, then how are we aware when we can show that our awareness is a result of using the same kinds of systems that are used by this photosynthetic unicellular alga? In essence, our capacities for awareness are processed and are molecularly similar to the "awareness" that must define all life once we realize how we come to be aware.

The environment for learning should be everywhere, and students can offer a rational explanation for how and why things are operational in the natural world by making the connection between themselves and other sentient and non-sentient organisms. Although students referred to the technical readings when talking about and designing their own experiments, they often got the same message from the literature assigned for the course. In thinking about algal vision, they take from Goodenough that "awareness is modulated by the receptors and their signal transduction cascades" (90) and from Dawkins "because photons travel fast and in straight lines, and they are absorbed or reflected by some material more than others, photons provide an opportunity for sensing technologies" (138-139).

To quote a student in this fall's science cluster, "although the subject material for both books is really biological, the books are written in a philosophical way." Both Goodenough and Dawkins gave this student perspective to try to understand how things work in biological systems. Group learning and exchange of ideas within the context of an experiential laboratory is a socializing experience. At the beginning of the semester, students don't even know the names of their group members. Then they get down to business, talk to each other and really begin to experience cooperative learning.

OUTCOMES AND EVALUATIONS

We provide instruction for all students enrolled in our *Bio 101* course so assignment of instructor is not a variable. We compared the course outcomes of freshmen enrolled in the Biology Science cluster, over a three-year period, versus the outcomes of freshmen interspersed within the remaining three laboratories during the same three years (Table 2). Table 3 (next page) outlines student responses to course format questions for General Biology laboratory. This biology learning community is an outcome of a National Science Foundation grant that we received in 1996 for "Improvement of Undergraduate Biology Laboratories in 'A Course Cluster

TABLE 2: FRESHMAN PERFORMANCE IN GENERAL BIOLOGY

How do the Freshman[1] Course Cluster Students compare, in course grades, to other freshman in the course?

Course Grade Average (%)

Year	Whole Class	Cluster	Other Freshman	Statistical Difference[2]?
1998	74	73	68	No
1999	77	86	72	Yes
2000	77	82	74	Yes

1. About 50% of students enrolled are freshman. In the three reported years, 42 of the 55 freshman in the biology cluster were biology majors while 38 of the 68 noncluster freshman were biology majors.
2. Two-walled t-test

Table 3: Student Responses to Course Evaluation Questions for the General Biology Lab

Scale: 1-5, 1 is a No and 5 is a Yes

A. Did the Instructor encourage you to think and to solve problems?

Year	Mean	Standard Deviation	N
1998	4.78[a]	0.456	63
1999	4.77[a]	0.721	60
2000	4.66[a]	0.617	67

a. Variation among means is not significant, $P=0.4453$ ANOVA

"This is a difficult class, anyone will tell you that, but it was conducted in such a manner that I felt what I learned for myself was the most important aspect."

"I think I learned more in this class than any other (college or H.S.) only because she made me WANT to learn and work."

"Thanks for not just handing us the answers."

B. Was this learning experience different from your previous learning experiences?

Year	Mean	Standard Deviation	N
1998	4.69[a]	0.589	62
1999	4.61[a]	0.842	61
2000	4.79[a]	0.478	67

a. Variation among means is not significant, $P=0.2747$ ANOVA

"This lab was different than most classes that I've had, the instructor encouraged us to take information we had learned and put it to use instead of just repeating it from memory. I thought it was harder, but in a good and challenging way."

"I learned a new way of looking at things."

"The instructors encouraged learning—something not many instructors do."

C. Did the instructor try to teach you in the same way scientists work in the field of biology?

Year	Mean	Standard Deviation	N
1998	4.40[a]	0.748	58
1999	4.70[a]	0.720	60
2000	4.61[a]	0.721	66

a. Variation among means is not significant, $P=0.0722$ ANOVA

"Excellent lab, really made me see how the scientific methods worked."

"Lab was definitely a learning experience—w/even more than just Science."

in the Sciences for Freshmen'." At present, the students in this learning community are enrolled in biology lecture, are clustered in biology laboratory as well as in courses in Library Skills (taught by Gordon Muir) and English Composition (taught by Lauren Kiefer). There is a great deal of coordination between the syllabi of Lauren Kiefer and Janice Marchut Conrad while Peter Conrad makes frequent visits to the English class.

Cellular Biochemistry Research Experience (Bio 490)

"Imagine that you are located at a relatively small, primarily undergraduate college and, during the spring semester, you share the teaching of a single upper-level biology course with an enrollment of about 15 undergraduates. Sound like heaven at a primary undergraduate institution (PUI)?" (Reiss, 2000)

Carol Reiss is writing about *Bio 490*, a course that we have taught for the last six years. Again, students work in research groups and are expected to develop and complete an original piece of research for presentation at the annual meeting of the American Society of Plant Biologists, Northeast Section. The class is presented with four or five suggested projects that represent original research. Within the context of this 15-credit course, a minimum of 27 contact hours per week, the students do everything for themselves. We teach them that success in research, and of course in life, requires the ability to ask the right questions and that information can be obtained through experimentation. The experience promotes the acquisition of information and application of knowledge to problem solving, hypothesis formation and testing, the collection and analysis of data and development of a convincing argument in defense of the work.

Students are given the space to recover from their failures and the opportunity to learn from them as well. A former student now in her fourth year at Cornell Veterinary School describes the experience this way: "It was an open and inviting experience and built one's confidence in one's own abilities. This is what carries you through graduate school and beyond. The most important skills that undergraduate research taught me were critical thinking skills and problem solving. Everything else flows from those skills."

Like a Family Breaking Apart

The most unexpected thing happens to these students every spring. They start out as a collection of strangers, somewhat aloof and thinking that they would do so much better if they didn't have to work within the team. They eventually realize that they could never have individually accomplished what they were able to achieve as a group (Table 4). At the end of every semester to date, they are visibly sad and to quote one student, "It's as though a family is breaking apart."

Teaching Science within a social context.

Bio 490 students and former students of *Bio 101* show a marked willingness to tutor or mentor a peer. These individuals form the cadre of students who serve as teaching assistants in subsequent *Bio 101* courses. They know that they got something from one or both courses and they clearly give something back to the students who follow.

Science Asks Why

Science addresses a basic question that every child asks and that is—why? Therefore, the learning experience should encourage the student to be creative, inquisitive and to color outside the lines. Does the process make sense even if the outcomes cannot be readily explained at the moment? Science should not be defined by a limited community, but should address community as a global concept. It should become clear to students that although we strive to understand and explain the natural world, we are not bound to act upon the information that we determine.

Sometimes students do not want to look beyond or ask the next question if they see no immediate value in what they have determined. We ask them to reevaluate information that they feel has no immediate apparent value in the context of a possible future value, that is, for example, the difference between basic science research and technology. Is it possible that we are not yet prepared to see its "usefulness?" Laser technology, used as a common medical tool, is a product of basic science in space exploration. There was no predetermined vision of a medical use of lasers when the national community funded the space program.

Conclusions

Assigned reading and results of a prior experiment is what the students know. To be able to synthesize and rearrange information in order to ask a new question is a significant measure of learning. It is only when they are doing their own experiments, whether in *Bio 101* or *Bio 490*, that they actually begin to understand the point of the experiment and what we were trying to achieve at the beginning of the semester. It is always amazing to find out that many students do not recall having initially received much lecture information that relates to the experiment. But after they become involved in the process of learning, they start to see the connections between information provided in lecture and experiments that address that information in lab. Along the way, they begin to understand

---

TABLE 4: THREE-YEAR SUMMARY FOR BIO 490 RESEARCH SEMESTER: 1999-2001

Question: The instructors motivated me to work independently.

ANSWER	YES	33
	NO	0

"…within a few weeks of the start of the course you have that tiny seed of confidence in yourself which you hang onto and work like hell to make it grow."

"Adapting to the class makes you a thinker by default."

"They gave you just enough to stimulate your mind but not enough for an answer. From there it was up to you."

"Seeing their enthusiasm, it makes it hard not to give this class 100% of your effort. I have never worked so hard in my life."

"They wanted us to work independently as well as working with others to find answers to difficult questions. I believe this was the best approach."

"Even when working on a group problem there was definite encouragement towards each individual to use critical thinking skills to brainstorm for the group."

---

what the knowledge means. Then they are surprised to find that the facts that they generate are often useful when they are considering other not seemingly related experiments. In the laboratory, students are encouraged to discover, to question, to rearrange and to defend or refute a position that they have taken, based on objective evidence.

We try to teach science as we have experienced it. Shermer (1997) sums up our philosophy of science teaching: "What separates science from all other human activities is its commitment to the tentative nature of all its conclusions. There are no final answers in science, only varying degrees of probability. Even scientific 'facts' are just conclusions confirmed to such an extent that it would be reasonable to offer temporary agreement, but that assent is never final. Science is not the affirmation of a set of beliefs but a process of inquiry aimed at building a testable body of knowledge constantly open to rejection or confirmation. In science, knowledge is fluid and certainty fleeing. That is the heart of its limitations. It is also its greatest strength."

Science and Technology

Students often confuse science and technology: the former addresses questions, and the latter is an application of answers. This is a bit analogous to the unknown versus the known. Some years ago, a biology major, who took our introductory course, tutored subsequent students in this course. She asked if she could do an independent-study for an anthropology project on the culture of our *Bio 101* course and the perceived effect of that culture on the students taking the course. We agreed. In her project report, she concluded that the students were very angry about the whole experience and very angry with us because we "broke the contract." They defined the contract this way: "Learning is about being taught facts [teachers' job], memorizing those facts [students' job], being tested on those facts [teachers' job] and getting the facts right [students' job] and fulfilling the contract defines the successful educational experience." From then on, we have been careful to acknowledge at the start of the course that the student-teacher contract, as they have probably experienced it, is likely to be broken by us.

CONCLUSION

In a paper published several years ago, good teaching is described as "a matter of living the mystery" and the original meaning given to the word *professor* "was not someone with esoteric knowledge and technique, but rather a person able to make a profession of faith in the midst of a dangerous world" (Palmer, 1990). We ask a lot of our students when we encourage them to move beyond the status quo, explore the unknown, open their minds to all the possibilities, and to then draw their own conclusions. They are asked to "live the mystery" of what's out there and what does it mean. They must be willing to let go of the familiar, to believe in themselves, and to move forward into an unknown world.

REFERENCES

Bello, S., Bogan, E., Prabhakar, K., and Fernandez, T. (2001). *Establishing Programmatic General Education Goals and Objectives by Faculty for the Improvement of Teaching and Learning.* Paper presented at SUNY General Education Assessment Conference. Syracuse, New York.

Bernal, J.D. (1962). "The Place of Speculation in Modern Technology and Science" in I.J. Good (Ed.), The *Scientist Speculates. An Anthology of Partly-Baked Ideas.* New York: Basic Books.

Cox, A. M. (2001). "Precipitating Classroom Change" in *The Chronicle of Higher Education*, **Volume XLVII**, Number 37:A12-14.

Dawkins, R. (1996). *Climbing Mount Improbable.* New York: WW Norton and Co.

Fuentes, A. (2001). "The Importance of Teaching Introductory Courses in Anthropology" in *The Chronicle of Higher Education*, **Volume XLVII**, Number 37: B16.

Goodenough, U. (1998). *Sacred Depths of Nature.* Oxford: Oxford University Press.

Goodwin, L., Miller J. E. and Cheetam, R.E. (1991). "Teaching Freshman to Think-Does Active learning Work?" in *BioScience*, **Volume 41**, Number 10:719-722.

Harris, E. (2001). "*Chlamydomonas* as a Model Organism" in *Annual Review of Plant Physiology and Plant Molecular Biology*, **Volume 52**:363-406.

Marchut Conrad, J. and Conrad P. L. (1993). "Small Groups and Research Projects in Science" in *College Teaching*, **Volume 41**, Number 2:43-46.

Palmer, P. (1990). "Good Teaching-A Matter of Living the Mystery" in *Change*, **Volume 22**:11-16.

Reed, R., Holmes D., Weyers, J. and Jones, A. (1998). *Practical Skills in Biomolecular Sciences.* Harlow, England: Addison Wesley Longman Limited.

Reiss, Carol. (2000). "Teaching Undergraduates to Do Research" in *Education Forum of the American Society of Plant Physiologists Newsletter.* March/April.

Shermer, M. (1997). *Why People Believe Weird Things.* New York: W. H. Freeman and Company.

Stokstad, E. (2001). "Reintroducing the Intro Course. Trends in Undergraduate Education" in *Science*, **Volume 293**: 1608-1610.

Tobias, S. (1992). *Revitalizing Undergraduate Science: Why Some Things Work and Most Don't.* Tucson: The Research Corporation.

White, T.H. (1958). *The Once and Future King.* Isle of Man, UK: Fontana.

It all started when I realized that I was almost personally acquainted with one of the world's most famous composers—Ludwig Van Beethoven! Don't get me wrong—I was born in the second half of the 20th century and after all, Beethoven was born in the 18th century. So while we had centuries, languages, cultures, and generations separating us, the connection was quite incredible.

As I recall, my father, a violinist, told me the following story, which he had supposedly heard from Jan Sibelius, the great Finnish composer. Sibelius was always dreaming of establishing a personal connection with Beethoven himself. One day as a very young man, he met Beethoven's aging music messenger who picked up and delivered manuscripts from Beethoven to the publisher. "Tell me," began Sibelius, "you are one of those few who has seen and touched the master. Tell me something from your encounters with the creator of the most beautiful music!" The old messenger scratched his forehead and said, "Oh, nothing really. Oh, yes! Beethoven had very hairy arms." And so through my father, I established a personal touch with Beethoven, who was born in 1770 and died in 1827. Today when I teach my college students about music, history and art, I tell them this amusing story. Through me, they are closer to the events of the 18th century, and once again I create this link that they take away from the classroom into their own lives to cherish and pass on to generations to come.

LINKING THE WORLD MOSAIC OR "BEETHOVEN'S HAIRY ARMS"

NINAH BELIAVSKY

TEACHING LANGUAGE THROUGH WORLD HISTORY

History is a universal experience. It is reflected in the arts, in music, in literature, in politics, in science and many other aspects of our lives. We shape, style and create history while our own lives are reflected in the times when history is a mirror of our experiences. We can learn about our own lives and the lives of others by reading famous literature, listening to musical compositions and enjoying the world's greatest works of art. When teachers and students explore interesting and genuine content by listening to music, viewing a film, reading a story, exploring the internet and doing exercises based on such approaches as cooperative learning, they are not simply engaged in an artificial or meaningless activity. Students have an increased opportunity to use the content knowledge and expertise they bring to class from their own backgrounds and cultures. They can explore complex information and become involved in demanding classroom activities, which may lead to intrinsic motivation.

LESSONS BEYOND THE CLASSROOM

The students who are exposed to authentic content in their foreign language classes are benefited in a large number of ways. Students have an opportunity to relay stories from their native countries and to marvel about how the pieces of the world mosaic all fit together. So let your students hear the music, admire world famous art, feel the history, and visit historical places as they are learning a foreign language. This approach to teaching not only creates the possibility of students expanding their horizons, but also allows them to look at world events, works of art, and music from multiple perspectives—thus creating a rich environment for learning.

I teach English as a Second Language (ESL) to students who want to learn and acquire knowledge beyond the grammar stage. I believe that teaching a language should extend beyond grammar and spelling. As I teach my ESL college students, I try to go beyond the realm of the usual and the standard. I attempt to enlighten them, to ignite their interests, to enrich them and create an experience that will be remembered and cherished beyond the classroom.

MULTIPLE REPRESENTATIONS OF KEY IDEAS

Howard Gardner claims that we process information in different ways. His theory of multiple intelligences (MI), which has had a tremendous influence and impact on my own teaching, sets forth eight intelligences: Linguistic, Mathematical, Logical, Musical, Spatial, Bodily-Kinesthetic, Interpersonal, Intrapersonal, and Naturalistic. He believes that all of us have these intelligences. However, no two people have the same combinations of these intelligences—not even twins. So if you teach only one way, you reach only one student while other students would suffer. Because there are many intelligences, there are many ways of understanding the world. Therefore, there should be multiple representations of key ideas. Ideas should be taught in more than one way. This will enable you to reach more students and teach your students what it is like to think in more than one way. Furthermore, according to Gardner, understanding is very difficult to achieve. Disciplines like physics, literature and biology are human inventions: mental vehicles or ways of understanding the world. Disciplines are key arenas for understanding. Understanding is not the same as parroting back—it is applying knowledge and concepts in new situations. If students can't use their knowledge flexibly, it is of no use. If they can't apply their knowledge, it is wasted. So I strongly agree with Gardner that we need to take advantage of our multiple intelligences and try to teach in such a way that students connect with the information that is presented in the classroom. Gardner believes that "teachers must be freed to pursue an education that strives for depth of understanding. Teachers should not settle for coverage, but rather for uncovering information in more depth. Teachers should move for uncoverage…embrace the principle of less is more" (Gardner, 1993, pp. 191-201).

BEETHOVEN AND NAPOLEON

So what do I do in my own classroom? I want to teach my students about a particular historical period through a lens that encompasses music, art, and politics. I want to build a multidimensional arena of the information I present. I want students to experience this new knowledge through music, art books, film and written text. The lesson that stands out most vividly takes us into 18th century Europe—the lesson is built around music, politics and art. The mosaic is created this time by linking a musician, a politician and a painter. The German composer Beethoven, the Emperor of France Napoleon Bonaparte (1769-1821) and the Spanish painter Francisco de Goya (1746-1828) will enable the students to establish a knowledge base that will help them think artistically and historically.

I usually begin by telling my students of how I am connected to Beethoven. While this story is entertaining and attention-capturing, it also provides a setting for my lesson. It immediately establishes a connection between 18th century Europe and my 21st century college students. Beethoven's name is no longer abstract, and no longer so far removed from the present times. After all, I, their professor, am almost personally acquainted with a figure three centuries removed from us. Then we listen to music in class. I always begin with the known. I will bring different selections, which I hope will be familiar to most students, such as "Für Elise". Most have heard this popular bagatelle (little piece) that was written around 1810, even if they do not know the title or the composer.

NATURAL LINKS IN AFFAIRS

Each piece of the information I teach has a natural link to another. For example, Beethoven wrote this piece for Therese Malfatti, a charming young lady he loved and was hoping to marry. The name—Elise—however, owes its existence to an error in deciphering Beethoven's terrible handwriting. By this time, my students begin to know the composer not as an abstract figure from past history, but as a man who not only wrote beautiful music but also had a sloppy handwriting and a romantic nature—something students can easily relate to. We then listen to the famous *Moonlight Sonata*, which Beethoven wrote in 1802 as he was realizing that his deafness was progressive and incurable. This leads us into a whole new avenue for discussion—the enormous strength, willpower, and the ability of not giving up even under the most difficult life conditions. This human quality of perseverance can be observed and studied in other famous individuals who have suffered from handicaps and made a mark on our history.

We slowly move to 1803 as we listen to Symphony No. 3 in E flat, *Eroica*, which Beethoven dedicated to Napoleon. This is our natural link to the politics and historical affairs of the time. In December 1804, Beethoven heard about Napoleon proclaiming himself Emperor of France. Beethoven reportedly became so infuriated that he destroyed the page containing the dedication of *Eroica* to Napoleon. Beethoven raged, "Is he, too, nothing more than human? Now he will crush the rights of men. He will become a tyrant!" *Beethoven, The Immortal*© <www.lucare.com>. And thus Napoleon is linked to Beethoven.

We begin to know Beethoven more and more not as a composer but as a human being with principles and ideals. How can we go on to understand Beethoven's music if we do not travel from Austria to France and learn about Napoleon Bonaparte, the French Emperor, who conquered much of Europe, who created an empire, and who has changed the course of European history. We read about Napoleon Bonaparte and his accomplishments and failures. We talk about the era of the French Revolution (1774-1815), the government, the Napoleonic Codes and his coronation on December 2, 1804 in Notre Dame cathedral in Paris in the presence of the Pope himself. I show clips from art videos *Art of the Western World—An Age of Reason, An Age of Passion* and *Grand Museum Series: A Tour of The Louvre*, and point out *The Consecration of the Emperor Napoleon and the Coronation of Empress Josephine,* a painting by Jacques-Louis David (1748-1825) that thousands of tourists come to view in the Louvre in Paris. We talk about Victor Hugo's novel *Les Miserables*, which has been adapted into a

Broadway Musical. We can then listen to some of the more popular melodies from the production, such as "Castle on a Cloud" and view clips from the movie *Les Miserables.*

ONTO GOYA AND SPAIN

We are once again forced to travel and this time—to Spain. We learn that Spain, an ally of France, was governed by an incompetent and corrupt government. It was not a threat to France yet it was an unreliable partner in Napoleonic plans. Napoleon managed to coerce the Spanish minister to allow the French army to march through Spain and into Portugal. Lisbon was taken in 1807. More French troops came into Spain and by autumn of 1808 they conquered the peninsula. For five years, the Spanish army had lost every battle but the French could not win a significant victory. Spain became Napoleon's "bleeding sore"—a struggle of terrible atrocities on both sides <www.galenet.com>. While Spain was burning, Francisco Goya was recording history. The painter recorded the war in his famous paintings "2nd of May of 1808" and "3rd of May of 1808". These paintings, among others, are displayed in the Prado National Museum in Madrid, Spain.

In the classroom, I show my students Goya's works of art in art books and in art videos. We "travel" to Spain and "visit" the Prado National Museum; we begin to learn about the famous Spanish painter whose art was influenced by historical events. We learn that Goya was a personal painter to Carlos IV and thus received commissions to paint the portraits of the most notorious people in Madrid. We study Goya's most important painting of the 19th century—the "Royal Family of Carlos IV." We also learn that in 1792, Goya became severely ill and was left deaf for the rest of his life. During his illness, Goya redefined himself as an artist. This applied not only to color and line, but also to the subject matter. Goya, in contrast to Italian masters' portrayal of beauty, used his art to depict the cruelty and madness of war. Goya's temperament of the 1790's is revealed in his two self-portraits, which depict a man with stern eyes and unruly hair. We now can compare two of the greatest personages of the 18th century—Beethoven and Goya—both deaf and ill tempered <www.galenet.com>.

Goya was in Madrid when the Spanish War of Independence erupted. Witness to uprising and executions, Goya created two paintings to represent the bloodshed—"2nd of May of 1808" and "3rd of May of 1808". The latter depicts faceless French soldiers firing at a man whose arms are outstretched; another man is on the ground in a pool of blood. We learn of Goya's special technique of applying the red paint with a spoon rather than a brush. Goya was recording history as he published another famous series of engravings called *The Disasters of War.* How can we begin to understand and appreciate Goya's art without understanding the situation in the world? How can we view Goya's art in isolation or Beethoven's music without Napoleon's rule? We cannot do justice to Beethoven, Napoleon or Goya without linking their lives and creating a world mosaic.

LEARNING THROUGH MULTIPLE DIMENSIONS

This lesson lends itself to teaching language though multiple dimensions—music, art and politics. Students can listen to recordings, view films, enjoy art books, and read biographies. Students can learn how lives of seemingly unrelated people are intertwined with one another, how they are influenced by one another and shaped by the events around them. This lesson lends itself to teaching the four traditional skills in language teaching/learning—listening, speaking, reading and writing. Grammar exercises can be easily developed based on the content. For example, after we listen to musical selections, students discuss in groups the mood of the music, the background information and other aspects related to the piece. When students read selections from biographies, they can work on scanning and skimming the passages, answer information questions and do further research on the subject matter. Writing activities can easily be developed as narrative, descriptive and argumentative essays.

WHAT IF?

Students can also write in their journals answering hypothetical questions such as "If you could travel in time, where would you go and what part of history would you like to change?" One of the students in my intermediate ESL class answered the question in the following way:

> If I could travel in a time tunnel and go back in time to 18th Century, and I had the power to change history, I would, of course, stop Napoleon to be an emperor and his conquer of Spain. This way, Napoleon could win back the respect from Beethoven and Goya. However, he would not be Napoleon anymore, and not a great and well-known person in world history. If he didn't have the ambition to conquer the world and to be an emperor, he would probably be an ordinary French general for all of his life and would not be remembered by the world, and we would not discuss him here. History is history! Can not be changed!

Another student wrote:

> Finally, I want to tell the leaders of the countries, the peace is very important. They had the responsibility to avoid the war. Moreover, I would persuade the leaders to give more democracy to people, in order to stress the important of human

right. Based on the terror war, I think what I can do is to change the leaders' thoughts. In conclusion, everyone have a dream to do something influencing the world. Every time when I read the story of history, I always wish I could change the ambition of the notorious war maker, it would save many lives in the world. People in the world have no fear to the threats of the war and they could enjoy the true life surrounding by music, love and peace.

Finally, I'll ask my students to write their reactions and share with me a surprising discovery that they have made during the lesson. This will open yet another door to creative teaching and learning while incorporating students' input.

During this class I have discovered the fascinating links between different heroes of the 18th Century: Goya, Beethoven and NapoleonÖ. These three prominent figures of the 18th Century were linked together in a way that I could not imagine before; I knew the story of these three persons but I never linked their life. This was a great discovery I made during this class: Goya, Napoleon and Beethoven were related! I also learned in this class…[that] Beethoven had very hairy arms!!!

REFERENCES

Abbruzzese, M. (1978). *Goya.* New York, NY: Grosset & Dunlap.

Gardner, H. (1983). *Frames of Mind, The Theory of Multiple Intelligences.* Basic Books.

—. (1993). *Multiple Intelligences, The Theory in Practice.* Basic Books.

—. (October 26, 2001). Remarks delivered at New Jersey City University's Fifth Annual Urban Mission Conference: Innovative Methods of Teaching in Higher Education: Engaging Multiple Intelligences.

Solomon, M. (1977). *Beethoven.* Prentice Hall International.

WEBSITES

Merriam-Webster Collegiate Dictionary On-Line, 10th Edition, 1994. Merriam-Webster.

<www.galenet.com>

<www.lucare.com>

VIDEOS

A Tour of The Louvre. 1983. *Art Collection Video.*

A Tour of The Prado. 1983. *Art Collection Video.*

Art of the Western World: An Age of Reason, An Age of Passion. 1989. The Annenberg/CPB Collection.

Beethoven Lives Upstairs. 1992. The Children's Group.

In *Intelligence Reframed*, Howard Gardner lays out three propositions that encapsulate the key implication of Multiple Intelligence (MI) theory for education: "We are not all the same; we do not all have the same kind of minds... and education works most effectively if these differences are taken into account rather than denied or ignored" (91). I had not heard of MI Theory until quite recently. In experimenting with my own teaching, however, I arrived at a point notably congruent with Gardner's ideas. I had developed a predominantly constructivist approach with an emphasis on collaborative learning methodology that took advantage of varied learning preferences and other characteristics implicit in the MI approach.

History connects past, present and future; thus its meaning depends entirely on context. In understanding history, students develop their own contexts to make the past meaningful. In fact, such individually conceived contexts are the only way humans can understand the past. All of this makes clear two things. First, the history classroom is especially well suited to take advantage of MI and allow students to learn in ways that reflect their individual intelligences profiles. Secondly, the constructivist approach best matches our natural process of "history making." History, then, as a discipline combined with collaborative constructivism, seems especially promising for exploiting the multiform nature of intelligence.

Traditional assessments in the field of history favored only students who were strong in logic and linguistic intelligence. This paper explores how the combination of discipline, approach, and method, helps students who may excel in different intelligences. Let us look first at constructivism, which refers to the idea that students learn by building their own understanding rather than by receiving someone else's knowledge. In constructing knowledge, students draw on their own particular mix of intelligences and their own set of experiences and prior knowledge (Sheurman 6). Thus constructivism fits naturally with MI theory: the special role of construction in historical understanding magnifies that effect.

CONSTRUCTING INTERPRETATIONS

History as a discipline is inherently constructivist. If we think of learning history as history-making rather than history remembering, the natural correspondence becomes clearer. While we often use the expression "reconstructing the past," in truth, history-making is more a process of construction than of reconstruction. History, in the sense of past events, can never be reconstructed: it is gone. The only history that we have is what we know and remember about those events. When we learn history, what we do is construct an interpretation of the past that allows us to function in the present and move into the future (Becker 239-44). This is always true, but it is especially so in the educational setting since a key purpose of education is preparation for the future.

COLLABORATION, CONSTRUCTIVISM AND MI: CLOSE ALLIES IN THE HISTORY CLASSROOM

GERALD CARPENTER

INDIVIDUAL AND SOCIAL MEANING

The constructivist approach assumes that all students build their own knowledge, and this is especially true in a field like history where interpretation so dramatically outweighs accepted *fact* because most *fact* is, in reality, consensual interpretation. Constructivism in history courses allows students freedom to approach and solve problems on the basis of their own strengths and to produce and demonstrate understandings both individually and socially meaningful. This fits well with MI Theory, since learning through a variety of constructivist-based exercises gives students—as much as possible—the chance to employ their favored intelligences and to construct their own understandings within individualized contexts.

COLLABORATIVE LEARNING AND THE MULTIPLE INTELLIGENCES

Added to the nature of history and the advantages of the constructivist approach, collaborative learning further exploits the multiform nature of intelligence. We are talking about a social, as well as an individual process. Although we each arrive at different understandings of the past, we also must share some common vision to function as a society (Becker 247-48). Recent controversies such as those over the appropriate way to commemorate the accomplishments of Christopher Columbus or how the National Air and Space Museum should display the *Enola Gay* aircraft fifty years after the Hiroshima bombing make that clear. Thus, collaborative learning techniques are natural to authentic historical understanding. Moreover, they engage intelligences that are usually slighted or ignored with more conventional methodologies.

Collaborative learning (1) maximizes the opportunities for students to develop further their constructed understandings in order to share them, and (2) provides for the exercise of Interpersonal Intelligence. Echoing the process by which societies arrive at a shared understanding of their pasts, collaborative learning is a natural and authentic part of any study of history. History, constructivism, and collaboration can work together to engage and stimulate multiple intelligences. Examination of case studies like the ones discussed below can help show us how.

CASE STUDIES

In question were upper-level American history courses: *Big Business and the Gilded Age* and *American Labor History*. Both were taught with the assistance of a participant-observer Paul Vermette, a colleague from the Niagara University College of Education. In Spring 1994, I accepted Dr. Vermette's offer to assist me in teaching the Gilded Age course. Because of his own research interests and expertise, his primary roles were to (1) create collaborative exercises designed to increase learning, and (2) observe the effects of that added element. Although his role evolved in a different direction, the addition of the collaborative approach was an immediate and obvious success.

We collaborated again in Spring 2000 in the labor history course, adding some new strategies while continuing the emphasis on collaborative learning. Our on-going discussion of the course's progress and our students' responses to the various activities produced a growing appreciation of constructivism's role in its success. The varied activities were designed to accommodate differing learning styles, but subsequent exposure to the work of Gardner on MI Theory convinced me that we had also taken advantage of the Multiple Intelligences of our students.

In the interest of brevity, the list of activities used in the two courses can be combined. We used role-playing simulations, game design and construction, graphic organizers, analogy generation, pictorial analysis, analysis of historical music and art, personal interviews, email journals, group problem-solving, and traditional essay writing. On reflec-

tion, these exercises seem to have created opportunities for the engagement of Logical/Mathematical, Linguistic, Visual/Spatial, Body/Kinesthetic, Musical, Interpersonal and Intrapersonal Intelligences. (Of course the ability of the instructor to anticipate or appreciate just which intelligences might be engaged, or how, is limited by his or her own profile of intelligences.)

Not all of the activities were collaborative, but most involved some collaboration. In both courses, after an initial assessment based on early class participation, we divided the students into heterogeneous base groups of four or five students each. Although the groups did not work together every day, we did average one collaborative activity per day in each course. In most instances group brainstorming or problem solving was followed by large group debriefing.

FIGURE 1:

This diagram was distributed to the students with no words filled in.

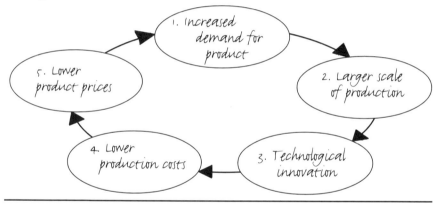

One example of a collaborative problem-solving activity used in both courses should suffice to make clear how constructivism and collaboration worked together to enhance student learning and to exploit the Multiple Intelligences of our students. The exercise was the completion of a flow chart representing the process of industrialization and, more specifically, the transition to mass production. Groups were given a chart like the one in Figure 1.

At the bottom of the page were listed five changes or developments needed to explain the transition to mass production: lower production costs, lower product prices, increased demand for the product, technological innovation, and larger scale of production. The groups were asked to arrange those developments in an order correctly representing the causal relationships. They were further asked to determine the logical starting point for this circular process.

Once the groups arrived at their answers, the entire class was debriefed, discussing first the correct order for the developments. Disagreement about the correct order created opportunities for groups to explain the rationales for their particular solutions. Depending on one's interpretation, technological innovation could take place at several points in the process, and in the discussion those alternatives were acknowledged. After examining the circumstances under which each suggested order could be correct, the class agreed on the following as the most likely order: lower product prices, higher demand for product, larger scale of production, technological innovation, lower production costs, lower product prices, etc.

Since the process is circular, the problem of finding the most likely starting point generated more disagreement among the groups. Granting that any of these developments could independently have begun the process, the instructor argued that the most likely starting point in the particular historical circumstances of the Gilded Age was increased demand for the product because of changes that began independent of the circular process: rapidly increasing population, urbanization, improved transportation and rising average incomes.

ADDITIONAL INSIGHTS

This exercise illustrates the manner in which students constructed their own understanding of the historical process and modified that individually constructed knowledge in light of additional insights gained through discussion. The process resulted in meaningful personal understanding of a key phenomenon, but in a way that assured a shared interpretation of the core understanding. The constructivist nature of the exercise was magnified and reinforced as the class revisited this model several times during the semester, elaborating on the initial understanding as they added further elements such as urbanization and regional specialization to the pattern.

RESYNTHESIZING IN CLASS EVERY DAY

The cumulative nature of the understanding that is gained illustrates well the potential of the constructivist approach. One of the most gratifying pieces of feedback occurred when a student was asked whether he had difficulty with a particular exam question requiring synthesis. His answer: "It was easy because we resynthesized in class every day." While this task would seem to draw primarily on Logical/Mathematical Intelligence, students might also bring to bear Linguistic and Visual/Spatial Intelligences. The intra-group and whole-class discussion called for the exercise of Interpersonal Intelligence, and several students reported a perceived benefit from that interaction.

ROBBER BARONS OR CAPTAINS OF INDUSTRY

Other collaborative assignments invoked other intelligences, but all gave opportunity to employ the Multiple Intelligences of individuals and the combination of intelligences represented among group members. For example, groups listed characteristics of today's economic globalization and examples of current government actions affecting the economy. Teams also took part in debates such as one on the interpretation of big businessmen of the nineteenth century as either "Robber Barons" or "Captains of Industry." Some of these activities were based on reading assignments while others depended upon the sharing of pre-existing knowledge of the students. Some involved student's analyzing visual representations of historical developments like a picture of pre-industrial craftsmen at work as compared to workers in a factory setting. Ultimately, student groups designed, built, and demonstrated board games based on their understanding of the historical processes that were the central focus of the course.

Since the purpose of the game assignment was to assess the students' understanding of the key processes rather than their recollection of past events, the instructions emphasized that players should not advance or win on the basis of specific historical knowledge. *Rather teams were encouraged to develop game rules that would demonstrate their own understanding of the processes of change.* Within the group—if not within every member—this project called for the use of Logical, Linguistic, Visual/Spatial and Interpersonal Intelligences and perhaps others.

All of this gives an overview of the direction we took in these two courses. We were able to observe the way individual students structured their learning through varied assessments, but especially through their email journals. These personal communications made abundantly clear the different mixes of intelligences the students brought to bear on their tasks. One of the most interesting examples occurred when a student produced contemporary song lyrics that she found analogous to developments a century ago. Fostering the construction of student understanding was significantly more satisfying for both instructors and students, and assessments indicated that student learning and understanding was, in fact, deeper. The correspondence with MI Theory also seems clear.

MULTIPLE ENTRY POINTS

Both constructivism and MI Theory are premised on the uniqueness of every person. We each construct our understanding differently because we each bring to the process a unique mix of intelligences and prior knowledge. The effort to facilitate historical construction by all students began with the use of multiple entry points similar to those advocated by Howard Gardner in *Multiple Intelligences: The Theory in Practice* (203-04). Narrational entry points are the heart of the historical learning. Not only are we likely to begin with inspiring or intriguing stories, but students create their own stories. Role-playing simulations are narrations completed by improvisation. Interviews and work histories offered students in the labor history course a final opportunity for story construction and story telling.

Exercises focusing on some of the quantifiable measures of social and economic change during the late nineteenth century provided quantitative/mathematical entry points although most students in college history courses seem disoriented when asked to do mathematical thinking. Many of the problems posed to the groups as discussion starters required logical thinking more than specific knowledge. Certainly that was the case with the flow chart about mass production and similar exercises.

FUNDAMENTAL QUESTIONS

Foundational questions generally arose only at the beginning of major divisions in the course. For example, students spent time discussing "What is work?" The emails following that discussion showed just how provocative such questions could be for some students. Excerpts from contemporary literature and art provided aesthetic entry points, while the games and simulations offered experiential entry points. Finally, many of the entry points were social because of the collaborative nature of the exercises. Beyond the entry points, we emphasized analogies as a means to fuller understanding since, like constructivism, analogous thinking assumes that understanding of the new subject must progress from more familiar ideas. In *Multiple Intelligences: The Theory in Practice*, Gardner emphasizes that the teacher is "challenged to come up with instructive analogies"(172) as a follow-up to multiple entry points, but in a constructivist setting it often seems better for students to create their own analogies whose aptness can then be critiqued in discussion.

Finally the constructivist approach seems to facilitate what Gardner refers to as "conveying the central understandings" of the topic (*Intelligence Reframed* 173) because it requires the teacher to think through the subject and plan the process of construction most likely to produce that fundamental understanding. Because constructivism and collaboration preclude broad coverage of all topics, they force the hard choices about where to concentrate. As in the case of the mass production flow chart, constructivism also encourages reiteration and resynthesis, further reinforcing those central understandings.

CONCLUSION

The correspondence between MI Theory and collaborative constructivism seems clear: (1) Learning is understanding which occurs when each person constructs his or her own knowledge by a process at some level unique to that individual. (2) This construction of knowledge is limited and guided by the individual's particular profile of intelligences and operates differently in different domains of knowledge. (3) The addition of collaboration amplifies the synergy of Multiple Intelligences and constructivism by engaging additional intelligences and requiring reiteration of individually constructed understanding. History courses taught with collaborative constructivist methodology illustrate how, to paraphrase Gardner, taking into account the different ways our different minds work makes education more effective.

REFERENCES

Becker, C. (1935 & 1966). *Everyman His Own Historian: Essays on History and Politics*. Chicago: Quadrangle Books.

Gardner, H. (1999). *Intelligence Reframed: Multiple Intelligences for the 21st Century*. NY: Basic Books.

—. (1993). *Multiple Intelligences: The Theory in Practice*. NY: Basic Books.

Sheurman, G. (1998). "From Behaviorist to Constructivist Teaching" in *Social Education*. Jan. 1998: 6-9.

Vermette, P. (1998). *Making Cooperative Learning Work: Student Teams in K-12 Classrooms*. Upper Saddle River, NJ: Merrill.

There are distinct benefits to using feature film analysis as a component of the undergraduate psychology curriculum. For example, feature film depictions may provide students with a situation or character that simulates a "real life" quality. Also the narrative power and complexity of film may serve as an entry point for students who may be turned off to abstract analysis of less stimulating, more impersonal, case material. Discussion of film may be used to encourage students to discuss their current level of understanding about concepts that will be investigated. Film analysis also encourages students to critically analyze the portrayal of complex characters in order to develop or apply an enriched understanding of concepts already learned. Moreover, film analysis encourages students with diverse learning styles and varied ethnic and cultural backgrounds to engage in connected learning experiences and critical thinking.

BACKGROUND

In many college classrooms, the communication of course content relies primarily on the lecture format. However, to encourage deeper learning and to reach all of our students, we would do well to integrate alternative teaching modalities and strategies that are sensitive to diverse learning styles. Since no one method or technique will work for every student population, the instructor must take into account students' backgrounds and interests. The integration of feature films in the psychology curriculum is one approach that may encourage students to become more active learners.

To be sure, the notion of showing an entire film, or even a film segment, to a college class does not summon up images of active learning. However, specific uses of feature film analysis may promote students' active mental engagement with material (Perry, Huss, McAuliff & Galas, 1996, citing Benjamin, 1991). The inherent drama and conflict depicted in feature films, when linked conceptually to the content of a curriculum, can increase student involvement in the course—a first step for higher-level learning processes.

My initial foray into the use of feature film as a teaching tool grew out of my experiences teaching college students at an urban community college during the early 1990s. The rule of thumb for student assessment in most classes was the multiple-choice exam. The majority of my students avoided classes where written assignments of any type were required. My goal in using film in the curriculum, then, was simply to provide students with some intriguing material that might ameliorate their initial resistance. The students' reaction was enthusiastic—both in terms of the quality of the class discussion and of the written work. Since that time, I have successfully integrated feature films in several of my psychology courses, to make material more relevant to my diverse student population, to facilitate meaningful student involvement with concepts I am teaching, and to encourage the development of higher-level cognitive strategies.

USING FEATURE FILMS IN THE PSYCHOLOGY CURRICULUM

CHERYL BLUESTONE

CRITICAL ANALYSIS AND TRANSFER OF TRAINING

The integration of feature film in the psychology curriculum can provide students with material that encourages active mental engagement with key concepts and ideas. Active learners think about the material they are studying and are willing to take risks and think critically about material (Perry, 1996). Critical thinking is multifaceted in nature, and includes the ability to evaluate evidence for differing arguments and to consider issues from multiple viewpoints (Chaffee, 1994; Ruggiero, 1996). Many films provide storylines with multidimensional characters, various levels of conflict, and complex situations—all of which may provide material that will encourage students to engage in a critical analysis of multiple perspectives (Anderson, 1992). These same qualities of film often provide a more meaningful context for concepts and ideas initially presented in the abstract. Verbal or text-based examples of concepts, situations, or characters may not fully provide such a context.

Sternberg (1987) argues that students benefit from educational experiences that facilitate transfer of critical thinking skills to assorted situations, as opposed to teaching in an isolated or decontextualized fashion. Students may also respond to the use of feature film because the narrative format promotes connected learning experiences (Belenky, Clinchy, Goldberger and Tarule, 1997). These approaches emphasize the importance of affective experiences and personal narratives. Belenky and her colleagues (1997) note that women and ethnic minority students may feel disempowered by the lecture/read/test format, or what they call "separate learning." This stresses the importance of abstract analysis, objective observation, and a focus on the mastery of factual material, and does not emphasize the sharing of ideas, personal experiences, and empathy with others (Clinchy, 1995; Enns, 1993). Film characters can provide an opportunity for students to understand the experiences and worldview of characters with whom they have little in common. Additionally, under-represented students may find that they can relate to the narratives found in feature films. Plots may center on issues relevant to students' daily lives and larger concerns (e.g., AIDS, community violence), and are more likely to include characters representative of their diverse ethnic and socio-cultural backgrounds (e.g., *Boyz in the Hood*; *Philadelphia*).

CONNECTED LEARNING

Connected learning provides students with opportunities to relate emotionally to course material. The use of films may allow students access to the characters' perspective thus making a powerful connection to their struggles. This may provide an opportunity for students to think more fully about the material and to make use of their experiences to consider the concepts presented (Anderson, 1992; Fleming et al., 1990). When we accept the validity of students' experiences and take them seriously, students will feel empowered to express their ideas and will be more likely to engage in a meaningful interchange about them (Clinchy, 1995). Thus, this modality may encourage critical thinking skills that can engage a range of students who may feel alienated from more traditional teaching formats.

Gardner (1991, 1999) emphasizes the notion that in order to nurture students' deeper understanding of material, we need to recognize diverse learning styles. Not all students are flexible learners. Thus, we must become flexible teachers. There are multiple entry points that will allow students to examine core ideas and concepts. The use of feature film may provide opportunities for students who prefer the narrative or experiential format to enter the dialogue necessary for meaningful learning. The emotional power of film may also bring together a class, encouraging more open and thoughtful class discussions.

FILMS AND BOOKS

I have shown entire films or film segments with relevance for a particular topic. I used film analysis for the first time when I was teaching *Child Development* at an urban community college during the height of the crack epidemic in New York City. The majority of students in my classes reported hearing gunshots at night, and otherwise experiencing direct consequences of the violence that grew

from the drug related issues and opened up class discussion of several important issues related to those themes. The film *Boyz in the Hood* (Nicolaides & Singleton, 1991) dealt directly with those issues. I chose to use a 15-minute segment of the film in conjunction with a book entitled *Children in Danger* (Garbarino, Dubrow, Kostelny, & Pardo, 1992). The film also depicts many interesting dimensions of father-son and mother-son relations. I introduced a discussion of Baumrind's (1991) parenting styles, opening up the topic of students' ideas about parenting and discipline. Following this, I asked the students to view the film segments critically, thinking about the parenting qualities and relationships depicted in the clips. An example of such a question follows: *Did these qualities seem to be indicative of what students feel is necessary for good parenting? If so, why? If not, why not?*

The characteristics that the students identified were then discussed and examined as they corresponded to the parenting dimensions of warmth and control identified by Baumrind. The students were then asked to place the film characters in the matrix that corresponds to Baumrind's parenting styles (e.g., authoritarian versus authoritative parenting). Students were also asked to apply these dimensions of parenting to other issues that arise when raising children. The discussion of the film may incorporate several other themes—including the role of the father in the family, or the effect of violence on child and adolescent development. Moreover, the film depiction of a strong, warm and involved African-American father may also contribute to deconstructing stereotypical notions about African-American families in general and African-American fathers in particular. Thus, one film sequence can lead to an extended, in-depth examination of several inter-related topics.

NEGATIVE REINFORCEMENT VS. PUNISHMENT

Alternatively, short film segments can be used as an activity to generate student interest or consolidate students' understanding of concepts already learned. An interesting way do this is to develop a library of media interpretations of psychological concepts—they are most often incorrect. Students enjoy applying their newly acquired knowledge to identify such inaccuracies. For example, the first several minutes of the film *Ghostbusters* (Brillstein & Reitman, 1984) consists of a humorous psychology experiment that illustrates common misunderstandings about concepts and terms that are important constructs in an introductory psychology class. Discussion of this film clip can provide a framework to engage students in thinking critically about and applying their knowledge of the terms "negative reinforcement" and "double-blind." Students commonly have difficulty differentiating the operant conditioning term "negative reinforcement" from "punishment," much in the same way it is incorrectly depicted in the film. Feature films may bring to life a wide range of psychology concepts (see Gregg et al., 1995 for a thorough listing of films and related psychological topics).

FILMS AS CASE ILLUSTRATIONS

Another approach is to use the characters depicted in film as case illustrations or as material for a more in-depth case analysis. When I teach a unit on psychological disorders in my *Introduction to Psychology* course, I use several film clips to illustrate specific diagnoses. For example, I show a five-minute clip of a series of interactions between the Glen Close character and the Michael Douglas character in the film *Fatal Attraction*. I ask the students to watch the characters' interactions critically, considering any behavior that seems unusual or atypical. The film character of Alex clearly depicts the erratic behavioral patterns and extreme emotional turmoil that often characterizes individuals with Borderline Personality Disorder (BPD). In this activity, the students are able to generate the major criteria for the DSM (Diagnostic Statistic Manual) category of BPD before these criteria have been introduced. The students' observations can then be linked to the terms and concepts found in the text. Textbooks and educational videos may economically and accurately show them these same criteria, but the film characters convey the clinical feel of diagnostic syndromes.

ABNORMAL PSYCHOLOGY

In my *Abnormal Psychology* class, I use both feature film clips and educational film clips throughout the semester to provide a familiarity with various concepts and diagnoses. After I have already introduced basic principles, major diagnostic categories, and concepts related to the DSM multi-axial diagnostic system, I show an entire film in class. (Note: a multi-axial diagnostic system requires consideration of several areas of functioning, and other factors that might influence the patient in addition to the clinical diagnosis). Most recently, I showed the film *Panic* (Bromell, 2001). After viewing the film, students were asked to make a Five-Axis DSM diagnosis of two of the characters. The main character does not display behavior that fits neatly into any one diagnosis. However, this is true in real life diagnosis as well. That is, one rarely finds real persons who display distinct, unambiguous symptoms where diagnosis is cut and dry. After watching the film, I place the students in collaborative groups to discuss the characters. They work together to identify behaviors that might be suggestive of any particular diagnosis. I then

ask them to write a paper in which they make the diagnosis and provide an argument for their decision.

This, like other feature films, portrays complex characters with symptoms that are depicted in the context of an intricate plot. Students must actively process concepts and diagnostic criteria that they have learned in order to see if they apply to the film characters. In this process, the characters provide opportunities for students to appreciate the shades of gray and overlapping symptomology characteristic of patients as they are present in real life. This exercise requires students to apply several concepts to simulated situations, to consider evidence that might support various hypotheses, and to weigh arguments from the differing viewpoints of others in the group. A more typical approach to this topic would ask students to demonstrate mastery by recognizing or describing what they have learned in a multiple-choice exam. Students may memorize the description of each of the 5 Axes of DSM, but still not fully appreciate how to use each of the five axes. Indeed, it was only after I read their papers that I was able to grasp what the students misunderstood. Once I am aware of the students' misconceptions, I can present information or activities to build more accurate and sophisticated understandings.

STUDENT RESPONSE

Students' level of interest and enthusiasm increased, but was the time in class that I spent on film analysis a worthwhile use of valuable class time? Students seemed to believe so. I conducted informal surveys that indicated that the majority of students felt the use of class time was positive. Approximately 73% of the students indicated that they felt that the films made them think more realistically about the issues discussed in class, and about 40% reported that the emotional involvement they felt for the characters contributed to their positive responses. In responding to open-ended questions, many students reported that they felt the use of films gave them an opportunity to examine the issues more in depth; they felt their learning had a more hands-on flavor; and they felt more a part of what was going on. This type of anecdotal data does not directly address the issue of whether these learning experiences actually increased students' higher-level cognitive skills. Nevertheless, these responses suggest that many of the students responded to and felt more emotionally involved with the course material

PRACTICAL CONSIDERATIONS

Despite the potential benefits, the use of feature films in a traditional psychology course may present some practical difficulties. In a 14-16 week semester, time is a valuable resource. One feature film, if shown in its entirety, typically requires the better part of a week of class time. There are several ways to deal with this, depending on the time constraints faced. One suggestion is to assign a film to watch as a take-home project (Anderson, 1992; Boytzis, 1994); another is to use selected clips, or to make a tape of highlighted segments of one or more films that illustrate topics of import. These methods allow the majority of class time to be devoted to the application of conceptual material to the film.

Although saving class time is an important consideration, watching an entire film in class may be worth the time spent. Both Sternberg (1987), and Gardner (1999) suggest that if we value meaningful learning, it is best to focus curriculum on a few topics that are examined in depth. For Gardner (1999), devoting enough time to teach topics in depth is necessary to undo the firmly engraved misconceptions held by students. His point about misconceptions may apply broadly to students misconceptions about learning and their relationship to learning. Many of the college students I teach have had learning experiences that have fostered a passive learning style. They seem to hold a deeply felt notion that "learning is rote, boring, and not something I am good at." The use of feature films may expose students to the pleasures and excitement some of us feel about learning and thus, is a valuable tool to smooth out misconceptions about the learning process.

CONCLUSION

Feature film, integrated meaningfully into the curriculum, can foster a variety of important skills for lifelong learning. Although I have only cited a few examples from the psychology curriculum here, distinct cognitive benefits can be reaped when appropriate films are selected within history, literature, sociology, social work, social welfare, and other liberal arts courses. Feature films often bring home topics more relevant to a diverse student body. The more realistic immediate quality of films further enhances students' ability to understand and apply concepts. Film analysis, when linked with key themes and issues covered in class, also serves to increase student engagement in the course while providing opportunities to develop connected learning experiences and critical thinking skills.

REFERENCES

Anderson, D., D. (1992). "Using Feature Films as Tools for Analysis in a Psychology and Law Course" in *Teaching of Psychology, 19*, 155-158.

Baumrind, D. (1991). "Effective Parenting during the Adolescent Transition" in P.A. Cowan & M. Hetherington (eds), *Family Transitions* (pp.111-163). Hillsdale, NJ: Earlbaum.

Belenky, M. F., Clinchy, B. M., Goldberger, N.R., & Tarule, J.M. (1997). *Women's Ways of Knowing: The Development of Self, Voice, and Mind.* New York: Basic Books.

Bromwell (Director) (2001). *Panic.* (DVD). (Available from Artisan Home Entertainment, CA).

Chaffee, J. (1994). *Thinking Critically* (4th ed.). Boston, MA: Houghton Mifflin.

Chambliss, C., & Magakis, G. (1996). *Videotapes for Use in Teaching Psychopathology.* U.S. Department of Education, Office of Educational Research and Improvement, Washington D.C. (ERIC Document Reproduction Service No. ED395243).

Clinchy, B.M. (1995). "A Connected Approach to the Teaching of Developmental Psychology" in *Teaching of Psychology, 22*, 100-104.

Craik, F.I.M. & Lockhart, R.S. (1972). "Levels of Processing a Framework for Memory Research" in *Journal of Verbal Learning and Verbal Behavior, 11*, 671-684.

Demme, J. (Director). (1993). *Philadelphia.* [film] (Available from Tristar Pictures, US).

Diagnostic and Statistical Manual—IV. (1994). Published by The American Psychiatric Association. 4th Edition.

Enns, C. Z. (1993). "Integrating Separate and Connected Knowing: The Experiential Learning Model" in *Teaching of Psychology, 20*, 7-13.

Fleming, M.Z. , Piedmont, R. L., & Hiam, C.M. (1990). "Images of Madness: Feature Films in Teaching Psychology" in *Teaching of Psychology, 17,* 185-187.

Garbarino, J., Durbrow, N., Kostelny, K., & Pardo, C. (1992). *Children in Danger:*
Coping With the Consequences of Community Violence. San Francisco: Jossey Bass.

Gardner, H. (1991). *The Unschooled Mind: How Children Think and How Schools Should Teach.* USA: Basic Books.

—. (1999). *The Unschooled Mind: What All Students Should Understand.* NY: Simon & Shuster.

Gregg, V.R., Hosley, C.A., Weng, A., Montemayor, R. (1995). *Using Feature Films to Promote Active Learning in the College Classroom.* U.S. Department of Education, Office of Educational Research and Improvement, Washington DC. (ERIC Document Reproduction Service No. ED 389367).

Jaffe, S., Lansing, S. (Producers), & Lyne, A. (Director). (1987). *Fatal Attraction* [film] (Available from Paramount, CA)

Malle, L. (Director) (1987). *Au Revoir les Enfants.* [video] (Available from Orion Home Video, US).

Mead, J.M. & Scharmann, L.C. (1994). "Enhancing critical thinking through structured controversy" in *The American Biology Teacher*, **56**, 7 416-419.

Nicolaides, S. (Producer) & Singleton, J. (Director). (1991). *Boyz in the Hood* [film]. (Available from Tristar, Burbank, CA)

Perry, N. N.. Huss, M.T. , McAuliff, B.D. , & Galas, J. M.(1996). "An Active-Learning Approach to Teaching the Undergraduate Psychology and Law Course" in *Teaching of Psychology*, **23**, 76-81.

Ruggiero, V.R. (1996). *Becoming a Critical Thinker*. Rapid City, SD: Houghton Mifflin.

Saxon, E. (Producer) & Demme, J. (Producer and Director). (1993). *Philadelphia* [film]. (Available from Tristar, Burbank, CA).

Sternberg, R. (1987). "Teaching Critical Thinking: Eight Easy Ways to Fail before You Begin" in *Phi Delta Kappan*, **68**, 456-459.

M uch like the recent revival of poetry and poetry groups across the United States, the emergence of the memoir—possibly the most controversial literary genre of our times—is characterized by the fact that its practitioners are not necessarily so-called professional writers. Indeed, the contemporary memoir proposes, with its life narratives of marginalized and previously voiceless people, a forum for unspoken issues and stories. My experience teaching memoir at New Jersey City University since 1997 has taught me that this genre has extraordinary potential in terms of community-building and the creation of an active partnership among students, and between teachers and students. In addition to producing memoirs that deal with issues that transcend the specificity of individual life experiences, my students have become articulate in commenting on the function of the memoir as a radical literary genre. Laura McKeon, a student in one of my memoir workshops, explains:

> We all suffer from certain degrees of historical, social, and familial amnesia. Through memoir-writing, one can learn to fill in the blanks and, in the process, reclaim his or her past honestly….the greatest gift I received from my course experience was the sense of validation, trust, and community I garnered from my fellow classmates…I came away with the sense that our personal struggles, although different in detail, bound us together as survivors of our own life experiences.

Another student, Anuradha Lazarre, sees memoir writing as a practice linked in vital ways to one's sense of self-assertion and one's search for legitimacy and recognition:

> Giving your experience a body, putting it down on paper, stakes out your little piece of reality, plants your flag on your territory of human experience.

Grace Guandique, another memoir student, writes:

> The memoir writing workshop let me finally tell the story that I have been carrying around for many years. A story that my family wanted to tell, to scream, to shout at the top of their lungs, but could not. My family could not speak English. We did not have a place to be heard because immigration officials said we did not belong in America. We were not legal residents and therefore, the United States did not recognize us. To them, we did not exist.

SESSION AT CONFERENCE

This session at the Urban Mission Conference came together as the result of work that I have been doing with my students of memoir and advanced memoir workshops. After taking these two courses, many have written Honors Theses that focused on memoir writing. Many have presented their work in public forums and published in the school's creative writing publications. A few have begun to publish in national venues. My memoir students have become actively involved in constructing the culture of the memoir

BUILDING BRIDGES IN THE CLASSROOM: MEMOIR, COMMUNITY, AND POWER

EDVIGE GIUNTA

workshop with extraordinary commitment and professionalism. In the egalitarian space of the memoir workshop, students experience what Melida Rodas, another student, describes as "the warmth and affiliation of community."

It is the collectively-created nurturing environment that makes the memoir journey not only possible but enriching—at times even life-altering. Singular life-narratives, it soon becomes clear, transcend their specificity to become public articulations, stories that resonate for the community. The session itself—and the two essays included here—exemplify the kind of collaborative work that teachers and students can engage in. Through the session, we hoped to prompt some reflections on the memoir and the creative possibilities it affords for personal growth, healing, and, of course, for one's writing power.

BREAKING THROUGH: REFLECTIONS ON MEMOIR WRITING
by April Sinisi

When I came to college in 1997, I had pneumonia twice within that same year. That spring, I turned gray at an Elton John concert in Madison Square Garden when the smoke-filled frenzy of cigarettes and marijuana catapulted me smack dab on a stretcher headed for St. Vincent's Hospital. When my doctor diagnosed pneumonia a third time, I felt devastated. Stronger rounds of steroids, with four alternating inhalers and seventy-eight pounds later, my asthma was out of control.

In the spring of 1999, I took a Women Writers Workshop at

New Jersey City University. I hadn't written since I was twelve and was hoping to improve my writing skills while trying to rediscover the writing I loved in my childhood.

In the privacy of my eighth grade book, I wrote about jasmine and sweet-smelling roses that contrasted against the jagged brick wall of my gray house in the bright sunlight. I wrote about ideals that would change my destiny as I leaped to heaven on puffy white clouds to ask God if it was O.K. to dream. Within the range of my pen, I took chances exploring the Arctic on a Viking ship, drank Mead with the men, and showed Christopher Columbus how to use a compass. I wrote about the distinct textures of grass that grew in my back yard, pressed the three different varieties in between the lined pages of my notebook, and penned off a note to the Museum of Natural Science about these unique findings.

I recorded the results of sticky balls experiments that fell from the big old Maple tree in my backyard, filled my blue-jeans pockets with them, to dissect the green almond centers with my pocketknife, hoping to find a miracle cure for cancer. I drafted stories about my first winter in Union City when I, a stranger on a new block, with no one to play with, explored the vast wilderness of my yard. As the wind swirled through my snowsuit, as the late afternoon sun stayed hidden behind thick purple white clouds. While snowdrifts filled the gray stairs of the left side of our porch, as our neighbor's door was covered halfway up to the doorknob, I wrote about the forgotten pioneer woman who pushed through the driving snow into the vast unknown wilderness separated from her wagon train, with only scraps of wood and dried leaves to kept her alive. Upstairs, in the my attic room, I penned away. Now I wanted to recapture the thrill of those experiences.

My professor wrote on my stories in red: "You are dancing April, get to the heart of your subject. What do you really want to write about?" I was flabbergasted. I believed I could mask and hide within new stories, the same way I had hidden all my life. But I couldn't deceive myself any longer. This thing, this need, wouldn't wait any longer.

I read stories about the strife of women who suppressed and forgot their abuse. I read Louise De Salvo's Vertigo and was completely captivated by her story. In Judith Herman's Trauma and Recovery, I discovered that I had been unable to move forward emotionally like a lot of other victims of violence and terror. Their stories reminded me of mine. Instead of accepting the personal challenge, I tried to build safe walls to harbor the inner me. And now this teacher wanted me to rip them down using my pen as a bulldozer.

By the fifth week of the semester, I was experiencing panic attacks: I trembled as my breast pulled and pushed against the rhythmic beating of my heart. I started to withdraw, the same way I did when I was twelve, despondent about my writing, my life, my secrets. All my life I hid from myself, became good at hiding, very good at it. I flatly refused to reveal. But now, I couldn't seem to hold it together. I didn't want anyone to know my underbelly. I couldn't raise my pen up without feeling a panic attack mounting, from the back of my mouth. My pen would shake in mid air.

Three days before class would meet I would start to sweat and cry, complaining that my teacher had no right to intrude on my world. I shut down the creative process. I scribbled on the blank page: "I Could Tell You Secrets." Two of our community writers were young girls that went to school with my children. I couldn't trust this community of writers with my secrets. It would have to wait. I couldn't take the chance of my children finding out.

She gave me sound advice one day after class, when she looked me squarely in the eyes and said, "Look April, we all have a lot muck in our lives. And it's only after you dive into the muck that you can see other colors and other dimensions." Now, I don't dive into anything. I wade; and with this I didn't even want to get my toes wet. She handed me pamphlets on therapy and counseling, I threw them out.

Two semesters later, I met another professor who specialized in memoir. I still harbored ill feelings for Professor Caronia and her teaching strategies. I walked into the Memoir Workshop uneasy and somewhat resistant, afraid of what she would push me to see. She introduced me to journal writing, a requirement for each of her classes. Every week we wrote five uncensored pages of how we felt or about any of our own memories. She explained that what we wrote in our journals would provide a safe private passage into understanding our feelings, our memories, our stories. As I explored my feelings in my journal, memoir started to emerge without the emotional chaos that haunted me before. For me it was the first step I took towards understanding myself.

Within the first two weeks of my Memoir class here, I found acceptance, compassion, and forgiveness, not directly from this professor, but from within me. I found acceptance from other students, who shared their own stories as I came to terms with my abuse. Within the community that I was now ready to join, I felt release, freedom, forgiveness. My pen became my tool, as I searched for my voice. Introduced to another book by Louise De Salvo, Writing As A Way of Healing, I started to find a way to write without anger. It opened up my mind, forged a way through my adolescent nightmares. I understood, from reading DeSalvo, that retelling trauma is necessary for healing.

Much later, I realized that this was the muck that Professor Caronia had tried patiently to tell me about. With my new tool I was able to vent the same emotions that offended my father. By digging through muddled mixed emotions of my self-imposed silence, I realized that I use my pen and notebook as implements to help the healing process begin, the same way I tried when I was younger. She explains that writing won't make the pain of incest and unprovoked beatings go away, but it will change the writer's relationship to these traumatic experiences. By retelling trauma, the writer takes the first step towards healing. I wanted more than *anything to begin healing. I wanted freedom from this pain. I had to let go, it was time to move on.*

However, writing through trauma is still difficult. I take small awkward steps towards healing, but it's still long, hard work. Sometimes I falter and get angry about the life I should have had. I cry thinking about all the lies and deceit that my family lived with. I am in the midst of that process now, and sometimes it's easier to backslide into a river of self-pity. I made reminders for myself, in muddy shades of green, brown and yellow. The bookmarker reads, "When writing I am diving. When diving, I'm discovering the hidden layers of me." I am anxious to see who I am hidden under the layers of so many yesterdays.

To deny writing now would be to die, for with writing I have stepped out of my pit of muck and mire, wet sticky, and excited to find new colors blending together in this pit. My anxiety attacks have almost disappeared. I've been able to stop all Predisone medication. The once 10-pill day combined medication has been reduced to 0. I no longer sleep with the "orange inhaler" in hand, nor do I use extraordinary amounts of support medication. Inhalers no longer line up next to my bed. My notebook sits on the end table now. When I am emotional or stressed, I write. It is here that I can see the parallels between my youth and my adult life. Do you know how much this has cost me? One 29-cent pen, two 99-cent marble notebooks, and two fantastic women to guide me through the most incredible journey of my life.

What follows are excerpts from my long memoir project.

RAINBOW

Miss Celenza writes my Mom complaining that I won't speak in class. She's right; I don't talk. Sometimes she stands in front of me and uses her pointer to push and prod me to answer the question. Sometimes I don't want to talk and I can't be made to talk by pushing, prodding, and yelling. Just plain simple: nothing comes out no matter what. At times it is fun watching her get all crazy but it is not fun when she writes to my mother. I hate that. Hate long letters inked in blue on white paper describing my "problem." My mother hates my problem. I am silent at home too, almost four years now.

"What is the answer April?" she screams standing over me with her brown hair that hides her face getting redder and redder, as she looks down at me. I don't see her any more, but hear her black high heels walking away from my desk, when she gives up in disgust. Peeking through overgrown bangs, she's flailing her arms up and down like a heavy bird unable to lift off. "Speak up, does the cat have your tongue?" Everyone laughs, as she slaps her hand down hard on mine to get her point across.

"Meow!" someone snickers. Everyone laughs again. I don't care what they say about me, because I can't hear any of the mean things they say behind my back. Instead, I watch the white florescent light over her desk jump up and down in the long glass

tube. It hums. I am drawn into colors that change and move. The white gets bigger with specks of black, black that will get eventually get bigger and bigger, if I'm not careful. I can hear the humming, buzzing, rhythmic humming above the clatter of my classroom. Quietly, the light sings me a song. I sit and smile, humming along. I no longer hear anything but sweet surges of soothing sound. Almost like bees searching for their beds, in a long white beehive content to be home. With any luck, I will be home before I am swallowed up completely. It is not smart to allow the black to engulf me in school. I am afraid that they will send me to the other school, the one with all the other retards.

Mom is mad at me today, but I don't care. She had to take off from work to see Miss Celenza, like the letter said. I want her to talk to me. But she doesn't talk; she just yells like Miss Celenza, "What the hell has gotten into you April? Why can't you just answer the questions in class? Why do you make your life so miserable?" She doesn't want to talk; she doesn't want to know anything. So I say nothing to her too.

On our way to see Miss Celenza I look at the cracks in the sidewalks that will break her back. I step on every crack I can find. I cry onto my shoes. I always cry when my parents yell. I can't get the words to form in my mouth, so I cry. Sandy, my older brother, calls me "a crybaby!" He laughs at me. Says I'm stupid. Can't answer any stupid questions in school cause I'm crazy. He says they're going to send me away and lock me in a dark room and throw away the key. I'm scared, too scared to talk.

I try to participate because I don't want to be retarded. Like I can be retarded one day and OK the next. I'm afraid of the dark and don't like small places that aren't mine. But my mother and father are furious. Angry because their plans aren't working. I'm just being stubborn and thickheaded like they said. This time dad goes to school, so that mom won't have to use another of her precious sick days. She's saving the rest to watch Sandy play basketball. While they talk, I won't look up from my dark wooden inkwell desk. Together, outside the door, they plot out a plan as the whole class watches the glass door. I can't see any colors, nor will the buzzing return. I hear the loud pounding of my heart, pushing through the bones of my chest. The pushing hurts. My heart hurts. But no black. I want black today.

They decide that he will come in every Friday before he goes to work to check on my "progress." She is determined to make me normal. For five weeks there is no change. My mother is crazy with worry. I can tell her why. But she won't sit long enough for me to get it out.

I started to talk in school, not on Mondays or Tuesdays but definitely by Wednesday. After two or three weeks, on Fridays I answer all of Miss Cleneza's stupid questions. Mom is happy, I guess. She smiles when she talks to her sister about me now. A couple of times Daddy comes in early to talk with Miss Celenza. She likes him. She laughs loud and smiles a lot whenever he is there. Tells everyone in my class that my Daddy is handsome and funny, so she lets me go home early with him, a couple of times. If we don't hit traffic or if Miss Celenza doesn't laugh too much it's early enough for us to play mommy before he goes to work. I don't want to go home. I look out the car window the white starts to fade into yellow. Yellow slowly turns to ochre, blue comes and turns into deep violet then dark gray is followed by warm black. Warm dark black, I am not cold anymore.

NAPKINS

The quiet was maddening. Just soft muffled sounds of me hopping from one leg to the other. How much time passed, I couldn't say. Why he stopped, I don't know. When he left, I could neither stand nor sit nor cry out for help. I stood there hopping on one beaten left leg and alternated to the bruised right one. It wasn't because he stopped that my cries were silent; it was because I reached a new level of pain. Past my limit of understanding, of accepting, my limit of knowing. "God help me," I whispered. Left leg jig, right leg wobble.

The simple truth is, I defied him by bringing home nine-cent napkins and five-cent sponges. It was a power of wills and he won. I no longer cared if I saw a napkin or a sponge again. The battle to have them in our house was over. Now I would feel the rage of my defiance. Till now, most of the beatings took place outside in the hallway, between my father and my brother. I know I pushed him, pushed too hard, knew it when I rounded the top of my block, shopping cart in hand. What was I thinking? I had hoped that they would give the appearance of normalcy to our home. Now I was hoping that he would hit me only a couple of times, just a couple of familiar belt marks a few red welts that usually appeared on my thighs. When he entered my room I knew, as he slapped his thick black belt repeatedly in his large callused hand harder and harder, the silver belt buckle bouncing up and down, I had gone too far. Rising my hands up in front of my face I begged him not to hit me. I promised never to bring home anything not on the list again. I promised to be good. One slap followed by another. A short pause. Then he hit me again. And again. And again. And again. I danced a jig I had never known. The sound of his belt slapping my skin bounced off the walls of my room, out the open window into the quiet undisturbed night. He was no longer beating his defiant daughter, you see. It wasn't about nine cent-napkins or five-cents sponges. He was no longer hitting me; he was beating out everything that he hated. His eyes grew narrow as this rage took over. He was no longer able to control himself striking out against his incomplete life, his past, his birth, the death of his mother, his absent father, his loneliness, his wife, his disobedient children, his drinking, his abuse, and the bus driver who wouldn't allow the drunk to board the bus this afternoon. Somehow we all became connected within that black belt in his massive hand. And I was the catalyst that drove him there and for that I was sorry.

MEMOIR-ISTICALLY SPEAKING
by Loryn Lipari

Bare legs. Bent at the knee. Feet, reluctant, under motel room's bed sheets. Left hand draped over stomach. Right hand lifted into the air that separates us. My fingers spread. Stop. I see the yellowing of the bed sheets and her thigh. The black cotton shirt falls just past the 'γ'.

This picture, taped inside my journal, is dated July 28, 2001. The flash of the camera brightens my skin.

Meadowlands Motel on Tonnelle Avenue, 5 AM, Room #57. The black nylon thong with the cotton crotch does not shield me from the bedbugs that push against the edges of my panties. Pubic hairs of strangers speckle the sheets in between the flat, the fitted, and the cheap polyester bedspread. The carpet is frayed at the edges of the walls. The hollow bathroom door is splintered in a long indentation, a fistful of anger—or angry sex. Only two of the four ceiling spotlights work. It smells of sex, like a garbage can used over and over again without a plastic bag in it. The air-conditioning unit clanks and spits out air like an open freezer box in a butcher's back room. The mattress is exhausted in the middle, its edges lifting into the air on either side when my body sinks in. I pull the cinnamon gum from my mouth, roll it between my thumb and index finger, and lob it across the room. It bounces off the paneling and rolls onto a brownish stain on the carpet.

There are three of us here tonight.

Are you with me? Have I taken you there? Do you want to know more? If I have, then I have done my job. I have given you a Memoir Moment. It came from my journal. Not all of it. Next to the snapshot that is taped inside my journal are words scribbled within the pages about the evening at Meadowlands Motel. Quick phrases. No order. Not intended to be read, just written down, these words, so I would not forget.

I write in my journal every morning. Like going to a gym. I have to make the commitment to exercise my brain, to joggle my memory. The only way I can begin the process of writing the memoir is to write. And I write. I complain about my girlfriend, my homework, my daily living. Nothing in my journal has substance in the beginning, its contents full of the static that is inside my head, but it clears a passage through which I can focus on writing, writing my memoir. Literally, with pencil in hand, the physical act of writing allows me to break through the surface of my memory.

To go back and read what I wrote about any given day and then WRITE about it, really write about it. Discipline, I was told. Structure. Revisions. Dedication. Writing partners. Editing. Re-writes. Re-writes. More re-writes.

Subject matter. Memoir is the writings of personal memories. I gave you a hot, sexually charged moment early on. Subject matter changes in time. Some of us go right to the most painful memories. An alcoholic parent. Drug Addiction. Child Abuse. Death. The process of digging is long and slow and because memoir writing is so personal, it can be emotionally draining.

Writing is a transitional process that pushes itself, as if I am bloodless and receiving a transfusion, my stories flow through me while I am writing. Images of rooms, favorite toys, clothing, faces fill my veins like the push of a nurse's thumb against the syringe. Only to have the words spew out into the computer, open wounds at my fingertips. Bleeding. By the time the piece is finally printed on 8 1/2" x 11" sheets of paper, I'm dry.

One of my first published pieces was about crack addiction.

"Debby lives across the hall. I can't guess her age. Her hair is knotted and held back with bobby pins. She smiles when she sees me, knowing that I will give her a hit in return for the favor of letting me hide here. Her teeth are rotten. Large gaps suck in the air as she opens her mouth to speak. Her gums are red and swollen, irritated where the teeth meets the flesh. Plaque embeds itself in the sides while a blackened mass attaches itself to the corners of her lower front teeth. Valleys and hills of neglect grow like moss across her smile. When she greets me at the door, the staleness of her breath floats towards my nostrils and sticks to the hairs in my nose. I close my mouth and run my tongue across the front of my teeth, wishing I had a toothbrush, but not knowing where I would trust myself to brush. The corners of Debby's eyes are crusty with late afternoon awakenings."

The piece in full is about six pages. It came out of me mid-semester, when discipline became a ritual. I wrote it without getting up from my computer. I placed myself back in time. I typed the details as they came to me, quickly. Debby's features so vivid in my memory. The details of not even an hour of my life stretch across six full pages. Before, a lifetime had barely covered six pages.

The classroom, on the third floor of Grossnickle looks like a vacant city lot. Torn bread thrown on the pavement. Someone feeds the pigeons. They gather in a small circle around tonight's offerings. Peck at the chunks, tap their beaks slightly, manipulate the food with their tongues and bounce long, narrow jointed feet towards the next piece. Dry mouthed and feathered with an urban grit that dulls any sign of color. I clench my paper in my hands tightly and cut my eyes towards the six or seven students who shift their bodies towards me. Tonight I present my first Memoir Moment. The faces of strangers, the unfamiliar sound of my voice towards them as I sprinkle myself out in the open lot. I am afraid of the dirt of my pages. The topic I have chosen reveals secrets about me. But this is what the beginnings of Memoir is. It is not just about writing. It is about sharing your work. It's about reading your work and getting a reaction. Building levels of community: Professors, students, audience

I sit, crimped to the beige, metal chair. Elbows rest on the simulated wooden desktop and begin to read "Cracked." My voice feeds into the air. Monotone. It speaks the words that I have written, like the sound of a heart monitor just as it catches death, in a long, low hum. My eyes do not drift from the pages.

I bring the audience inside. I take them across imaginary streets and up into real buildings in the Bronx, into the features of characters like Debby. Enter her mouth, the corner of eyes, the smell of her breath, in order to visualize how I lived. It is with the attention to detail and imagery that memoir writing becomes inescapable to the reader and challenging to the writer. My writing doesn't expel outward, it pulls the reader into my memory. At first, shyness lowers my voice. My ability to detach from my audience turns out to be an important key in presenting my work. By sheer accident, I realize that my written word is half the power and my spoken voice completes the circle, because not only do I need to write, I need to read my work in front of others. Any awkwardness in a sentence, any holes in the story I've left out or choppy transitions, any interesting facts that I haven't provided to the reader, all come out when I read my work aloud.

"What do you like? What don't you like? Where is the hole in the narrative? What would you like to know more about?" The Professor breaks the silence in the classroom. She asks the class to consider these four questions when critiquing my work. I listen carefully to the suggestions of my fellow writers. I jot down everything each one says. Actually, that is a lie. I make notes within the margins of my paper. Discarding certain suggestions that didn't feel "right." I need to remain open minded, but true to my writing. Suggestions are necessary, but changes in the story are not mandatory.

How can we possibly write it all, when in fact it is the process that leads us deep within ourselves and creates revelations that we didn't even know existed until we write about them.

It is March 10, 2000. The Barnes and Noble bookstore is buzzing with familiar faces. Professors from New Jersey City University, Edvige Giunta, her husband, her daughter, Emily. Memoir students accompanied by friends and family. The Dean of Arts and Sciences.

It is a week night in Hoboken, but the weight of the traffic tricks outsiders into believing it may be a weekend. The title of tonight's event is "Celebrating the Voices of the Women of Hudson County" sponsored by the Collective of Italian American Women. I have been asked to come and read "Cracked" at the event.

Folding chairs line the opening at the back of the store, next to the Children's Literature section. A small desk sits on a slant and holds some flyers for tonight's event, and a vase with assorted flowers. I'm not sure of the kind. A steel microphone stand causes the carpet to indent at its base, its emptied bracket droops towards the floor. I am not the first to read, I am perhaps the second or third. I hear my name split through the speaker system like the beam from a naked light bulb through the peep hole of a darkened hallway door. I make way my up to the podium, weaving in out of the crowd huddled in front of the microphone.

In a subway station. Alone. Thick, warm air brushes against my cheek bone. It tickles my forehead, just above my eyebrow. The approaching train rumbles the floor against the balls of my feet. The vibration creeps up into my calves, pauses in my knee caps and intensifies in my torso. The papers shake in my hand . I grab the microphone. I do not stand. I sit down behind the desk and begin to read.

The applause at the end sounds muffled. I aim my eyes into the crowd, but cannot see a single face. My first experience doing a public reading. I will continue to write full force, the clapping acts as some spiritual assembly. It urges me on.

Some writing comes easy. Some stories are told without walking away from the computer every half an hour to re-evaluate direction. "Cracked" in its original form was just that. A story that was written in one sitting with very few edits. A publishable piece. But what about the story that is written that gets rejected? The thirty pages that are not accepted? When a deadline is just days away and the writing is not there?

Inhale. Exhale. Look at the blank computer screen. An anthology on Italian American women and food. Based on "Cracked," I'm asked to be a contributor in this upcoming book. I'm thrilled, but when I sit at my computer to expand this piece and keep in mind the basis for the book, I am confused. I begin to write about my grandmother. I am in my father's car, a red convertible Elderado driving on the Garden State Parkway South towards North Bergen. I am climbing the steps of her house on 43rd Street. I am in her kitchen, her living room, her back yard patio. I am in the wrong place. Thirty pages later, it is not the story my editors are looking for. My submission gets rejected. The thirty pages gets saved on a disk and pushed aside, for now. Nothing I write gets thrown out.

Inhale. Exhale. Look at the blank computer screen. Italian American women and food based on my piece "Cracked." It is about drug addiction, not food. Starvation, not nourishment. I start brainstorming. I write down everything that comes to mind, whether it pertains to the topic or not. I'm bound to hit on something, to unleash a story.

Where do I get the instructions for preparation, the measurements of crack to ashes, the cooking procedures that make sure I get a good hit? I don't think I found them in my great grandmother's notebook of recipes, in between pizza dough and butter cookies. Her daughter, my grandmother, Nanny, didn't write it down for me on her slanted handwriting, the number of handfuls of crack marked in script on a loose leaf paper with the corner torn off. Olive oil stains at the bottom where it instructs me to knead.

Crack

1 Serving

Preheat mental state to 450

Prepare pipe for smoking Crack (see Pg. 136, "Pipe Making Techniques")

Combine:
*   2 to 3 Parliament filter sized scoops of cigarette ashes (preferably whole)*
*   2 or 3 small rocks of Crack/Cocaine (May have to break down by hand)*
Heat:
*   Using a lighter for best results*
*   Inhale slowly*
*   Repeat as needed*
★hint: re-use foil package

I write a fourteen-page memoir that speaks about the distance between me and my family. The detachment of tradition. The gaping hole between us that is filled with my drug abuse. It was a hard piece to write because I am asked to write it. I found that to be the hardest challenge out of all my writing. To not write what I wanted. To dig for the story. One without the original "Cracked" memoir at all. It was edited out in its entirety.

My fingers open onto my shaved head pulling the skin of my forehead up. The palms of my hands prod my eye sockets. I glance at the keyboard. Drag my index finger just above the keypad collecting white dust particles. I roll them between my thumb and forefinger. Let out a long sigh. To someone else looking from the doorway into my office my eyes are fixed onto the keyboard. But, they're not. They're not even focusing on any one letter. I'm bringing myself back in time. Trying to find the place where the story lies. The children's voices calling to their parents downstairs trickle into some space in between the wooden boards and plaster of this house. I am no longer in immediate reality. I begin to type. Just one moment. I'm not sure where it will lead. Where it will take me. Where it will take you. I type and type and type.

Challenging Institutional Thinking

The Criminal Justice system is described as a juggernaut, a mammoth structure composed of law enforcement, the courts and the penal system that moves slowly and is fiercely resistant to change. Education for the imprisoned is but one small spoke on this machine's wheel of justice. Customarily, it has been designed to provide Basic Skills or G.E.D., with little or no room for change or innovative approaches to providing inmates with sorely needed behavioral or social skills.

The authors, John Kerwin and Roberta Davidson, taught at the Washington State Penitentiary in Walla Walla, Washington, (the infamous "Concrete Mama") for a combined fifteen years. During that time, they created and then taught a class in *Gender Differences and Communication* which was a bold approach to change in the corrections education. The concept was unprecedented in a prison: a woman and a man together in the classroom, teaching convicted murderers, rapists and thieves about sensitivity to gender differences. The language they used to connect with the inmates did not follow traditional pedagogical guidelines as it was conversational and jargon-free, and their classroom "texts" included stories and themes in contemporary films. Their goal was to encourage more effective communications between the inmates and their families and female friends and, ideally, with society at large.

The Premise: Imaginative Reasoning

John Kerwin had been teaching for five years at the Penitentiary. His courses were in basic communications skills using television technology—two cameras, a switcher and videotape machine—as a conduit for inmates to express themselves, as well as mediating inmate-to-staff communications, and staff-to-inmate communications. This program experienced considerable success as John observed that if he allowed the inmates to "talk the talk" of the prison culture and then guided them through production lesson plans and course subjects, he could "raise the bar" in terms of inmates learning more effective communication techniques. But he also needed to be willing and able to "talk their talk" to facilitate this kind of communication.

During this time, John observed that numerous inmate video projects had, as their theme, men and women in relationships, sex and love. This observation caused John to approach Dr. Roberta Davidson to see if she was willing to venture from the security of a quiet, liberal arts college environment in order to cross-town and enter Concrete Mama to co-teach a course in *Gender Awareness and Communications*. Roberta had been instrumental in creating the Gender Studies Minor at Whitman College and, perhaps most importantly, believed in the effectiveness of incorporating non-traditional texts and techniques in the classroom, particularly when addressing issues of gender. John and Roberta, therefore, were compatible in their basic teaching philosophy and their belief that gender awareness and

Gender Communications behind Bars: Non-Traditional Classrooms and Teaching

John Kerwin and Roberta Davidson

sensitivity were issues of crucial importance both in the classroom and outside it.

The authors initially had difficulty convincing the Walla Walla Community College, which chooses the courses taught at the Penitentiary, that gender studies was viable for inmates. These classes would be the first in the history of the Penitentiary, which had not offered any form of gender studies in the past. Nor had most of their students—who came from predominantly economically and educationally underprivileged backgrounds—been previously exposed to the idea of gender as a cultural construct. Both the methodology of the class and its ideology would break new ground.

The Hypothesis: "It's a male/female thing."

There were two institutional challenges, therefore, that had to be addressed before John and Roberta stepped into the classroom, as well as one personal one. The personal challenge was to convince themselves that their approach could work. Their first task was to create a convincing argument in the form of an hypothesis that would sell prison and education authorities that the course would be successful. They hypothesized that in a gender communications course, if a male and female team teach the course and express viewpoints in an open discussion format that represents their different sexual identities as they explore issues and themes of relationships, sex and love by using contemporary films as "outside voices" and other classroom exercises that spoke the language of the inmate students, then the result would be the most effective method of teaching these non-traditional students [inmates] in this non-traditional classroom [prison]. The course was approved. Then the real challenge began.

NON-TRADITIONAL STUDENTS

The students who took the class over the five-year period were consistent only in their diversity. The prison population contained a disproportionately large number of minorities, including African-Americans, Latinos and Native Americans. The men ranged in age from sixteen-years-old to mid-fifties, with an average age of twenty-seven. The class had an average of a seventh-grade educational level, although several students had G.E.D.s. Many had been convicted of crimes of violence toward women, including assault, rape and murder, and some were themselves survivors of maternal and paternal child abuse. The challenge for John and Roberta was to facilitate a constructive and *united* classroom environment, to find ways to effectively communicate across class and racial lines, and effect changes in these men's attitudes, language and behavior patterns with women.

CONTEMPORARY LANGUAGE IN CONTEMPORARY FILMS

John and Roberta used a variety of methods to encourage their students to make their own connections between gender theory and actual practice. Because of the poor educational preparation their students had received in the past, the written word tended to alienate and alarm some of them. Therefore, they depended heavily upon contemporary films to document current societal attitudes toward gender. This allowed the class to address the most contemporary examples of the marketing of gender and to satisfy the students' expressed desire for "keepin' it real." They were also assigned weekly journals in which they were evaluated on the quality of their ideas more than the smoothness of their prose. Some of the films and themes used were:

The Wood	The struggle of surviving and making it on the streets. Male-to-male relationships and male-female relationships.
Mi Familia	Exploring the foundations of family, love and pride in the Latino community. The strength of family to overcome trauma and tragedy.
The Best Man	The questions, concerns and uncertainties that must be overcome to find trust and commitment in relationships and marriage.
Brothers McMillan	Working class men exploring the full gamut of male/female dynamics and honesty in relationships.
Love Jones	A group of young, artistic African-American friends try to restore their belief in love and relationships.
Breaking Up	The pain and healing process of a failed relationship.
The Last Seduction	A powerful and manipulative woman moves the men around her like game-pieces by playing on their gender stereotypes.
Slam	An African-American poet in prison finds non-traditional ways to protect himself without resorting to stereotypical "male" behavior.
Romeo and Juliet	The modern-day remake of this four hundred-year-old play is still one of the most powerful stories about love's power to ennoble and destroy. The gang violence between the families was an easy point of identification for our students.

The following brief examples of inmate journals, written in response to two of these films, provide valuable insight, not only as to their grasp of the assignment, but also to illustrate the range of attitudes and values of the inmates.

RESPONSES TO *THE LAST SEDUCTION:*

"Rashid," twenty-eight years old, assault with a deadly weapon
"Anyone in a relationship has to draw lines. A person has to step back and take a look and realize when he or she is being used. Bridget got men to cater to her ego by catering to their egos. This is using. The men who loved her loved her like a drug. Any drug is going to take you down in the end. All the other stuff that went down between Bridget and her men went down because they were all blind to this reality. Treat love like a drug that gets you high and it's going to kill you. It don't take a genius to see it!"

"Shawn," forty years old, illegal possession of drugs and firearms
In a way, I admire Bridget. She is only doing what millions of men have done for years. Those men in the

film think she's their partner, but they don't really think she's their equal or she couldn't get away with playing them. But she steps over a line, even if they deserve it. I have known a couple of lady's [sic] who were very close to Bridget's character. They were fun for a while, but soon wore me out. It is fun to run on the fence for a while, but you must know when to step down and to which side to step, main stream or extreme. That's when you have to get real, with a woman, and with yourself.

RESPONSES TO *ROMEO AND JULIET:*

"Tommy," thirty-three years old, bank robbery

Love at first sight, what a concept! In my youth I thought I was in love on a hundred different occasions. As I grew older I realized that love is a series of compromises and sacrifices. True love is not based on physical attraction alone, although that is certainly a primary catalyst for bringing two people together. I think that love, true love, in this day and age is a rarity. The generation of ME, ME, ME has turned the phrase "I love you" into something like "How you doing?" or "See you later." Can we still love like Romeo and Juliet? I think they make it because they believe that true love exists. They love like kids, they're so naive it works. We try to love like adults, with all the compromise that love takes, and in the end we don't really find true love. We know too much about love for it to exist for us.

"Dave," twenty-nine years old, murder

I love my wife and kids. Life without [parole], trying to forget, the hardest part about trying to forget my love is the remembering forgetting brings back. I thought love was made up of the things that had happened, things and thoughts I could put away. How privileged of me to think of love as a thing or a thought. The more I don't think about my family the more I miss them. Trying to forget makes me know I can only define love as emotions shared in a spirit's heart. The love is still in my heart as I sit in a living tomb and wonder what went wrong. I wonder if I'll ever stop feeling this way even if I can make myself forget everything. I know why Romeo didn't want to go on living after Juliet died.

"Paul," twenty-three years old, murder

Love is trust, devotion, dedication. Love is caring, joy, security. Love is warmth of the heart, deep feeling for another. Love is missing that special someone when they are there. Love is grief when that special someone is gone for good. Love is family and friends. Love is the heart filled to capacity and overflowing. Love is the attachment a mother has for a newborn. Love is Cupid and love is Jesus. Whoever feels any part of love feels all the parts of love, even if it's just for a moment or a week. As the saying goes, love is what conquers all, even death, even prison.

PLAYING ROLES IN MOCK TRIALS

John and Roberta also experimented with role-playing and debate in the classroom. One class, for example, was set up as a mock trial in a sexual harassment case, using John as the accused and Roberta as the accuser, with inmates playing the roles of counsel, jury and judge. Such creative methods were new in the Penitentiary. Their success was dependent, of course, on the willingness of the students to cooperate with the experiment, which they largely did. Several factors contributed to the students' willingness to—literally—play along. Most of them felt privileged to be involved in the class, and they were willing to reward the teachers' trust in their maturity with supportive behavior. On the whole, the hypothesis that the students would respond favorably to "raising the bar" of expectations was a success. When treated as adults, most responded in an adult fashion.

A HIGH RISK EXPERIMENT—FREE WORLD LANGUAGE IN PRISON

One of the many drawbacks to teaching gender in a Maximum Security environment is that despite the diversity, there is one key group who is largely absent—women. In particular, the inmates tended to treat Roberta as a spokesperson for all women, as though her gender allowed her insight into all other women, regardless of difference in age, class and race. Roberta attempted to address this problem by gaining permission to bring her gender studies class at Whitman College, made up of both men and women, to the Pen. In the end, both sets of students shared a single classroom, seated in a circle, as they addressed their common concerns in a free-ranging discussion. What emerged from this discussion was a positive energy. Both sets of students realized, despite the differences in their class demographics (Whitman is a small, liberal arts college, predominantly middle-class and white, with the most common minority population being students of Asian ancestry, the smallest ethnic group found in the Pen) they shared many common interests and concerns regarding love and trust, and the problem of knowing what goes on in the mind of the "Other." Moreover, through the experience of seeing themselves through the other student body's eyes, both inmate and Whitman students were given the opportunity to reflect about their own attitudes and self-representation in ways that they would have resisted without that outside stimulus. Moreover, the realization by both groups of students that they had more in common in their attitudes and mental processes was a stunning one for both groups. They were moved to question how much of the difference between them was one of opportunities, self-presentation and attitude, rather than genuine intelligence and ability.

Conclusion

Although it has been five years since John and Roberta began and finished the teaching of Gender Communication at the Penitentiary, the majority of their students are still behind bars. It is not possible, therefore, to judge whether or not the class had any real impact on the men's behavior toward women in the free world. Nor would it be fair to assign all the praise or blame for their subsequent behavior to a single class. In Division of Correction terms, therefore, it is not yet possible to determine whether or not the class made these students into "better" men in the long run. In the short term, however, its benefits were many and the class, deemed a success, was repeated for several years running. Inmates were introduced to the idea of gender as a cultural construct. They were encouraged to examine their own behavior and attitudes, as well as those of the society around them. They engaged in conversations about love and relationships with students from a different world, and found startling affinities of interest and attitude. They gained confidence in their classroom skills. They even discovered that the educational process could be fun. And finally, in an environment in which the man with nothing to lose is a danger to himself and others, they decided for themselves that they valued the experience of going to a class above the dubious pleasures of disruptive or aggressively individualistic behavior.

Male-female team-teaching in gender courses, "talking their talk," innovative approaches and "raising the bar of expectations," worked for the hardened criminals in maximum security. It is not beyond the bounds of probability that it works equally well or better in free classrooms.

While dramatic attention is being given to engaging K-12 learners in more effective lesson delivery, higher education often lags sorely behind, bogged down in a tradition of lecture-based instructional practices. The old adage says, "What's good for the goose is good for the gander." It is a perfect analogy for instruction at the post-secondary level. Many of the pedagogical techniques, strategies and approaches used in K-12 education can be adapted to enhance instruction at the college level. This paper suggests specific methods that are designed to foster higher levels of student engagement for the college classroom, supporting the premise that active, cognitive and constructivist processing is critical to learning.

BACKGROUND

Is lecture the preferred mode of information processing by post-secondary students? Or is lecture the logical result of content-area specialist's limited pool of instructional variety? Usually college and university professors begin their careers in higher education immediately after graduate school (Borra, 2001). Although they have a depth of content—that is, subject specific knowledge—their pedagogical training is less than adequate to support the complex learning environs of the university setting.

Studies over the past thirty years de-bunk passive models of learning, opting for more hands-on and experiential engagement of students in the process of learning (Eggen and Kauchak, 1997; Brophy, 1992; Brophy and Good, 1986). Learning is defined by Kauchak and Eggen, (1998) as "a natural process…of discovering and constructing meaning from information and experience…"(p.10). Thus, learning may be viewed as a by-product of cognition and the lived experience. The constructivist perspective focuses on *what* students know and their thought processes or *how* they think.

INDUCTIVE MODELS

Anderson and Krathwohl (2001) support the constructivist perspective stating that, "Learners are not passive recipients, nor are they simple recorders of information" (p.38). More active models of lesson delivery serve to provide students with multiple opportunities to engage in active ways with the material to be learned. Although factual knowledge comprises the traditional ethos of learning, Anderson and Krathwohl identify three other types of knowledge as *conceptual*, *procedural* and *meta-cognitive* (p.63). These other types can be developed and assessed most appropriately when students are allowed a participatory role in lesson delivery.

Models of inductive teaching embrace the premise that students should be actively engaged in the learning process. The approaches to instruction are learner-centered or student-centered. Instructors using inductive teaching models plan lessons that link the concept to be learned with what students already know. They prepare instructional tasks or experiences that help students make the connection

WHAT'S GOOD FOR THE GOOSE: USING K-12 PEDAGOGY TO TEACH POST-SECONDARY LEARNERS

CATHY GRIFFIN MUSSINGTON

between the abstraction of conceptual information and concrete or procedural tasks. Questioning skills play an integral role. Probing, higher-order, and open-ended questions strike at the core of identifying both prior and newly introduced knowledge and students' ability to cognitively process information.

DISCUSSION MODEL

One aspect of engaging students that is used effectively in college classrooms is the Socratic method. The art of questioning requires specific skill in using probes, context/content clues and prompts. These serve to foster deeper understanding of concepts. Ultimately, the goal is to stimulate the development of higher-order and critical thinking skills. According to Gunther, Estes and Schwab (1999), an effective teacher should pose a variety of *types* of questions throughout discussions. The types are categorized as *factual*, *interpretive* and *evaluative*. Too often the emphasis—especially in assessment of learning—is on the factual knowledge base of the learner. The interpretive and evaluative types of questioning techniques allow students to formulate and demonstrate higher levels of understanding through their classroom dialogue. Also stressed is the importance of encoding the theoretical constructs into meaningful, applicable and relevant information that students can apply to real-life situations.

In framing effective discussion questions, the following aspect must be considered: wording the questions should be precise, discussion questions should not be too broad, and the question must reflect a "rational" doubt" (Gunther et. al. 184). In wording, the question must be clear and specific. Vague questions with multiple possible responses confuse and frustrate students instead of providing clarity for understanding of the concept. In terms of reflecting rational doubt, a possibility of other correct responses is desired. This form of query, used in both interpretive and evaluative questioning, adds intellectual ferment to class discussions providing a more thought-provoking atmosphere.

MASTERY MODEL

Mastery learning allows students to progress through a lesson or unit of instruction at a pace set by their own mastery of the content (Hunter, 1984; Guskey and Gates, 1986; Slavin, 1987, Slavin, 1995). The mastery teaching model follows the premise that time spent and time needed to learn are key. It is an instructional paradigm based on reductionism. Reductionism postulates that given sufficient opportunity to learn and appropriate instruction, the vast majority of students can achieve mastery of content (80% or higher). According to Slavin (1995), the empirical research on this approach to instruction is very positive for low achievers, especially when the assessment criteria is specifically covered in the lesson. The down-side is related to the time and individualization needed to meet the needs of all learners when using this model. Perhaps coupled with lecture and experiential activities, this approach or model can provide the needed pacing for synthesizing complex concepts covered in college level course work.

MULTIPLE INTELLIGENCE MODEL

Learning style is the preferred medium by which information is processed. It involves the neural pathways or sensory channels individuals use to receive, process, store and retrieve new information. Teaching to the specific learning styles of students holds great promise for assisting the learner in reaching optimal understanding of concepts taught. An outgrowth of brain research, it is supported by the research of Gardner (1983) and Lazear (1992) on multiple intelligences. Their data suggest that the rate of learning is directly related to the modality or medium by which the information is taught or presented and that there are at least eight forms of intelligence. Evoking the senses to teach is fundamental across K–16 education.

The data from multiple intelligence research suggests that incorporating them into class activities, assignments and assessments adds the following:

1. A variety of instructional modes for assessing student understanding of complex concepts,
2. An opportunity to engage in developing the lesser used intelligences and strengthening those preferred,
3. An opportunity for students to think deeply about the concepts,
4. An opportunity for the instructor to assess student's demonstrated competencies through a variety of formats,
5. A critical assessment tool for understanding the depth and breadth of individual student understanding.

Multiple assessment strategies allow students to work from a position of their learning style strengths. It also gives the instructor varied "looks" into the students' cognitive-processing abilities. Students who may not excel on standardized formats of testing may demonstrate competency and understanding of the information through other formats. Multiple intelligences assessment strategies support the premise that students have preferred conditions or learning styles for information processing. It is important that these strategies be included in assessing student learning and their demonstrated competence. Other instructional activities that assess student ability needs to be included beyond the traditional "paper" assignments. Creative planning and ingenuity can both enliven and flesh out the sleeper student, whose cognitive abilities are not apparent in essay-type assessments.

MODALITY TEACHING

Modality teaching engages the five senses. It incorporates a variety of strategies, activities and hands-on engagement for the same content or concepts. The research suggests that engaging a student's preferred learning style strengthens the learning connection at the neural level. The linkages between integrating new information into existing schema are greatly enhanced using sensory modalities. Stored in short-term memory through the process of mental rehearsal, newly introduced concepts interface with the neural pathways through sensory reinforcement, which assists in long-term memory formation and learning.

Thus, refining pedagogical tools may mitigate the complexity of teaching post-secondary learners. Using what is known from Best Practices research coupled with sufficient opportunities to learn (OTL) and opportunity to practice (OTP), the following are considered key aspects for effective teaching, especially in college and university settings:

Keys to Effective Teaching in Academe

- Knowledge of subject matter
- Knowledge of clientele
- Creation of a positive and productive classroom climate
- Utilizing a variety of instructional modalities
- Flexibility in assignment formats
- Creating a "safety net" for discovery and exploration
- A process-product orientation
- A Constructivist orientation
- Weighting assignments equitably
- Using multiple assessment strategies

Cronin (1992) determined that the most effective college instructors use activities that are relevant and challenge students to think critically. These activities include providing continuous feedback and reinforcement, encouraging student interaction and participation, and fostering a classroom climate that is conducive to positive dialogue and student learning. These strategies, which are quite familiar in the K–12 arena, may be perceived to be of lesser importance in a setting dominated by the traditional lecture format. Essential to learning at all levels—especially post-secondary—are activities, strategies, and approaches that assist in connecting the instruction or concepts to theory and prior knowledge that is relevant to the task at hand. Additionally, several other factors play a key role in effective teaching: Instructors' professional and content area knowledge; flexibility in assignment formats; student engagement; and the use of multiple assessment strategies.

ASSIGNMENT FORMAT

The format of required assignments must be re-assessed to insure that it is not prohibitive or restrictive for the student. It is widely held that structure is preferable to significant variance on key criteria when making assignments. However, within the parameter of the assignment, the instructor would be prudent to allow for student ability and learning style variations. For example, an assignment on the major components of a particular subject can be amended to accommodate a variety of student ability and preferred learning styles. Students should be prompted to include charts, graphs, photos, computer-generated graphics, and even to add lyrics and music where appropriate. A standard research paper or project then becomes more of a product of the students' ability to synthesize information and present it in a coherent fashion, than a writing exercise. This higher level of cognitive processing and synthesis should be the ultimate goal of instruction, rather than the recall and assemblage of discrete facts.

CLINICAL EXPERIENCES

Clinical experiences are used to assist in the understanding of complex theory. Practicing a concept or aspects of a concept—actually walking-through or utilizing the theory in a classroom setting—is a powerful learning tool. Practicing with a safety net is inherently value-added to the clinical practice of complex theory. Students are allowed to engage with their classmates, and intimately examine theory in a non-threatening, peer-based setting. Instructor feedback and critique, peer evaluation, and video analysis give an excellent vantage point from which to understand the intricacies of a particular subject, topic or concept. Additionally, clinical experiences provide the following:

Benefits of Clinical Experience

1. An opportunity for students to engage in hands-on activities related to the theory or concepts studied,
2. A safety net for practicing complex concepts,
3. An opportunity for students to think deeply about the concept,
4. An opportunity for students to share with classmates ideas for implementation of the concepts in real classrooms,
5. An opportunity for the instructor to assess student readiness for fieldwork and practicum,
6. An opportunity for students to re-think or modify problematic areas in their understanding of concepts before the fieldwork begins,
7. A critical assessment tool for evaluating students' demonstrated competence in specified areas.

Clinical practice may be used to provide deeper understanding of newly introduced concepts. It may reinforce application, analysis, synthesis and evaluation as students move up the taxonomy of educational objectives, delineated by Bloom et.al. (1956). Clinical experiences may even serve to reduce the number of practicum hours students need to understand and attain proficiency at field sites.

CONCLUSION

In the final analysis, effective teaching methods transcend student type, age and cognitive ability. The methods, strategies and approaches described within this paper represent a sample of the research from Best Practices that serves to inform the knowledge base of currently-trained teaching professionals. It is recommended that university teachers seek to improve their teaching through professional development activities if they are to provide an optimal learning experience for their students. The commitment to strengthening pedagogical knowledge should be real. A nation "at risk" can ill-afford to be taught by those who have not received the best instruction that our post-secondary institutions can offer.

REFERENCES

Anderson, L. and Krathwohl, D. (2001). *A Taxonomy for Learning, Teaching, and Assessing: A Revision of Bloom's Taxonomy of Educational Objectives.* New York: Longman Publishers.

Bloom, B., Englehart, M., Furst, E., Hill, W., and Krathwohl, O. (1956). *Taxonomy of Educational Objectives: The Classification of Educational Goals. Handbook 1. The Cognitive Domain.* White Plains, NY: Longman.

Borna, J. A. (2001). "From K–12 School Administrator To University Professor of Education Administration; Similarities, Differences, Risks & Rewards" in *Education.* **Vol. 122** Issue, Fall.

Brophy, J. (1992). "Probing the Subtleties of Subject-matter teaching" in *Education Leadership.* **49** (7) p. 4-8.

Brophy, J. and Good T. (1986). "Teacher Behavior and Student Achievement" in Wittrock, M. *Handbook of Research on Teaching.* 3rd Ed. p. 328-375. New York: Macmillan Press.

Crowin, T.E. (1992). "On Celebrating College Teaching" in *Journal On Excellence in College Teaching.* **Vol. 3**.

Eggen, P. and Kauchak D. (1997). *Educational Psychology: Windowson Classroom* (3rd Edition). Upper Saddle River, NJ: Prentice Hall.

Gardner, H. (1983). *Frames of Mind: The Theory of Multiple Intelligences.* New York: Basic Books.

Gunther, M.A., Estes, T.H. and Schwab, J. (1999). *Instruction: A Models Approach* 3rd. Ed. Boston: Allyn and Bacon.

Hunter, M. (1984) "Knowing, Teaching and Supervising" in Hosford, P. (Editor) *Using What We know About Teaching.* Alexandria, VA: Association for Supervision and Curriculum Development.

Kauchak, K, D. and Eggen, P. (1998). *Learning & Teaching: Research–Based Methods* (3rd Edition). Boston: Allyn and Bacon.

Lazear, D. (1992). *Multiple Intelligences.* Bloomington, IN: Phi Delta Kappa Fastback Series.

Slavin, R. (1987). "Ability Grouping and Student Achievement in Elementary Schools: A Best-Evidence Synthesis" in *Review of Educational Research.* **57**, 293-336.

—. (1995). *Cooperative Learning.* (2nd Edition). Needham Heights, MA: Allyn and Bacon.

Wittrock, M. (1986). *Handbook of Research on Teaching.* 3rd Ed. New York: Macmillan Press.

"What is the role of the Professor in a classroom that honors Multiple Intelligences (MI)?" In this article, we attempt to make observations that constitute part of an answer to this question. Central among these observations is that the construction of collaborative classroom experiences can either inhibit or facilitate the recruitment of the multiple intelligences, affinities, and skills present in any group of students. It is this point that schools of education are trying to instill in future teachers—those students now sitting in college classrooms. Viewing models of solid pedagogical techniques and philosophies is of utmost importance for these developing educators. It is our responsibility as educational leaders to provide those models. When considering the importance of modeling good teaching, one of the multiple intelligences rises above the rest: interpersonal intelligence. Simply put, the skills necessary for good teaching can be demonstrated and taught. It is the application of the interpersonal intelligence that elevates teaching to an art.

BACKGROUND

Another perspective of our question concerning the Professor above is, "What is the role of MI in post-secondary education?" That is part of the question we have been asking ourselves during much of the last decade as standards-based reform and constructivism have begun to influence higher education. These concepts have had their greatest impact in K-12 school systems that embrace viewpoints acknowledging the diversity of their student populations and the variety of learning profiles accompanying that diversity. Now that the graduates of these successful secondary schools are filling our collegiate classrooms, we periodically need to assure ourselves that our teaching techniques are consistent with the best that these students have already experienced. Even more important is the need to assure the effectiveness of our instructional techniques for those students who might otherwise experience more difficulty than necessary.

A few years ago, we embarked on a large project, seeking to develop a unique approach to interdisciplinary and integrated curriculum based on the work of Howard Gardner and others. As we led thousands of teachers in professional development and field-testing experiences, we found ourselves adjusting our instructional techniques to better accommodate the varied learners before us. One of our central findings was that teaching through multiple intelligences (MI) is not a technique or approach. It provides a theoretical framework/philosophy around which we can structure meaningful interactions with course content. We have therefore grown to prefer the phrase "instruction that honors multiple intelligences" rather than "teaching toward multiple intelligences." When coupled with pedagogical tools that lead toward understanding rather than simple mastery of isolated factual knowledge, we feel that MI Theory—properly employed—can contribute to a vibrant, engaging, and collaborative classroom environment.

THE ART OF GROUPWORK: HONORING MULTIPLE INTELLIGENCES IN THE COLLEGE CLASSROOM

PATRICK K. FREER AND CHRISTINA CRAIG

The core of this article is an examination of one method of honoring multiple intelligences in higher education classrooms. While our subject matter is visual art and music, the instructional process is the key element.

COLLEGES AND IN-DEPTH LEARNING

Many college instructors now recognize the need to provide hands-on, collaborative learning experiences within the normal class schedule. Research routinely makes it clear that good teaching is about providing just enough information to spark interest and inquiry in students, and then allowing students to engage with the material in whatever way seems appropriate to their interests and motivations. Whenever inquiry-based learning and classroom projects are discussed, the question of breadth versus depth emerges. In line with Gardner's views, college classrooms must be about providing in-depth learning opportunities around a few broad issues. Instructors must plan carefully enough to ensure that the foundations of content mastery and research methods are established. While students work with this foundational information in collaborative work, the instructor is no less important—monitoring the ensuing learning activities to track what understandings occur. In this view, the college teacher functions as a facilitator rather than a mere pedagogue. The role of an instructor is, then, to promote methods and strategies that encourage understanding of essential information. Students subsequently acquire deeper understandings as new information is interwoven with prior information and individual interest areas.

THE MI CLASSROOM

All too often, well-intentioned instructors attempt to apply the theory of MI by teaching one lesson in a way that emphasizes one area of intelligence (e.g. Music), and then another utilizing a different intelligence (e.g. Kinesthetic) during the next class meeting. While laudable for rising above the traditional lecture mode, this approach may result in a scattershot approach toward both instruction and MI that does little to advance either one. Another common approach utilizing multiple intelligences occurs when instructors valiantly try to teach toward all eight intelligences in the same lesson—but, often, the result is a completely bewildered group of students just trying to keep up.

Every individual possesses a range of intelligences and aptitudes that are represented in an array of relative strengths. A classroom environment that *honors* MI differs from one that *teaches toward* multiple intelligences. Honoring multiple intelligences (and diversity in general) necessitates a constructivist approach toward instruction wherein students build individual understandings through guided practice and inquiry. Whenever practical, instruction should be structured to allow strengths in various intelligences to present themselves naturally within the classroom and then be utilized as springboards toward increasingly focused and targeted content and methods.

At the center of this approach is the building of a collaborative classroom environment in which instructors trust their students almost more than students trust their instructors. There will be times when these young adults will be unable to articulate what they need to know or to express their own lines of inquiry. In these moments, the instructor will be given an opportunity to teach toward the development of cognitive skills that can enable the discovery of interests, the posing of meaningful questions, and the recognition of multiple learning pathways.

OUR PROCEDURE

Our session at the Urban Mission Conference at New Jersey City University in 2001 was designed to provide participants with specific content and then allow them to engage with that content in a variety of ways, using several of the intelligences. As they explored photographic slide images of everyday life and artworks found in West Africa, participants were asked to focus on the various components of patterns as represented in the images—components such as motif, repetition, and interval. A discussion ensued about the sociological significance of the patterns, the ways that patterns can be represented visually and aurally, and the various intelligences that could be employed when perceiving and responding to these patterns.

We then divided into four groups, each with a different set of instructions or questions. The four groups corresponded to the four ways in which group work is often structured in classrooms. Although such groups are often created in response to an instructor's wish to assign content and determine outcomes, this well-intentioned method of creating group work may not always fully honor multiple intelligences. This seminar was an attempt to explore the ways in which the construction of group work either inhibits or invites the engagement of MI.

Participants in each of the four groups dealt with the same design in Figure 1.

FIGURE 1:

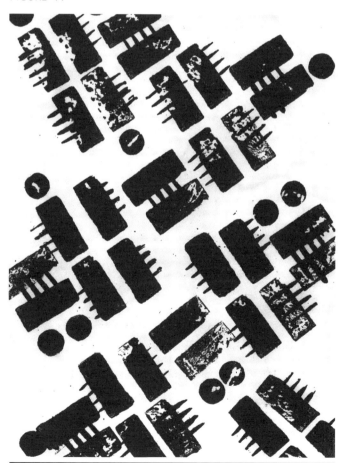

Textile Design: This abstract design was used by each group as they explored different approaches to group-work. The design was printed on a textile sample similar to those viewed during the whole-group instruction.

Using information derived from the just-completed discussion on pattern, participants were given directions or a focusing question and a time limit for exploring the information. Participants were told that there would be a conversation about this instructional experience following the activity. A presentation of these directions/questions and a brief discussion of the results of this workshop activity appears below. The elements that varied in this activity follow:

KEY ELEMENTS

a = Teacher-Directed Content
b = Teacher-Directed Method
c = Student-Directed Method
d = Student-Directed Content

GROUP A

Teacher-Directed Content	Teacher-Directed Method
a	b

The following are directions for a musical activity based on the design in Figure 1.

1. Look at the textile, and verbally describe what you see.
2. Identify examples of pattern, interval, motif, rhythm, and/or interval.
3. Notice that the patterns are made up of individual markings.
4. Have each person in the group choose a different mark.
5. Choose a sound to represent your individual mark. Use any object that makes sound (by striking, scraping, shaking, or by verbalizing) to represent mark.
6. Notice how your mark is incorporated into the larger patterns and motifs on the textile.
7. Practice "playing" your sound, and see how it fits with the other sounds represented in the textile (utilizing the other members of the group).
8. Reading the textile as a musical "score," turn the page so that you can read from left to right.
9. Read the score, remembering that each mark represents an individual sound.
10. Figure out where each member of the group should make their sound (according to the score).
11. Determine if you want your group's piece to performed just once, or if the entire piece should be repeated.
12. Practice for a group presentation, remembering to figure out how you will begin and end the presentation.

RESULTS

The specific procedure prescribed for this group dictated the outcomes: sequential thinking, a carefully organized final product, and a lack of conversation about content. The individuals in this group worked especially well together, negotiating responsibilities and tasks throughout the process. One group member expressed annoyance with the inflexible, step-by-step directions and ultimately left the group despite attempts by others to gain his cooperation. Group members discussed the possibility that specific directions may be comfortable for teachers and some students, but other students may rebel and exhibit off-task behaviors.

GROUP B

Teacher-Directed Content	Student-Directed Method
a	c

The following is a focusing question on design in Figure 1 requiring the elements of Bodily-Kinesthetic Intelligences.

Question:
Using this textile as a point of departure, how could you explore the elements of pattern through the bodily-kinesthetic intelligence?

RESULTS

This group was given the opportunity to explore possible interactions between the components of pattern and bodily-kinesthetic intelligence. The lack of instructor-defined procedures encouraged divergent thinking—with the result being an examination of the movement and choreography possible when producing a musical interpretation of the visual prompt. This was exemplified in the group presentation that focused on a call-response approach between a leader and other group members. Also explored were the exploitation of physical space and the manipulation of energy levels. This group was by far the most enthusiastic during groupwork, and reported high levels of cognitive engagement.

GROUP C

Student-Directed Content	Teacher-Directed Method
d	b

The following are focusing questions on the design in Figure 1. They explore patterns through one of the intelligences.

Question:
Using this textile as a point of departure, how could you explore the elements of pattern through one of the intelligences?

- Which intelligence did you choose, and why?
- Make certain to record the responses of each group participant in writing, and determine how you will present this information to the class.
- You will have 90 seconds for this presentation.

- Be sure that each group member is involved in some way with the presentation.

RESULTS

The strict procedures of this group's assignment did not set well with these individuals. Members ultimately presented a project that was a conglomeration of individual mini-projects rather than a unified group presentation. Members reported that the method seemed reductive and oriented toward assessment while the lack of specified content appeared too expansive in comparison. This group concluded that the content and method seemed contradictory and led to elevated levels of frustration.

Group D

Student-Directed Content	Student-Directed Method
d	c

This focusing question was exactly the same as that of Group C. What differed was the absence of teacher direction.

Question:

Using this textile as a point of departure, how could you explore the elements of pattern through one of the intelligences?

RESULTS

Two phases were clearly evident in this group's work. The first phase was characterized by rapid-fire conversation and brainstorming. The second contained a more measured discussion of how projects like these could be used early in a semester to gauge levels of student motivation, identify content affinities, and predict which intelligences might emerge as strengths in individual students or the class as a whole. The open-ended content and method afforded this group the opportunity to entertain divergent possibilities, prompting a line of discussion that demonstrated high levels of understanding.

COMMENTS

As groups proceeded thorough their various tasks, it was interesting to note that each needed direction from us (the instructors) except Group A, the group having the most scripted assignment. We had confidence that the scripted group would accomplish its goals, but the depth of learning was less certain owing to the lack of instructor involvement. Our predictions proved to be accurate: the scripted group had less spontaneous conversation and reported lower levels of higher order thinking than any other group.

Groups B, C, and D each took the task and created outcomes very different than those we could have foreseen. Our basic objective of enhancing knowledge about pattern

through various intelligences was accomplished in each group. The freedoms built into each of the tasks allowed ideas to emerge in ways that resonated with the particular interests of the participants.

QUESTIONS FOR ELABORATION

Based on the information presented in this article and elsewhere in this volume, we would like to pose the following questions related to the engagement of MI in the higher education classroom. Each of these presents many opportunities for further study and comment.

TASK APPROPRIATENESS

- Under what circumstances might the set of directions labeled "D" be more appropriate than those labeled "A"? How might factors such as subject area, age of students, and classroom environment contribute to your decision?

PRELIMINARY EXPERIENCES

- What types of preliminary experiences are necessary to support constructivist activities in ways that ensure expansion of knowledge rather than result in projects lacking curricular focus?

ASSESSMENT OF LEARNING

- How do we assess the student learning that occurs during group work? Since "A" is most similar to conventional teaching methods, we can rather safely predict the outcomes of that experience. How will we be able to discern student learning in groupwork situations like those in "B," "C," and "D"? Does making a distinction between formative and summative evaluations provide clues?

We encourage you to return to your students and make an art of teaching as you listen, observe, and respond, honoring the intelligences these young people bring to your classroom.

In a newsletter named *Inbox* (2002) published by the National Council of Teachers of English (NCTE), the following statement appeared: "Effective teaching strategies are essential to the intellectual growth of all students, but they are especially critical to the success of linguistically and culturally diverse students." NCTE's Task Force on Racism and Bias, according to the writers of that article, suggest that teachers of writing should "introduce classroom topics and materials that connect the students' experiences with the classroom. [They should also] introduce writing activities which promote discussion, encourage contributions from all students, allow peer interaction to support learning [and] provide frequent, meaningful opportunities for students to generate their own text…acknowledging and validating their experiences, feelings, and ideas."

One empowering and validating experience shared by young persons in virtually all parts of the world is their participation in hip-hop culture. Many of our students creatively produce elements of this youth culture, or they are passive participants who buy hip-hop records, wear hip-hop gear, and attend hip-hop activities and events. In fact, we found that hip-hop music was playing in 98% of the cars which exited from the parking lot at Bergen Community College in Paramus, New Jersey, on one morning several years ago. Even more interesting is the fact that only about 15% of the students are from the African Diaspora or of Latino ancestry, in whose communities hip-hop has its origins. Furthermore, because of its widespread popularity, elements of its culture include writing to communicate messages, and because students who participate in hip-hop culture often bring knowledge of the writing process to the classroom, aspects of hip-hop culture can be utilized with great effectiveness in the writing classroom. After an introduction to the origins and development of hip-hop, we will explore this contribution to the understanding and practice of writing by teachers as well as surprisingly disciplined students.

II. Origins of Hip-Hop Culture

Kool Herc, the father of hip-hop, who was born Clive Campbell in Jamaica, migrated to the United States with his family in 1967 in the midst of a national social revolution. This revolution had grown out of the 1955 boycott of public transportation organized by the African American community in Montgomery, Alabama. That boycott soon became the National Civil Rights Movement, out of which by 1966 the Black Power Movement had developed. While the emphasis in those movements was on equity in all civil and social matters pertaining to African Americans, a broad based coalition of many other groups at the grass roots level, beginning in the mid 1960s, addressed issues of inequity of all racial, ethnic, gender-oriented, and special interest groups. Lyndon Baines Johnson, President of the United States during the decade of the 1960s with the exception of the first three Kennedy years, was building the Great

HIP-HOP CULTURE MEETS THE WRITING CLASSROOM

JON A. YASIN

EDITOR'S NOTE: *In tour-de-force fashion, Yasin sketches the origins of hip-hop culture and describes specific elements of a relationship between that movement—which has swept much of the world—and the academic writing that is required in colleges across the USA. He perceives that this powerful youth culture represents a focus on the dynamic exchange of information that is possible between both informed and uninitiated teachers and students. According to Yasin, the involvement of music, dance, poetry and rhythm demonstrates the value of the concept of multiple intelligences.*

Society while J. Edgar Hoover, Director of the Federal Bureau of Investigation, was determining which citizens would participate in this Great Society. Because the origin of the social revolution was in the African American community, Hoover "mobilized the FBI to smash the vanguard (black political activists of liberal and radical views) and to keep track of the masses (the everyday people who lived in black communities" (O'Reilly 261). By the beginning of the next decade, 1970, the FBI had caused disruption in all these movements and had established systems of surveillance of African Americans. Large amounts of heroin appeared in the African American and Latino communities. The numbers of homeless citizens began to multiply, and disco, a new music from New York City's Greenwich Village, was heard across radio air waves.

This music did not appeal to all African American and Latino youths in New York City (Keyes). Therefore, these youths, including Kool Herc and other early hip-hop deejays, resisted disco. They continued to listen to and be educated politically by those musicians who sang rhythm and blues soul music, such as James Brown's "I'm Black and

I'm Proud" and the Temptations' "Message to Blackman", as well as the Black Acts Poetry recited over drums and music by such poets as Nikki Giovanni and The Last Poets. Kool Herc, whose bedroom in his family's apartment was next to the recreation room in the building, gained a reputation for playing soul and other types of music loudly, so that neighborhood youths gathered in the adjacent recreation room to hear it. At the end of the summer of 1973, according to Herc, his sister persuaded him to provide music for a back-to-school party. That party, deejayed by Kool Herc, is deemed by many to be the event which spawned hip-hop. One reason Kool Herc's deejaying skills were unique was because of his stereo system. In the article, "The Birth of a Nation" published in *The Source Magazine*, it is written that, "Herc…used his father's two turntables to spin records at neighborhood parties in 1973. Calling himself DJ Kool Herc, he played the instrumental breakdown section—or the breaks—of his favorite funk, soul and reggae songs, sending partygoers to the dance floor in droves…Kool Herc is unequivocally recognized by one community as the father of hip-hop music." (137)

Since 1980 when it was commercialized, hip-hop, although not universal, has become a global youth culture. In addition to deejayin', other elements of hip-hop culture include b-boyin' and b-girlin' (dancing), wearin' oversized clothin', taggin'/writin' (graffiti art), and emceein' (generally, writing lyrics and reading them aloud in public). These elements consign hip-hop to common culture, of which Willis writes:

> …there is a vibrant symbolic life and symbolic creativity in everyday life, everyday activity and expression—even if it is sometimes invisible, looked down upon or spurned… We want to recognize it…Most young people's lives are not involved with the arts and yet are actually full of expressions, signs and symbols through which individuals and groups seek creatively to establish their presence, identity and meaning. Young people are all the time expressing or attempting to express something about their actual or political cultural significance. This is the realm of living common culture. (1)

Indeed, the continuous cry of all hip-hoppers is that active participants producing elements of this culture should **"keep it real."** This **"keeping it real"** entails communicating messages about "everyday life, everyday activity and expression" (Willis 1). For example, Chris Miles, a student in my writing class, remarked during an interview that the emcee writes:

> …to…remind the people once in a while on what's going on in the world. Say a little rhyme here, a little rhyme

there…just tell the people what's going on in the world; give them little hints…Give them a little spark, you know; some people wake up and smell the coffee before it's too late…You rhyme about somebody getting smacked up…People in the ghetto can really relate to that because they've been through that…Rhyme about what's going on in that community; they can really understand what's going on and it's real deep, rap is real…

Chris is an emcee. Emcees or "MC's", also known as mike controllers, write and recite hip-hop lyrics which some identify as rap lyrics or rhymes. Emceein' is probably the most relevant element of hip-hop culture to the writing classroom because it entails communicating a message, although the message is spoken over music. However, it is important to understand the other elements of this culture.

THE ELEMENTS OF HIP-HOP CULTURE

After Kool Herc publicly deejayed the back-to-school party for his sister in 1973, he began giving parties in the streets, in the parks, utilizing any available space—public or private—deejayin' anywhere he got free electricity. Other youths studied Kool Herc's stereo system with the two turntables, his style of lengthening the instrumental break in the songs, mixing two songs together and other elements of this novel culture. Afrika Bambaattaa, another of the three major pioneers of hip-hop, attended Herc's parties and studied Herc's techniques. In time, Bambaattaa began deejayin'. Bambaattaa was a member of the Black Spades, a gang around the Bronx River Projects, who was very much influenced by the Muslim community and the Last Poets. The Last Poets are a group of African American and Puerto Rican men who use drums as background over which they recite poetry with positive messages designed to educate people. Afrika Bambaattaa organized his gang and other local gangs into the Universal Zulu Nation, which, today, is an international community–based organization that works toward social action and change. When Bambaattaa organized Zulu, members of the various gangs soon began to battle each other on the dance floor as b-boys (break boys), rather than on the streets in physical fights. According to Melvin McLauren, these b-boys had to protect their knees and other anatomical parts of the body. Thus, they bought pants and shirts several sizes too large to cover knee pads, etc., used clothesline rope in lieu of belts to hold the large pants in place and wore large shirts to cover the rope. Eventually, the fashion industry appropriated the over-sized clothing. Wearing of oversized clothing is the element of hip-hop in which most non-hip hoppers participate.

Illustration A

Illustration B

Figure No. 1. "A" is a "tag," which is a graffiti artist's signature. This style of "writin'" is used to announce competitive events. "B" is a "throw up."

GRANDMASTER FLASH

A third pioneer of hip-hop, Grandmaster Flash, attended Herc's early street parties and soon began deejayin'. Grandmaster Flash, who was born Joseph Sadler, was a student of electronics at Samuel Gompers Vocational High School in the Bronx; therefore, he utilized his knowledge of electronics to bring additional technology to deejayin'. Such techniques as backspinnin' and scratchin' are attributed to being created or popularized by Grandmaster Flash.

As more youths began deejayin', they began organizing competitions or deejay battles to allow the participants to determine who had better skills. Because hip-hop was an underground culture, battles were not announced on television nor radio community service programs. Taggers (graffiti artists) were enlisted to design posters and flyers announcing a given deejay battle with all pertinent information—deejay participants, date, location, time, and admission fee. Eventually, Africa Bambaattaa and the Universal Zulu Nation popularized the b-boy and b-girl battles, whose organizers enlisted the skills of the taggers in the local 'hood (neighborhood) as well, for advertising. Although there are three types of "graf," the tag was commonly used to announce battles.

Illustration "A" is an example of a "tag", which is like a signature. Illustration "B" is a "throw-up", which has bubble style letters that are colored in. My students, Maureen Perez, also an emcee, is the artist of the tag, while Miguel Sanchez did throw up. The third style is the "piece", which is a wall painting. Initially, the piece was created on the sides of subway cars during the night when the cars were in garages. Now, many people contact graf artists for pieces to be created on their property.

RHYTHM TALKING TO THE MUSIC

While traveling to their parties or to battles, deejays enlisted friends to secure their stereo equipment and records. These friends were and are known as "the crew" or "the posse" of the deejay. In the early days, b-boys and b-girls often traveled with specific deejays as part of the crew or posse, as well. According to Kool Herc, three young men, members of his posse, at some point began talking rhythmically in time to the music, so that the syllable of each word they pronounced corresponded with a beat or a portion of each beat in the music played by the deejay (Yasin 1997, 1999). These emcees were Koke La Rock, who was later joined by Klark Kent and Timmy Tim. Apparently, Melle Mel, Flash's emcee; the Sugar Hill Gang, and others studied these three emcees, and eventually they became mike controllers as well. Grandmaster Flash and his emcees, Melle Mel and the Furious Five in 1981 released "The Message", the first sociopolitical hip-hop recording. All of these hip-hop activities, according to Chuck D of Public Enemy had developed into a million dollar neighborhood business, controlled by the African American and Latino youths in the 'hoods of New York City before hip-hop was commercialized by Sugar Hill Gang in 1980 with "Rapper's Delight". Actually, Rapper's Delight was the second recording released after a recording by Fatback, earlier during the same year.

Before 1970, certain, elements of hip-hop—deejayin', taggin', emceein', b-boyin' and b-girlin'—"were there, but they came together in a certain way," recalled Fable, the legendary poppin' and lockin' b-boy and Vice President of the International Rock Steady Crew, who remembers growing up in Spanish Harlem and participating in the hip-hop parties in 1976. For instance, the origins of poppin' and lockin' can be traced to dances on the television program *Soultrain*. Young people are attracted to hip-hop and they add to it in turn. "Hip-hop [has] emerged as a source of alternative identify formation and social status [where] older local support institutions have been all but demolished along with large sectors of its built environments" (Rose 34). This identity is not shed when youths enter the classrooms in our various educational institutions. Because hip-hop identity is a catalyst for many social experiences of certain youths, it can be a catalyst for certain of their educational experiences as well.

III. Using Hip-Hop in the Writing Classroom

Writing instructors are charged with assisting students in understanding the writing process in order to develop the necessary skills to become fluent expository writers, i.e. to be able to explain some aspect of reality through written discourse. In addressing this charge, writing instructors often overlook students who are hip-hop emcees and who bring knowledge about the writing process and writing—although in another genre—to our classes. These emcees, who are our students, in some cases, have been writing hip hop lyrics for more than five years. They are known by their classmates for their expertise as a result of performing at hip-hop cultural activities on campus or in the local neighborhood. In addition, many are known as a result of underground media—hip-hop journals, newspapers, radio programs, and related cultural activities. Utilizing hip-hop emcees who are students in our writing classes and hip hop lyrics which these students have created have several distinct advantages:

- It establishes the immediate relevancy of the relationship between subject areas and classroom activities and the larger world outside of the academy.
- It motivates other students who participate in hip-hop to focus on class activities and to mentally attend to everything that transpires in the classroom.
- It allows all students who actively and passively participate in hip-hop culture to integrate what they know already about writing (and how hip-hop emcees write lyrics) with the additional information to which they are introduced in the writing course.

Instructors have curriculum objectives to meet and often relegate hip-hop to insignificance. On the other hand, an awareness of the scope of this movement and the depth of its influence on younger generations can contribute to a dynamic relationship between teachers and their students. Below are suggestions for its occasional use in the writing course. To ease apprehensions, it is not necessary for instruc-

tors to be knowledgeable about hip-hop because their students are; furthermore, collaboration with students provides an atmosphere where everyone is a student, and everyone is a teacher. For specific lessons, invite students to bring their creations, their lyrics, to class. However, from past experiences, I have found it necessary to establish certain rules initially, which include the following: (1) no profanity; (2) no disrespect to women, homosexuals, other ethnic groups or races, and religious groups; (3) no glorification of "thug" life. Students, generally, have adhered to these restrictions.

Steps for College Writing

Early on, instructors introduce students to the writing process. As an instructor is assisting students in understanding that process, these students are developing their procedural knowledge, i.e., how to perform all of those specific activities (Anderson) whose final product is a piece of writing. Reynolds, in *The Introduction to College Writing*, identifies the steps in the writing process as prewriting, discovering, planning, drafting, revising, and editing. However, for developmental writers in college as well as high school, Langan, reduces these steps in the writing process into their constituent parts that include the following four steps.

1. Begin with a point.
2. Support the point with specific evidence—facts, examples, statistics.
3. Organize the specific evidence into emphatic or chronological order, and connect the specific evidence with the appropriate transition signals.
4. Write clear sentences, which are error free. (47)

Although Langan, in the above steps, does not include the starting point which is prewriting, nor the revising of one's work, he does emphasize very strongly these important activities in which the writer must engage. For beginners, I include two additional steps. At Step 4, the student physically produces the required piece of writing. This step may continue over a period of several days. Once it is completed, I add steps, 5 and 6.

5. Relax, which includes "stepping back from the paper" and doing something that is unrelated. Ideally, this should be for one twenty-four hour period, but it can be for as little as one hour depending upon the student's schedule.
6. Revise, proof-read, edit.

As students develop fluency in written discourse, they, as many of us, revise continuously. And this complete process becomes more broad based and inclusive to reflect the steps as put forth by Reynolds.

Steps for Writing Hip-Hop Lyrics

Generally, the self-discipline and the above sequence of procedures are utilized by many of our students who are hip-hop emcees to create their rhymes. Furthermore, other students in our classes, who participate in hip-hop culture in other ways, understand this process as a result of their contact with local emcees. For example, during the fall semester of 2000 in a two session, three-hour-long discussion at Bergen Community College in Paramus, NJ, a class of basic writers that included fifteen students, from diverse ethnic, racial, socioeconomic backgrounds, generated the following steps in the process used by hip-hop emcees to write hip-hop lyrics.

1. **Think of topic.** What the writer wants to talk about.
2. **Rehearse.** Practice putting together words, that rhyme [repeat certain sounds] about the topic.
3. **Organize the words.** The rhyme must make sense and support the beat to which the emcee will recite the rhyme. [Some begin writing the rhyme on paper at this step].
4. **Combine everything.** Make sure the rhyme is in the order that the emcee wishes it to be/sentences, phrases, words, etc./and put it on paper [that is write down the completed lyrics].
5. **Drink a cup of water.** The voice is fatigued at this point from continuous recitation during the composing process.
6. **Revise.** Make sure everything [words] rhymes/that is sounds good and goes with the beats of the music/ "fixes it", if necessary.

This class of students included only one emcee, but there were three taggers/graffiti artists, who are, ironically, called writers. All other students in the class, in one way or another, participate in hip hop culture, the least of which wear "hip-hop gear" and listen to hip-hop music. A close look at these two sets of steps suggest that they are similar, and by reason, so are the two processes. *Thus, we can conclude that many students enter our classrooms bringing information about the writing process although they use this process to produce a different genre of writing.*

Classroom discussion about the process that student-emcees utilize to create hip-hop rhymes can be an introduction to the topic including the nature of the writing process, its purpose, and its importance. Such a discussion allows the student to lead the discussion and to collaborate on identifying the steps in the process. It also affords them the opportunity of becoming aware that learning activities in the classroom are not to be isolated from their outside activities and experiences because, in reality, they are related.

Understanding and utilizing the writing process to write paragraphs and essays, as well as hip-hop lyrics, eventually requires less attention, and becomes an automatic cognitive process, allowing students to focus on controlled cognitive processes (Anderson 56), which include thinking critically about the point or idea being explained in the writing selection.

Prewriting Activities

A primary objective of prewriting is to assist students in generating a point which they will develop in a paragraph as a topic sentence or in an essay as a controlling idea or thesis statement. Langan suggests utilization of any of the following techniques as prewriting exercises: freewriting, answering questions, brainstorming, and idea mapping. Students who write hip-hop lyrics can be allowed to generate a set of lyrics as a prewriting activity.

In a discussion at Gompers Vocational High School in Richmond, California, Joaquin a seventeen-year-old junior, wrote the following hip-hop lyrics.

The Big Money Blues (The Lyrics)

Let me buckle up my seatbelt and take a trip through yer mind
And see what your thinking cause me I'm thinking all the time
About my friends I used to kick it with after school
I knew this guy name Craig and yo! he thought he was cool
He use to stand up on the corner
Slangin the rocks
Dodgein the cops
When they patrolling the block
Until one day my friend got caught
I guess he didn't know he was sellin coke to a cop
And now my friend Craig is 19 years old
Doing 5 months man
Ain't that cold
5 months passes now he's fresh outta jail
And he was thinking to himself I'm a go back to the block and sell
He jumps out the car steps into his house
Grabs his stash and ready to bounce
Walks through the hood says wassup to his folks
Chills for a minute
Ready to smoke
20 minutes passed now he's ready to ball
He bounces with his friend walked straight through the hall
Then all of a sudden something went wrong
Craig seen these new cats selling dope to everyone
Craig got mad and so so
Then the other cat I think his name is David
Ohh well he punched him in the face and kicked his head into
*   the pavement*

It was a very bloody scene
Craig got up and destroying everything
He cocked back his pistol and started bustin shots
David got hit, he was pleading for his life
Hours passes and David dies
That's just tha way I gotta end it bye.
<u>*PE@CE MUCH LOVE!!*</u>

To Joaquin and many other youths "rhyming" or writing one's lyrics is one way of coping with certain experiences, especially the negatives ones. When asked about these lyrics, Joaquin identified the main point and the details about that point, which was the information he needed to write the paragraph below.

The Big Money Blues (Analysis of the Lyrics)

The Big Money Blues is a rap about this guy named Craig. Craig is a drug dealer and a thug, like many, many people I know that have been through the same thing that Craig has been through. About his experiences on the streets, one time he sold drugs to a cop and got busted. When he got out five months later he went back to the block expecting to take up where he left off before he went to jail. When Craig got back to his old spot, this dude David had already taken his place. Craig was furious and attempted to reclaim his turf. Then things got really, really ugly. David got shot and killed. Life is not a game and we are accountable for what we do to ourselves and others, because when you are hurting others you're hurting yourself too, and many of us don't know that this is true.

At this point, appropriate is a discussion about the purpose for which one writes and how purpose determines genre and format, tone, word choice and other features of writing. Also at this point, this student can be assisted in learning the dialect of English necessary for success in the academy.

REVISING FOR BETTER COMMUNICATION

People who have been writing over long periods of time often realize that the necessity of revising one's work is the result of not having communicated exactly what one wishes in a way that the intended reading audience will understand. Novice writers often are not convinced of the importance of revising one's writing. Hip-hop emcees including our student emcees, revise continuously. Showing classes written versions of students' lyrics and having them explain why they revise these hip-hop rhymes is most effective. Figure 2 below is a revision of "Masterpieces" by Michael Hasan Heller, known in the world of hip-hop as Pinnacle. Note the number of cross-outs and rewritings. Emcees in the class whose writings are used can discuss why they revise. In an interview, Pinnacle made the following comments:

Pinnacle:	*After I finish the piece, I feel good until I feel that I've got to write it over again.*
Jon:	*You mean, to revise…*
Pinnacle:	*I revise—most of the people I rhyme with, they get sick of me, because I revise a piece, like twenty times, I'm my worst critic…I like every single word to flow with each—like, I like them to connect perfectly, like if, a "the" isn't perfect before the word, then I'll take out the whole piece.*
Jon:	*…Okay! Now, why is revision important to you?*
Pinnacle:	*…[T]his person, he puts his whole self, his whole heart, his whole mind, his whole body and soul into making the best work possible, so that you can feel exactly what he's feeling at the time, when he's writing.*

Although he said he revises his paper for his college classes fewer times than his hip-hop lyrics, Pinnacle and other student lyricists can communicate the urgency of revising one's writing.

DOCUMENTING

For twenty years now, I have heard students say that they did not know the necessity of documenting the reference source when they take ideas from published materials and "put the information in their own words." This serious purloining of another's intellectual property is a lesson members of the hip-hop community learned some twenty years ago, when commercially, they used sections of other artists' music for their recordings without permission. Court suits were brought against them. These hip hoppers already had experienced others "biting" (stealing) lyrics, and they had devised methods of protecting themselves. Some emcees write the rhyme, memorize it, and tear it up, so there is no written record. Other's, like Pinnacle, write in a script so that their words are not decipherable. (See Figure 2). Pinnacle, the creator of these lyrics, is a graffiti artist, as well. His mother's garage wall is proof! He deliberately wrote in this script to protect his intellectual property.

A discussion of stealing hip-hop lyrics and how emcees protect themselves can be beneficial to students in writing classes. After emcees in the class share their experiences, the notion of documentation and an introduction of at least one documentation system is in order. Also, discussing the various institutional policies regarding plagiarism are beneficial to students, who at this point, are extremely receptive.

CRITICAL THINKING

It is important for students to think about the reasons why some things are more important than others. It is useful to discuss controversial hip-hop artists and their

MASTERPIECES

by Pinnacle (Michael Hasan Heller)

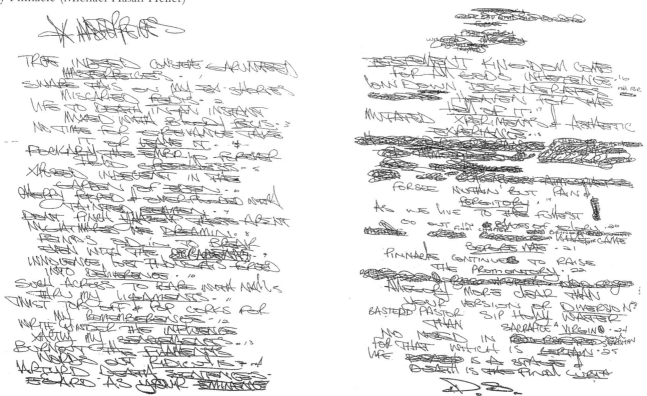

The importance of revision is seen in this hip-hop manuscript by a rapper named Pinnacle. Often these manuscripts are written so that they will be legible only to the writer, thus discouraging plagiarism.

work. Issues such as artist's responsibility and censorship generate lively discussions. Yolanda Whitaker, known as Yo-Yo in the entertainment and the hip-hop community, related in a private conversation, that only when some ten-year-old children recited her commercial lyrics to her (which were meant for adults only) did she realize the necessity for artists being responsible for their messages. Discussions about issues important to them with comments from professional artists like Yo-Yo, whom they respect, foster critical thinking in our students.

IV. CONCLUSION

Hip-hop is not the only contemporary youth culture; however, at the present it seems the most widespread. Graffiti is world wide, and hip-hop music can be purchased in nearly every language in existence today. Hip-hop has permeated mainstream American and other traditional cultures in a plethora of ways. Because of its relative newness, many experienced instructors have no appreciation nor under-standing of hip-hop. However, many young instructors entering the profession have been socialized in hip-hop culture since childhood, as have our students. Both groups of teachers can use hip-hop in different ways as a focus of information exchange that establishes rapport. Also, because it is a culture of resistance, it reaches out to some students who have been marginalized in the academy and society, in general. Finally, identifying students who are active partici-pants in hip-hop culture allows instructors, early on, to gain insight into certain skills that the student possesses.

Hip-hop emcees, for example, clearly exhibit what Gardner identifies as the linguistic intelligence. At the "5th Conference on Urban Education" at New Jersey City University, he stated that linguistic intelligence is the "capacity to use languages, one's native language, and perhaps other languages, to express what's on one's mind and to understand other people. Poets really specialize in linguistic intelligence, but so do any other writers, orators, speakers, or lawyers for whom language is an important stock in trade." Graffiti artists, deejays, b-boys and b-girls have developed one or more of the other seven intelligences as defined by Gardner. As instructors, we must exploit these intelligences to assist our students in acquiring the skills necessary for academic success.

Note: This research was partially funded by the National Academy of Education and the National Academy of Education/Spencer Postdoctoral Fellowship.

REFERENCES

Anderson, J. R. (1990). *Cognitive Psychology and Its Implications.* New York: W. W. Freeman and Co.

Andrade, J. Personal Interview. 13 March 2002. "The Birth of a Nation." (2002). in *The Source Magazine of Hip-Hop Music, Culture, Politics:* March, page 137.

Chuck D. Public Address. Hip-Hop Symposium. Columbia University, New York. 15 March 1994.

"Expanding Opportunities: Academic Success for Culturally and Linguistically Diverse Students." NCTE Inbox Newsletter. 15 May 2002. http://www.ncte.org/positions/exp-opp.html

Keyes, C. L. (1991). "Rappin' to the Beat: Rap Music as Street Culture among African Americans." Diss. Indiana University.

Kool Herc. Personal Interview. 23 March 2002.

Langan, J. (2001). *English Skills.* 4th Edition. New York: McGraw-Hill.

McLauren, M. Personal Interview. 15 November 1996.

Miles, C. Personal Interview. 15 November 1990

O'Reilley, K. (1989). "Racial Matters:" *The FBI's Secret File on Black America, 1960-1972.* New York: The Fress Press.

Perez, M. Personal Interview. 7 May 2002.

Pinnacle. Personal Interview. 20 March 2000.

Reynolds, J. (2001). *Introduction to College Writing.* Englewood Cliffs: Prentice-Hall.

Rose, T. (1994). *Black Noise: Rap Music and Black Culture in Contemporary America.* Hanover: Weslayan University Press.

Toop, D. (1984). *The Rap Attack: African Jive to New York Hip-hop.* Boston: South End Press.

Whitaker, Y. Private Conversation. 13 May 2002.

Willis, P. (1990). *Common Culture.* Boulder: Westview Press.

Yasin, J. A. (1997). *In You Face! Rappin' Beats Comin' at You: A Study of How Language is Mapped onto Musical Beats in Rap Music. Diss.* Teachers College, Columbia University.

—. (2001). "Rap in the African American Music Tradition: Cultural Assertion and Continuity" in *Race and Ideology: Language, Symbolism and Popular Culture.* Ed. Arthur Spear. Detroit: Wayne State. UP. 197-223.

*R*eal learning gets to the heart of what it means to be human.

Peter Senge

RThinking about a task while one is performing it often results in improved performance. That is the basic hypothesis of a recently completed pilot program in a large community college in California. The task was learning itself, and the broader goal was retention. The program required immersion in metacognition—thinking about thinking—as well as intentional learning and various reflective practices. This unusually creative Interactive Learning Model (ILM) paid off in terms of a dramatic increase in student retention and a cultural transformation for all concerned—faculty, staff and students.

Near the center of this undertaking was the perception of a needed paradigm shift described by educator Ernest Boyer (1987). He saw student learning as a crucial link between student success and institutional success. Boyer's report warned of a gap—a "disconnect"—between the expectations and the realities of student learning, curriculum and academic standards. It found that institutions were ignoring an important correlation between a positive sense of student achievement and high retention.

The culture of higher education did not explicitly promote student learning. Instead, the underlying assumption was that instruction—but not necessarily learning—is the primary function of a college. In that culture of instruction delivery, the purpose of the college is to offer courses and degree programs. When the students don't "get it", the systemic assumption is that they should change their major or their institution. Typically, 56% of entering students fail to graduate with their class (Tinto, 1993). In other words, the culture of instruction delivery did not imperatively link the college's success to the student's success. This is the crux of the "disconnect" that Boyer unmasked and that led to the experiment in learning at Foothill College.

FAILED MISSIONS

Since 1987, many colleges that adopted learning-centered mission statements never succeeded in implementing them. Several authors suggested that this failure in achieving a transformation from the model of instruction delivery could have been prevented by the adoption of *intentional* learning (O'Banion, 1997; Barr & Tagg, 1995). Intentionality means the deliberately thoughtful exploration of a given discipline (Senge, 1999); in this case, the discipline is learning itself. Promoting student success means shifting the intended institutional outcome from teaching and course creation to learning. Realizing Boyer's vision requires a culture shift at the primary level of connection: the classroom. The question to begin with is not how instruction is delivered, but how learning occurs, and how to use understanding of that process. At Foothill College, these questions provided a lever for cultural change that promoted *real* student success.

THINKING ABOUT THINKING: A DYNAMIC KEY TO LEARNING

KATHLEEN M. PEARLE

DESCRIPTION OF THE STUDY

Foothill is a community college with 17,000 students, 600 faculty members, and two campuses, located in Los Altos Hills, California. At Foothill, degree completion and transfer readiness figure prominently in the institution's statement of goals. Yet the college's institutional data told another story. In 1996-1997, for example, an average of 68% of students completed courses and 35% persisted from Fall quarter to Spring quarter. These figures may have been consistent with national data (Astin, 1993; Tinto, 1993), but they were inconsistent with a mission statement that calls Foothill College a "learning organization best described as a large community classroom" (Foothill College 1998-1999 Course Catalogue, p. 7).

Facing the apparent disconnect between goals and reality, the college's leadership had to ask hard questions about the quality of education at Foothill. How strong and successful is a community of learners when only 68% of them remain enrolled in courses each quarter? How can the college create communities of students who continue to achieve? How can those successes be measured and improved upon? How can faculty be enlisted in the change process?

Foothill's leaders began with the assumption that student engagement in meaningful academic and non-academic dialogue—with both faculty and other students—makes a critical difference in the development of their sense of self as learners and in their sense of belongingness. These assumptions are drawn from studies on learning organizations (Senge, 1994), learning communities (O'Banion, 1997; Barr & Tagg, 1995; Matthews, 1994), and student retention (Tinto, 1993; Astin, 1993; Pascarella & Terenzini, 1991). Both factors contribute significantly to the student's success in completing courses (retention) and programs or degrees (persistence). In 1998, the college's leaders decided to adopt Johnston's Interactive Learning Model (ILM) as a tool for promoting student success. In previous studies, the Model had effected the active engagement of students and faculty in the intentional construction of knowledge, leading to increased self-efficacy and belongingness.

FOUR LEARNING PATTERNS

The ILM is a brain-based learning model that uses a reporting instrument, the Learning Combination Inventory (Johnston & Dainton, 1997), and a metacognitive process (Johnston, 1996) to frame and facilitate individual and group learning. The theoretical basis of the ILM is a set of constructs establishing cognition, conation, and affectation as the touchstones of the brain's synchronization of the learning process. The ILM suggests that how an individual learns manifests itself observably in four learning patterns: *Sequential, Precise, Technical and Confluent.* These patterns represent how the learner sees the world, takes in stimuli, integrates the stimuli and formulates a response to it. An individual can begin his or her learning with a particular pattern or patterns, use patterns as needed, or avoid them. Table 1 summarizes the basic indicators of each pattern.

The Learning Combination Inventory (LCI) is a 28-item self-report instrument that quantitatively and qualitatively captures the degree to which an individual uses each of the four learning patterns. Nationally and internationally validated, the LCI has test-retest reliability as well as content, construct, and predictive validity. It has a track record as an effective learning tool in K-12 classrooms and for building teams in industry in the United States and abroad.

TABLE 1: ILM LEARNING PATTERN CHARACTERISTICS

PATTERNS	COGNITIVELY	CONATIVELY	AFFECTIVELY
Sequential	• I organize information • I mentally analyze data • I break tasks down into stepse	• I make lists • I organize • I plan first, *then* act	• I thrive on consistency and dependability • I need things to be tidy and organized • I feel frustrated when the game plan keeps changing • I feel frustrated when I'm rushed
Precise	• I research information • I ask *lots* of questions • I always want to know more	• I challenge statements and ideas that I doubt • I prove I am right • I document my research and findings • I write things down • I write long e-mail messages and leave long voice mail messages	• I thrive on knowledge • I feel good when I am correct • I feel frustrated when incorrect information is accepted as valid • I feel frustrated when people do not share information with me
Technical	• I seek concrete relevance—what does this mean in the real world? • I only want as much information as I need—nothing extraneous	• I get my hands on • I tinker • I solve the problem • I *do*	• I enjoy knowing how things work • I feel good that I am self sufficient • I feel frustrated when the task has no real world relevance • I enjoy knowing things, but I do not feel the need to share that knowledge
Confluent	• I read between the lines • I think outside the box • I brainstorm • I make obscure connections between things that are seemingly unrelated	• I take risks • I am not afraid to fail • I talk about things—a lot • I might start things and not finish them • I will start a task first—*then* ask for directions	• I enjoy energy • I feel comfortable with failure • I do not enjoy having my ideas criticized • I feel frustrated by people who are not open to new ideas • I enjoy a challenge • I feel frustrated by repeating a task over and over

UNIQUE COMBINATION OF PATTERNS

The basic assumption of the ILM is that every individual's combination of learning patterns is unique, *and* that every person has a unique approach to learning that is interconnected with the way he or she thinks and feels during the task. So, for example, when Johnston's model of interactive learning patterns is used to inform Gardner's work on multiple intelligences (Gardner, 1993, 1999), it provides an explanation for the range and diversity with which all learners exercise those intelligences (Both Winton Marsalis and John Cage express their musical intelligence through a combination of learning patterns that is unique to each artist). Equally important, the ILM assumes that through reflective practice (Osterman & Kottkamp, 1993), the conscious understanding of every individual's unique actions, thoughts, and feelings can be used with intention by both the student and the instructor.

Rather than being acted upon as a passive recipient of information, the learner takes control of the responsibility for making learning work, for co-constructing knowledge. For example, the ILM helps the instructor to become conscious of the degree to which the delivery of instruction, the construction of assignments and the assessment of student work are driven by the instructor's own combination of patterns (Our tendency is to represent our knowledge and to teach through our pattern combinations. For example, an instructor, whose high confluence and avoidance of sequence leads her to shift gears frequently, is not likely to stick to a syllabus or a lecture outline). The ILM affords the student both a process for deconstructing instruction delivery and assignments, strategies for helping him or her succeed in formatting and completing assignments, and a vocabulary to use when asking an instructor or peer for assistance. Using the ILM, the instructor and the students gain insights into the subtext of classroom discourse and are able to communicate about the construction of meaning and knowledge by the diverse community of learners in a given discipline.

THE RESEARCH DESIGN

Over the course of the first year at Foothill College, from 1999 to 2000, a group of 26 faculty members volunteered to implement the ILM as part of their classroom instruction. During the second year of the study, another fourteen faculty members were recruited and mentored by the first faculty cohort. Before the ILM was implemented, a research team collected baseline data on the *faculty* using the following tools: a questionnaire that captured information about expectations, mental models of learning, teaching, students, and Foothill culture; samples of course construction and evaluation standards.

Likewise, at the beginning of each quarter, baseline data was established on *student* sense of self as learner and sense of belongingness using the following tools: survey that collected information about mental models of higher

education, learning experiences, the faculty as deliverers of instruction, other students as co-constructors of learning, collective learning, sense of self-efficacy, and commitment to retention or persistence.

TEAMS AND PROJECTS

Faculty participants and the students in their classes took the Learning Combination Inventory. Facilitators used data on individual learning patterns to build collective class learning profiles and to construct teams if the specific course required group projects. The profiles became tools for launching a dialogue about how to communicate and collaborate, based on the diversity of learners in the room. Students learned to decode lectures and assignments and to use knowledge of the learning patterns to approach and complete course work. Students were coached by their instructor to develop individual and collective strategies to help them navigate course requirements with intention.

During the first year, as the faculty engaged in 33 hours of professional development workshops and classroom activities focused on the ILM, a research team monitored and measured their interaction as faculty members. Likewise, the research team periodically monitored and measured the students' sense of self as learner and sense of belongingness as they used metacognition to approach and master learning tasks.

These were the primary questions that the research addressed:

1. How does the implementation of the ILM affect the student's perception of his or her competency to learn? Or motivation to learn? Or responsibility to learn?
2. How does the implementation of the ILM affect the student's perception of his or her value as a member of the class? Or motivation to learn from and teach others in the class?

ONGOING DISCUSSION OF METACOGNITION

Using both the framework and the dialectics of an ongoing discussion about metacognition, faculty also engaged in reflective practice (Ostermann & Kottkamp, 1993), examining the process of teaching and intentional learning in their classes with the goal of fostering the construction and practice of a learning community. The research intention, based on an action research approach, was to capture and record the change as it evolved and to use the data as part of a reflective feedback loop.

Through interviews and participant-observation in meetings and classrooms, researchers gathered data on student-faculty interactions in creating classroom learning communities. They triangulated data with information from the following work by faculty and students: reflections on strategies for the effective use of the ILM in the classroom; reflections on assignments which did and did not measure up to expectations; learning portfolios that contained sample assignments, student work product, assessments, faculty and student reflections on assessments, and student self-assessment of knowledge construction. The data were used to help the learning community assess and improve learning.

At the end of each quarter, the researchers generated data on student course completion and intention to persist in degree or program completion. These were additional questions that the research addressed:

1. How did the rate of retention in the pilot group compare with institutional data on retention?
2. What reasons did students who had considered dropping out have for staying in courses? Were the reasons linked to changes in: measures of self-efficacy, sense of connection with the instructor, sense of connection to other students, sense of personal growth or value as a member of a class?
3. Had the students begun to use metacognitive processes outside of the pilot courses? In other courses? In their professional or personal lives?

FINDINGS

While the ILM was implemented to promote student success, its successful integration in the classroom was far more difficult than anyone had imagined. The culture of instruction delivery has powerful structural barriers, such as the time constraints of a twelve-week academic quarter, as well as attitudinal barriers, such as the mental model that faculty is responsible for expertise but not learning. Where faculty succeeded, they often found themselves outside of their level of comfort, confronting issues of the relationship of traditional course requirements and assessments to learning. If, for example, there was a strong positive correlation between the learning patterns of the instructor and the "good" students in the course, what, exactly, was the instructor assessing? What could be done about the "disconnect" between two learners whose patterns were near opposites? Understanding themselves as learners and using reflective practice to study and guide their teaching enabled faculty to reframe their concepts of successful teaching and learning. Faculty who successfully implemented the ILM reported that they "couldn't go back," that their teaching had been changed, not only because of their understanding of metacognition, but also because of their students' responses to their teaching. The students, less vested in the culture of instruction delivery than the faculty, "got it" more quickly. Student success fuelled faculty success. And—

just as frequently—faculty success fed student success. They represent inseparable components of a cultural change from instruction delivery to intentional learning.

YEAR ONE OF THE ILM

During the first year of the project, 50% of the original group of faculty members did not complete the pilot project. Faculty retention rates were worse than Foothill student retention rates. The majority of those who did not succeed were adjunct faculty who reported that structural factors had contributed to their lack of success: it was too difficult to balance their fragmented existence (teaching more than four courses at more than one college) with the additional work required to implement the model in the classroom. On the other hand, 50% of the original group of faculty members successfully implemented the ILM in the classroom. In those classes, faculty introduced the ILM in incremental steps. For example, to introduce the ILM, a photography course used an assignment for a self-portrait-as-learner that integrated knowledge of learning patterns with requirements for mastery of photographic techniques. The instructor added her self-portrait to the metacognitive critique. After modeling the assignment with their own personal reflections, professors in several ESL and English Composition courses asked students to utilize knowledge of themselves as learners in a range of writing assignments. In a Spanish II class, the instructor and her students completed written and oral assignments about how their learning combinations affected their ability to learn and speak a foreign language. The instructor reported that the assignment created trust and a level of engagement and productivity unknown in the same group's Spanish I class.

SUMMARY OF RESULTS

In courses in which the ILM was successfully implemented, 88% of the 469 students enrolled completed the courses; 89% of that group received a grade of A, B, or C (transfer-ready grades). In addition, 8% in the pre-survey, as compared to 60% in the exit survey reported that an increased sense of self-efficacy was critical to succeeding in the course (survey questions elicited multiple measures of self-efficacy to capture data on sense of self as learner). For example, in this quote from a pre-survey, the locus of control for student success lies with the instructor:

A helpful instructor doesn't give up on me because of the way I learn.

In the exit survey, the same student said:

Understanding patterns is an opportunity for growth, not an excuse for lack of performance.

Here, the locus of control for student success has shifted

from instructor to student. For students and their instructor, the culture in this course shifted from that of instruction delivery to intentional learning. Student surveys from Year I also demonstrated a shift in student sense of belongingness in the classroom: 7% in the pre-survey, as compared to 26% in the exit survey claimed that being able to learn from others in the learning community—in addition to the instructor—was critical to succeeding in the course. An example of this shift in student attachment to the learning community appears in the exit survey of one previously disconnected student: "Lately I have been studying with a partner, and that has been very helpful. I am able to learn more with the help of other people's patterns."

Among students there was also a realization that the ILM had transferability, both to other courses and to work situations. Students reported that in courses where the instructor had no apparent awareness of the ILM, they were able to get good grades because they had learned how to use metacognition to "decode" the lectures and the course assignments. Dental Hygiene students developed strategies for educating patients based on their understanding of learning patterns. Among faculty, the experiences of the first year were useful for revising the second year's recruitment and training processes, as well as for creating a core of six "veterans" who agreed to mentor new participants.

YEAR TWO OF THE ILM

During the second year of the pilot, fourteen additional faculty members, recommended or recruited by the first year faculty, joined the project. Nearly 70% of the faculty succeeded in implementing the model in the classroom. Those 30% who did not succeed were new faculty who felt overwhelmed by first-year responsibilities; the ILM was an added burden for them. In courses in which the ILM was successfully implemented, the students reported an increased sense of self-efficacy (12% in the pre-survey, as compared to 70% in the exit survey) and sense of belongingness in the classroom (6% in the pre-survey, as compared to 34% in the exit survey). Both were linked to student retention. Of the 769 students enrolled in the second year of the pilot, 87% completed their courses, and 92% received transfer-ready grades. Student exit interviews affirmed the transferability of the ILM, both to other courses and to work and life situations. Adult students in Life Skills courses in Foothill's Transition to Work Program were able to identify and prepare applications and interviews for jobs that were suitable to their "use first" patterns. Faculty recognized the individual and collective benefits of several, cumulative experiences with the ILM. In one notable case, student success could be measured in terms of

national achievement. The cohort/learning community of Dental Hygiene students who had been using the ILM for two years with the same instructor ranked 2nd in the nation on National Board Exams. The instructor credited the ILM, among other factors, for the excellent outcomes:

"I wanted you to know that the 2nd year just graduated. They took their National Board Exams and were ranked 2nd in the entire nation, including several dental hygiene programs that are based in Universities. This was the first class I introduced the ILM model to. Of course the excellent outcomes were a result of many factors, including the ILM. Thank you all for the opportunity to participate in this research project."

CONCLUSION

The ILM process requires and promotes intentionality, which in turn leads to the development of components that foster retention and persistence. While change and growth are shaped by the way in which both faculty and students achieve mastery in individual and organizational learning, intentional faculty commitment to the process is crucial to the initial and the sustained success of the ILM. At Foothill College, the faculty learning curve moved from (1) academic information accumulation about the ILM (consistent with the culture of instruction delivery) to (2) individual metacognition (understanding the use of patterns in one's own learning) to (3) organizational metalearning which engaged faculty and students in a dialogue about the use and meaning of the learning process in their classroom communities. These are the hallmarks of cultural change. Yet, some significant challenges lie ahead, similar to ones that Ernest Boyer raised in 1987. They are the challenges of remaining intentional and reflective while Foothill evolves as a learning college.

REFERENCES

Astin, A. W. (1993). *What Matters in College: Four Critical Years Revisited.* San Francisco: Jossey-Bass.

Barr, R., & Tagg, J. (1995). From Teaching to Learning: New Paradigm for Undergraduate Education. *Change, November/December,* 13-25.

Boyer, E. (1987). *College: The Undergraduate Experience in America.* New York: Harper & Row.

Gardner, H. (1993). *Frames of Mind: Theory in Practice.* NY: Basic Books.

—. (1999). *Intelligence Reframed: Multiple Intelligences for the 21st Century.* NY: Basic Books.

Johnston, C. (1996). *Unlocking the Will to Learn.* Thousand Oaks, CA: Corwin Press.

Johnston, C., & Dainton, G. (1997). *The Learning Combination Inventory*. Thousand Oaks, CA: Corwin Press.

Matthews, R. (1994). Enriching Teaching and Learning through Learning Communities. In T. O'Banion (Ed.), *Teaching and Learning in the Community College*. Washington, D. C.: American Association of Community Colleges. ED 368 416.

O'Banion, T. (1997). *A Learning College for the 21st Century*. Phoenix: American Association of Community Colleges/Oryx Press.

Osterman, K., & Kottkamp, R. (1993). *Reflective Practice for educators: Improving Schooling through Professional Development*. Newbury Park, Ca.: Corwin Press.

Pascarella, E., & Terenzini, P. (1991). *How College Affects Students*. San Francisco: Jossey-Bass.

Senge, P. et al. (1994). *The Fifth Discipline Fieldbook*. New York: Doubleday.

Senge, P. et al. (1999*). The Dance of Change*. New York: Doubleday.

Tinto, V. (1993). *Leaving College. Rethinking the Causes and Cures of Student Attrition*. Second Edition. Chicago: The University of Chicago Press.

The Eldridge Perspective

As a professor of reading methods in a college setting that prepares undergraduate and graduate pre-service teachers to teach in the New York City schools, I am often conflicted by my goals. On the one hand, I want them to have certain *skills and techniques* at their disposal before they assume ultimate responsibility for a classroom full of youngsters. The literature on literacy supports this emphasis (Pressley et al, 2001; Ruddell, 1997). On the other hand, I believe that these pre-service educators need to develop a *vision* of themselves as teachers and of what is possible in an increasingly prescriptive climate. Underscored is the value of teachers' abilities to reflect upon their own practices and to integrate their practices with a personal vision of their students' life-long engagement with literacy (Roskos, Vikelich, and Rizko, 2002). So, are skills more important? Or vision? These dueling methodologies wage a silent war inside my head each semester. Skills? Or vision? I go back and forth between the two, stronger in skills and techniques, and endlessly experimenting with the vision piece of the formula.

Out of the Comfort Zone

Enter Lincoln Center Institute (LCI). In the fall of 1998, the School of Education at Hunter College began a collaborative association with LCI to infuse principles and practices of aesthetic education into teacher preparation. The work of Maxine Greene (2001) and Howard Gardner (1985) inspired some of us to seek out ways to enliven the imagination of our students while experimenting with the presentation of course material to model differentiated instruction for a variety of student strengths. Early on, I was fascinated with the opportunity that the Lincoln Center Institute collaboration offered me to have my students experience what it was to have a "vision of possibility." Through the collaboration with LCI, I hoped to quiet my inner methodological war by weaving together skills and vision—ultimately creating students who became "visionaries with excellent skills." To do that, I wanted to take them out of their "comfort zones" in thinking about reading and the process of learning to read and write. I wanted to challenge their beliefs about what it means to teach. And I wanted them to experience that challenge in a new way, not as an intellectual exercise.

What follows is a narrative recreation of the collaboration between myself and Heidi Upton, one of the talented teaching artists associated with Lincoln Center Institute. Heidi and I became collaborators because I had chosen to challenge the graduate students in my course on *The Advanced Teaching of Reading* with a musical performance. Trained at The Juilliard School as a concert pianist and possessing a doctorate in music as well, Heidi brought to our collaboration a love of music, an understanding of the LCI music repertory and aesthetic approach, and a broad knowledge of the finer points of composition and

Skills, Vision, or Visionaries with Excellent Skills

Deborah Eldridge and Heidi Upton

performance. I brought my knowledge of literacy pedagogy and my own love of teaching. Together we integrated Nurit Tilles' performance of 20th century piano compositions by Samuel Barber and Charles Ives into my graduate course in advanced reading. We did this by agreeing on a line of inquiry that would hopefully guide the aesthetic experiences in my course. For Heidi the central question was: *"How might an exploration of a concept such as texture and its application to musical sound create a pathway to a deeper understanding of the piano sonatas of Ives and Barber?"* For me the thread that tied it all together was: *"How might an exploration of the textural sounds of these two piano sonatas lead us to new understanding of the process of reading?"* Although partnering with LCI means putting a work of art at the very center of the exploratory process—in this case Nurit Tilles' piano performance of sonatas by Ives and Barber—this paper discusses the impact of that process on the context of a college reading methods course.

Shape, Texture and Moods

The participants in our workshop were present and future teachers. We encouraged them to leave their comfort zone and experience a new way of thinking about something they intuitively and experientially know a lot about (reading). We needed to warm them up. Heidi passed around a bag of articles and asked everyone to choose something without looking at the article. They were to handle it, experience it, feel it for its shape and texture. She then asked for volunteers to describe their articles. And we created a list of the textures and shapes they named. For example, one brave person described his object as pointy, yet smooth, dangerous but soothing. (He held a small sprig of a plastic pine branch).

Next, participants were asked to think about their mood that morning and to describe it in terms of texture, shape, color, and/or sound. One woman noted that she felt round, and dark, opaque, sonorous like a gong. Following this exercise, Heidi played excerpts from a CD containing a variety of disparate musical selections. Odd pieces. Hurried. Slow. Dissonant. Disconnected. Jagged. Soft. Mournful. Elusive. The workshop participants described the sounds they heard in similar terms of texture, shape, color, and mood—an example of the LCI practice to "describe, analyze, interpret." If interpretation was the first response, we would ask: "What about the music led to your ideas?" We would ask them to listen again.

As Heidi and I took the participants through this warm-up, we each had a goal. Heidi hoped to create a lens to help them experience the music and to have some organizing factors with which to make a personal connection to the music of the performance. I hoped that they would make a connection between preparation to hear a musical performance and preparation to read literature. I wanted the warm-up experience to open a vision of pre-reading activities as aesthetic experiences. Our efforts to relate reading and music were beginning to find realization. The preparations seemed to share a common element—anticipation of an emotional experience.

THE UPTON PERSPECTIVE

At this point in the undertaking, I called their attention to a table in the center of the room. There, I displayed a collection of musical instruments similar to the ones we used in our workshop at Hunter College: a set of claves, a triangle, a cow bell, a tambourine—and an amorphous green object in a plastic tube that emitted a characteristically functional sound when manipulated. (We teaching artists will do anything to keep participants interested). Under my guidance, the group explored the sounds of these instruments through the lens of texture. Would it be possible, I asked the workshop participants, to use instruments in combination to evoke different kinds of texture? How might this work? Would it be possible to have a series of sounds that would evoke a series of moods? The group wandered through the sounds of their instruments for a few minutes.

I then proposed to the group that they were to imagine they were part of a new music movement called the Texturalists. This movement was known to focus on the shapes of sound and—through a process too esoteric to explain—make it into great music. Not only was the music

of the Texturalists popular, but other people wanted to play it too. In the original workshop, I explained to the presentation participants, the students had to create their own system of notation—one that would allow other "musicians" to read and reinterpret their Texturalist work (see Figure 1). And as with the student group, in order to facilitate the present workshop's participants' understanding, we brainstormed about what would be necessary to have in place when creating a notation system. Would there have to be some key or legend established first? What else would have to be notated? They mentioned finding a way to denote time, what instruments to use and how they should be played. Once these parameters were established, we shared with them the student notations. One of them is recreated on the next page.

At first, there was intense discussion about how to decipher what they saw. Once the system had been decoded to everyone's satisfaction, an attempt at performance (using the exact instruments as notated in the piece) was made. It took awhile. After a few tries, discussion in the room was active and rich regarding how this "Texturalist interpretive" experience related directly to the experience of learning to read. The deepest part of the imagination of the participants had been called on, and it yielded a remarkable variety of relationships between sound and reading.

SKILLS OR VISION

Together we had created an experience that felt powerful and empowering. The presentation participants were curious: How had the graduate students responded to these experiences? At this point in the presentation, we shared students' journal responses to the LCI aesthetic experience that exemplified a number of "levels" of response. On the first level were the students who do not "get it" at all:

I just don't know how this experience relates to the reading classroom. I have tried to expose my students to music and art in a more traditional manner by playing classical music during the day and highlighting an "Artist of the Month."

At the second level were students who thought of the LCI aesthetic experience in terms of what to do with their own students in their own classrooms.

I feel that I may have taken it for granted that students were exposed to print, when in reality they aren't. They need to learn to appreciate the written word just as they appreciate any possessions they may hold dear to themselves.

At the third level were students who saw the aesthetic experience as a "how to" manual for teaching.

For my students, it would be a fun activity to take them on a walk around the block and have them listen to the

Figure 1: Novel Notation of Music

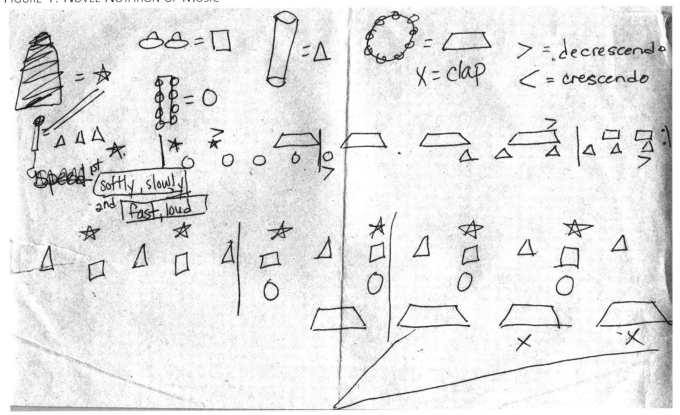

This is an example of a new way developed by students to denote time, the instruments to use, and the manner in which they are to be played.

sounds and write down the texture they associate it with. It is also a wonderful way for them to learn new words. They can even paint a picture to go with it. They can listen to sounds at home and write about it. It is a great tool to learn listening skills and creativity at the same time.

Then there were the students who took the experience to heart and gained some insight into children and learning.

It did, though, make me think of how frustrating it must be to look at something and have no idea what it is. As I walked around the room looking at the other groups' pieces, I did not know what their symbols meant. I was not supposed to know! My two children, the ones really struggling with reading, must feel such nervousness and embarrassment, because it is expected that they DO [emphasis in original] know by 3rd grade.

At the fifth level, some students reflected upon the reading process and connected it to their teaching.

I think that reading is a very personal experience, for the

most part. There is 'basic' reading—sounding out the words plus basic comprehension. Then there is bringing your whole self, your experiences and dream(s), to a work and it resounding with you. I think you have to be willing to let the students help guide you here. What one person considers perfectly clear, another may feel is oblique. I think that the notation exercise is key to understanding this, but to transfer that lesson from music to words is a tricky lesson. Whatever someone writes, someone else brings different experiences / knowledge that colors this. In accepted musical notation, if I know the language, I can follow along. Granted as a performer, I have my own interpretation, but the notes remain the same. With words, the exercise could help a writer to learn how to define things more fully and precisely.*

What Next?

Perhaps the intention to make methodological peace between skills and vision in graduate teacher education courses can only go so far. There is a point where the students' experiences, beliefs, imaginations, and priorities intervene. Some students respond by turning the aesthetic experience into a skill—something for them to do with the children. Some students respond by envisioning the possibilities of working with children in new ways as they learn to read, write, listen, speak, and represent their world visually. Perhaps, like the composers Barber and Ives, instructors in higher education can write the notes (diversify the experiences in a course in higher education). But whether or not our "music" makes a personal connection with our students has more to do with the student and his/her readiness to "hear." Thus, despite the intention to create a course in which skills were set aside and vision was possible, we had put together a constructivist experience in which the graduate students created their own knowledge and understanding of the interplay between aesthetics and literacy. Our agenda was not necessarily their agenda, and that is at it should be.

Perhaps, on the other side of the coin, the teaching and learning process takes time. In the Hunter College graduate and undergraduate courses that collaborate with Lincoln Center Institute, we've only just begun to glimpse the outcomes of innovation and the nuances of collaboration and integration. Our collective challenge is in the adaptations, recreations, and negotiations that create opportunities for empowering visions and expanded skills. It is a mindful process, and a challenging one. And that's what keeps us innovating in higher education.

REFERENCES

Gardner, H. (1985). *The Mind's New Science: A History of the Cognitive Revolution*. New York: Basic Books.

Greene, M. (2001). *Variations on a Blue Guitar*. New York: Teachers College Press.

Pressley, M., Wharton-MacDonald, R., Allington, R., Block, C. C., Morrow, L., Tracey, D., Baker, K., Brooks, G., Cronin, J., Nelson, E., & Woo, D. (2001). A Study of Effective First-Grade Literacy Instruction. *Scientific Studies of Reading,* **5**, 35-58.

Roskos, K., Vukelich, C. & Rizko, V. (2002). Reflection and Learning to Teach Reading: A Critical Review of Literacy and General Teacher Education Studies. *Journal of Literacy Research,* **33**(4), 595-635.

Ruddell, R. B. (1997). Researching the Influential Literacy Teacher: Characteristics, Beliefs, Strategies and New Research Directions. In C. K. Kinzer, Hinchman, K. A., & Leu, D. J. (Ed.),

Forty-Sixth Yearbook of the National Reading Conference: Inquiries in Literacy Theory and Practice (pp. 37-53). Chicago, IL: National Reading Conference.

One key factor impeding effective application of Multiple Intelligences (MI) in schools is that teachers tend to teach mainly in the intelligences in which they are strong. On the other hand, we found that students can be encouraged to work with intelligences they are not naturally inclined to use. This article explores a program that attempts to make education students widen their understanding of teaching and learning, thereby better preparing them for their future classrooms. We will attempt to apply Howard Gardner's theory of MI to a single case study of a recent graduate and propose a program that prepares teachers to create curricula that respect every child's strengths.

Education students generally arrive at pre-service and in-service teacher-education programs with extensive knowledge. Their 12-plus years as students in public and/or private schools result in strong assumptions about the roles of teachers, students and curriculum. Surprisingly enough, however, when they come to the university, they can be taught to consciously develop new expectations regarding the purpose of education and appropriate teaching and learning strategies. We will begin by considering Mary, a graduate student and herself a teacher, and some of her assumptions.

A CASE STUDY OF MARY

Mary considers herself to be a good learner. She enjoyed her own public school experience, which focused on the basics: reading, writing and arithmetic. Mary excelled in these areas and was recognized for it. Although she often took a passive role in math and science classes, she feels she was able to gain adequate content knowledge by watching others conduct science experiments without engaging in the discovery and problem-solving process herself.

Mary has taught fourth grade for two years and considers herself to be a good teacher. She feels comfortable with her classroom and curriculum. She implements teaching and learning strategies that prepare her students to succeed on statewide standardized tests, which concentrate on linguistic and mathematical skills. Her students score high on these tests, and Mary has been recognized by school administrators for this achievement. Mary reports having little time in her jam-packed curriculum to consider art, nature, music, and/or the democratic classroom approach.

MARY'S ASSUMPTIONS

Mary's first assumption, which she bases on her own experiences as a student and a teacher, is that instruction focused on reading, writing, arithmetic and exam preparation will result in good learners who are prepared to succeed in school and life. Contrary to this notion, Gardner asserts that all human beings have at least eight different intelligences: Verbal-Linguistic, Math-Logic, Spatial, Bodily-Kinesthetic, Musical, Interpersonal, Intrapersonal, and Naturalist. Applying this theory of MI encourages teachers to think about educating the whole child.

In his keynote address at the Urban Mission Conference at New Jersey City University, Gardner emphasized

USING MULTIPLE INTELLIGENCES TO BROADEN TEACHING METHODS

DINA ROSEN

that the interaction of all of these intelligences is conducive to genuine understanding in students. Each individual has a unique profile of intelligences that consists of dominant, less dominant, and perhaps dormant intelligences. Furthermore, no two people have exactly the same profile of intelligences. The modern classroom teacher can prepare children for success by developing and celebrating all of these intelligences, from dominant to dormant.

Mary holds a second assumption, also supported by her own academic experiences: incomplete curricula are a "necessary evil." Mary's curriculum is incomplete in that it focused on developing skills in two areas: verbal-linguistic and math-logic. According to Gardner's theory, instruction focused on a limited number of intelligences is flawed. Gardner stressed in his keynote speech that if you teach only one way, you will take advantage of some students' strengths but will ignore the strengths of others. The clear lesson here for Mary is that if she uses several different ways to present information to her students, more intelligences will be tapped, and more students might reach true understanding. Incomplete curricula often result from an intense focus on testing and identification of students' weaknesses. The theory of MI, on the other hand, celebrates children's strengths and does not seek to identify weaknesses.

POSSIBLE EXPLANATIONS OF MARY'S MISCONCEPTIONS

There are at least two possible explanations for Mary's assumptions described above. The first is that Mary teaches as she was taught. Mary has many misunderstandings about teaching and learning, a result of the twelve-plus years she participated in education that was focused on two of the intelligences: verbal and mathematical. A second explanation is that Mary's dominant intelligence is verbal-linguistic so her instruction is focused on reading and writing. Teachers tend to teach the way they are most comfortable. Certain teachers, such as Mary, have particularly dominant verbal-linguistic intelligence, and their classroom instruction tends to rely heavily on verbal-linguistic methods. (The particular dominant intelligence varies from teacher to teacher and may have arisen from a natural strength or schooling.) When Mary does not explore and use all of her intelligences in her teaching, her students do not reach their potential. She also fails in that she does not address her own weaknesses. Although the application of MI Theory is not a quick fix, it can contribute to Mary's success—and to that of all other professional educators. Pre-service teachers' tendency to teach only according to their own dominant intelligences can be lessened by making them aware of their MI profiles. The problem that teachers tend to teach as they were taught can be addressed by involving them in alternate teaching experiences; that is, by helping them plan curricula that respect diverse MI profiles.

MI AS A FRAMEWORK
FOR CURRICULUM DEVELOPMENT

A program that guides pre-service teachers to consider MI when planning instruction and assessment can prepare them to help children achieve deeper understanding. The remainder of this article will focus on a Multiple Intelligences Teacher Education program this author has implemented. The following four-step process is described:

Step 1: Understanding MI theory and Profile
Step 2: Identifying and Accepting
     One's Personal MI Profile
Step 3: Indulging Students' Intelligences
Step 4: Planning for Curriculum and
     Assessment with Multiple Intelligences

STEP 1: UNDERSTANDING MI THEORY AND PROFILE

First, pre-service teachers must understand that each person possesses many types of intelligences. In three years of experimenting with MI and pre-service teacher education, I have found it helpful to allow my students to examine the concept of Multiple Intelligences by having them create lists of famous people and consider which intelligence is dominant for that person. For example, the famous dancer Alvin Ailey most likely had strong kinesthetic intelligence and the mystery novelist Steven King is likely to have strong verbal-linguistic intelligence.

Next, students must examine the concept of the MI profile. Each person has his or her own mix of intelligences, which can be referred to as his or her "MI Profile." Pre-service teachers need to understand that each child's profile is a unique combination of all eight intelligences in varying degrees, from dominant to dormant. Even twins have different profiles.

To further explore the concept of the MI profile, students can examine two fictitious students. Both student A and B have dominant Verbal-Linguistic Intelligence. However, their second most dominant areas are very different: student A's strength is Intrapersonal Intelligence and student B's strength is Interpersonal Intelligence. The combination of each student's two strongest intelligences may result in different learning preferences and behaviors. For example, student A may be excellent at writing stories (an activity completed independently) while student B excels in plays and performance (an activity completed with others). Furthermore, pre-service teachers must be made aware of the need to respect the great variety within a single intelligence. I share with my students the following situation that I observed in an urban fourth grade classroom. The teacher asked her students to write an essay. Many students began writing. Surprisingly, a few students who the teacher considered to be verbally-linguistically dominant were having difficulty writing the essay. Recognizing that these students favored oral communication, the teacher decided to give them an option of sharing their ideas for the essay orally. The students did so successfully.

Finally, it is important to help pre-service teachers consider factors that can alter the impact of a child's multiple intelligences profile on their learning. I start this discussion with a story. Jill, a second grade teacher, attended an in-service program on MI Theory. During the workshop, she conferred with other teachers about a child she considered to be a Spatial/Visual learner. The teachers all agreed and were intrigued by the fact that the student was blind. Jill and her colleagues appreciated the fact that sometimes limitations prevent students from relying on their dominant intelligence.

STEP 2: IDENTIFYING AND ACCEPTING
ONE'S PERSONAL MI PROFILE

After gaining understanding of each intelligence, students need to identify their own MI Profiles—which indicate their dominant, secondary and dormant intelligences. To achieve this, students make graphic representations of their Profiles, write about the learning strategies they use, and share their written reflections with peers. For example, John wrote the following reflection: "I always tapped on my desk during class. I drove my teachers crazy. I did not realize until now that I frequently created my own rhythms to accompany the ideas I was learning—as a way to improve my comprehension. Musical Intelligence is dominant for me." After sharing this reflection with some peers, another student asked John to consider what other intelligence may be associated with tapping the pencil. John thought for a moment and replied, "Kinesthetic, I guess. Yes, I do my best thinking on the move."

Based on their individual, self-designed MI Profiles, I asked students to break into eight groups. Most students joined the group that represented their most dominant intelligence. Each group represented on poster board strategies used by particular students with dominance in their specific intelligence. For example, the spatial learners indicated they used the following tools: graphic organizers, color-coding, multi-color highlighting, charts, and diagrams. The intrapersonal learners indicated the following learning preferences: they like choices, self-paced activities, and knowing the big picture (that is, a reminder of what they have learned and indication of what and how they will add to this knowledge).

STEP 3: INDULGING STUDENTS' INTELLIGENCES

The class discussed the importance of indulging students' intelligences. For example, students with dominant Intrapersonal Intelligence often need to know where they have been and where they are going. They will thrive better in the classroom having this knowledge; thus teachers should provide them with an agenda. If, as a teacher, you do not like or do not use agendas or advanced organizers, then you are ignoring students who like an overview of how learning activities connect before actually engaging in such activities.

Indulging students' intelligences can lead to fewer classroom management problems and to improved learning, both for a student exhibiting inappropriate behavior and his/her peers. The following is an example of a teacher missing an opportunity to indulge a child's intelligence:

Jason's teacher called his parents in for a conference. Instead of looking at the teacher when she taught, Jason doodled in his notebook. Jason's father respectfully listened to the teacher's issues and asked several key questions.

Father: *Does Jason seem to be learning from your instruction?*
Teacher: *Yes.*
Father: *Is Jason's learning considered sub-par?*
Teacher: *No.*
Father: *Are Jason's actions disrupting other children's learning? Does the doodling impede the learning process of his peers?*
Teacher: *No, his behavior is not impacting on other students' learning.*
Father: *Then I am not sure I see the problem here. He is learning. He is not disrupting other children's learning.*

The teacher had missed important clues suggesting that Jason excels in the Visual and/or Kinesthetic Intelligences. To reduce Jason's alleged behavioral problem and support his learning, Jason's teacher could have formally required all children in her class to "doodle" about what they were learning, for example, in a graphic organizer.

STEP 4: PLANNING FOR CURRICULUM AND ASSESSMENT WITH MI

In his keynote remarks, Gardner discussed the difference between understanding and parroting. He suggested that understanding is not achieved until knowledge is applied "in authentic ways." This concept—that true understanding is performance-based—underscores the importance of requiring pre-service teachers to apply their knowledge of MI Theory to the design and implementation of thematic curricula. To do so, teachers should plan instruction that respects more than one intelligence. Gardner said, "Not every lesson should be taught in eight ways, but the teacher should be ready to teach in more than one way." Specifically, I require pre-service teachers to work in groups to plan and implement lessons. The students are not told which or how many intelligences to include in their lessons. Since they work in groups, lessons usually include each students' own dominant intelligence and at least two others. Using a popular computer software program, *Inspiration*, students map out their lessons. I require pre-service teachers to demonstrate that they understand and can integrate MI Theory by asking them to teach their lessons twice: once with children and once with adults (class peers).

IMPLICATIONS OF MI THEORY FOR SUCCESS IN SCHOOL AND LIFE

The teacher education program described in this article has been beneficial to my students. The four-step process combats misconceptions and gives students an opportunity to explore teaching and learning. Despite current emphasis on accountability in education, no curriculum can be truly accountable without respecting each child's multiple intelligences. Gardner's theory is not just pie-in-the-sky. Applied with true understanding, it can bring the following benefits to any classroom environment: fewer classroom management problems, more well-rounded students, truer understanding by students of complex concepts, a more balanced and integrated curriculum, expansion of teachers' skills set, and better preparation of teachers to be life-long learners.

The purpose of this study was threefold: the identification of a pre-service teacher's Multiple Intelligence (MI) strengths, the identification of group MIs to determine best-practice teaching and assessment strategies, and the correlation between teachers' identified MI strengths and their preferred teaching and assessment strategies. A community-based action research design was utilized and included surveys, individual interviews and a focus group interview. Data were collected through literature review, observation of teachers, focus group interviews, individual interviews, and surveys.

The results of the data analysis indicated that pre-service teachers had preferred learning styles that could be based on MI Theory. The second result indicated that an understanding of group intelligences and an application of strategies and assessments supporting group intelligences facilitated both learning and teaching in a college classroom. The third result indicated that in-service teachers knew very little about the theory of MI. They had developed teaching strategies based on teacher education programs and observations, and they utilized a variety of teaching strategies to meet the needs of a diverse student population.

ACCOUNTABILITY IN EDUCATION

Accountability is a national concern in education today. The content that is taught in the schools is constantly under scrutiny as states adopt standards for curriculum. Teachers' concerns that they will be evaluated based on their students' achievement of objectives is a national focus. At the same time, teacher education programs have been targeted as the most critical programs in universities, and the content of those programs is given close attention. Concomitantly, the reform movement in education has many facets at the present time, least among which is recognizing how children learn. During the last decade, the theory of MI has become a prominent educational reform issue. That theory is a pluralized way of understanding the intellect. Recent advances in cognitive science, developmental psychology, and neuroscience suggest that each person's level of intelligence—as it has been traditionally considered— is actually made up of autonomous faculties that can work individually or in concert with other faculties. Gardner (1999) originally identified seven such faculties, which he labeled as "intelligences": musical, bodily-kinesthetic, logical-mathematical, linguistic, spatial, interpersonal, and intrapersonal. Recently, two additional intelligences have been added: naturalistic and existential. Much of the focus on the theory of multiple intelligences has been in elementary schools and with gifted and talented children. Little has been done to determine if the theory of MI can be implemented in other contexts.

NATIONAL LEADERSHIP CONFERENCE

Teachers who believe in the MI theory have developed lessons, assessments, apprenticeships and interdiscipli-

AN INFORMAL OVERVIEW OF MI THEORY IN TEACHER TRAINING

KATHLEEN GORMAN-CARTER, DIAN D. DUDDERAR, AND PAMELA A. ATCHISON

nary curricula addressing more than one or two intelligences at a time. They agree that one of the central tenets of a great program is that a school is responsible for helping all students discover and develop their talents and strengths. In doing this, the school not only awakens children's joy in learning but also fuels the persistence and effort necessary for mastering skills and information and for being inventive (Campbell, 1994). The examination of the topic of engaging MI in higher education was the focus of a national leadership conference at New Jersey City University in October, 2001. Thus, it is evident that the application of the theory of Multiple Intelligences might well be useful in educational settings on a continuum of pre-K through adulthood.

METHODOLOGY USED IN THIS STUDY

The methodology used in this study is primarily community-based action research and quasi-ethnographic study (Stringer, 1996). This method of research focuses on ways to improve practice through an "interpretivist paradigm" (Glesne, 1999, p. 13). The process includes gathering qualitative or quantitative data, interpreting the data as it relates to multiple viewpoints, and discussing the results with stakeholders. The action phase—what is actually done with the data—involves stakeholders in better understanding their situation. The results gained from this study were used to introduce MI Theory to undergraduate and graduate students and in-service teachers, to enhance classroom instruction and assessment, and to further explore MI Theory possibilities at the post-secondary levels of education.

PRE-SERVICE TEACHER EDUCATION

Current application of MI Theory in teacher education is not limited to the Harvard Graduate School of Education. A telephone survey of teacher education departments in two universities and one college in Delaware revealed that MI Theory is addressed in teacher education methods courses, but it is up to the individual instructors to incorporate the theory into their courses. One university representative indicated that MI Theory is usually a part of a *Theories of Education* course, but is not the focus of the teacher education program. In Maryland, the extent of MI Theory integration into teacher education courses and/or programs is focused in educational psychology courses and methods courses. Professional development opportunities for in-service teachers are similar to those in Delaware. According to the Delaware Department of Education Professional Development unit, teachers interested in MI Theory usually seek information due to personal or professional interests or at the professional development programs level. The Delaware Learning Resources Network offered workshops in MI Theory during the summer of 2001 to teachers in that state. The Harvard Graduate School of Education currently offers a summer institute as well as distance learning projects.

DIFFUSION OF MI THEORY THROUGH A TEACHER CERTIFICATION PROGRAM

Pre-service teachers are introduced to Gardner's MI Theory in an educational foundations course during their freshman year at St. Mary's College of Maryland. The course requires student groups to read and report to the class on one of 12 instructor-selected texts. The texts are all education-related and written by recognized theorists or philosophers. The student groups present their book review in any form they chose with the exception of a straight lecture format. The MI Theory presentation is based on Gardner's (1983) *Frames of Mind:* this presentation is always audience interactive and very creative in format. The student group presentations focus on simulating Gardner's concepts through implementing different instructional activities to demonstrate to the audience how the MI's differ in instructional approaches.

In the pre-service teachers' sophomore year, they view MI Theory through the psychological lens. They are given the opportunity to explore and identify a child's predominant MI in the field experiences component of the *Educational Psychology* course. One of the required readings for

this course is Gardner's (1993) *Multiple Intelligences: The Theory into Practice.* The pre-service teachers' observation activity for MI is to administer a child/adolescence MI Survey to one special-needs student at their field experience placement site. When they have identified the student's predominant MI, they then need to develop a series of activities based on the student's identified MI that will enhance content acquisition in a specific curriculum area in which the student is having difficulty. The teacher keeps a record of the student's progress using instructional activities that meet the student's identified MI. The pre-service teacher then reflects on the student's outcomes and draws conclusions based on Gardner's other works and supporting references. Many pre-service teacher's anecdotal reports from this project—which are shared with their cooperating teachers—have resulted in classroom teachers taking a closer look at their students' learning styles and their own teaching styles.

As the pre-service teachers enter their junior year, they cycle through a series of educational methods, techniques and materials courses facilitated in specific content areas. All of these courses require an extensive field experience component in which the pre-service teacher facilitates instruction with small groups of students in the classroom. Before the teacher begins the instructional planning for these small groups, the child/adolescence MI Survey is administered. The results of this survey assist the pre-service teacher in determining appropriate instructional strategies for each child in the group. During the planning and writing of instructional outcomes for student performance expectations, the pre-service teacher is encouraged to use Campbell's (1994) *Multiple Intelligence Handbook: Lesson Plans and More,* while integrating Marzano's (1992) *A Different Kind of Classroom: Dimensions of Learning* into their framework for instructional design. Using these resources as well as a number of others, the pre-service teacher is becoming more proficient in delivering quality-differentiated instruction to meet the needs of the diverse classrooms.

MULTIPLE CONFIGURATIONS OF MI

In a senior level elective course, *Educational Assessment,* pre-service teachers explore Gardner's (1999), *Good Work: When Excellence and Ethics Meet.* Finally, during *Teacher Intern Orientation Workshop,* which occurs during the pre-service teachers' fall semester of their senior year, they analyze their own MI through taking the MI Adult Survey. After identifying their predominant MI, they are put into groups of like MI participants and asked to brainstorm and list on chart paper the teaching strategies that would best help them to learn through their MI. The whole group is then reconfigured and each new group is assigned a different MI. The new group configuration and the new assigned MI should not have anyone assigned an MI that is their own. These new groups will now brainstorm and list on chart paper the teaching strategies that they think would best enhance learning for that MI type. The two groups match their chart organizers and orally present their rationale for selection of specific instructional strategies. The rewards of implementing this activity after three years of developmental acquisition of knowledge of MI Theory are twofold. First, the new teacher intern has had experience in prior field placements implementing MI into practice; and second, it helps to focus the new teacher interns on the necessity of teaching beyond their own MI at that critical juncture before they enter the classroom for their final phase of teacher preparation.

USING MI TO RECOGNIZE LEARNING STYLES

At the beginning of all methods courses, one researcher administers a battery of surveys collected in educational journals or textbooks. These quick tests provide opportunity for discussion of learning styles, personality characteristics, and communication patterns. They also provide an opportunity to focus on classroom management and student-teacher responsibility when discussing individuals' locus of control.

One survey instrument in the battery entitled *Where Does Your True Intelligence Lie?* (Gutloff, 1996) was voluntarily completed by one hundred pre-service teachers—a community of learners—in four methods courses during the Spring, 1998 semester. The course, *Effective Teaching Strategies*, was the first methods course for students in a teacher education program. More than 75% of these students were in an elementary education program; 10% were enrolled in an early childhood education program; and 15% were beginning various content-area secondary education programs. Prior to completing the assessment, the students-teachers were asked to list the strategies that their own teachers used that made them better learners. Then students-teachers were asked to list their one preferred traditional form of assessment and their one preferred form of alternative assessment. After completing the self-scoring survey instrument, students participated in a presentation and

discussion on MI Theory and then compared their survey results with their preferences for learning and assessment.

The results of this exercise are presented in Table 1. It is interesting to note that across the four classes, there were no distinctions by gender or ethnicity. Interpersonal strengths led to successful group work, group presentations, discussions of ideas and theories, and feedback from students on peer presentations. Scores on mid-term and final examinations in the form of multiple choice and essay questions did not reflect, as a group, the success of oral performances.

GROUP MULTIPLE INTELLIGENCES AS A TEACHING/ASSESSMENT TOOL

The MI Theory can serve as a useful tool for teachers in determining the predominant learning preferences of the class at large. Utilizing the action research model similar to the "interpretivist paradigm" (Glesne, 1999), three different groups of college students voluntarily completed the MI survey. One class was a group of undergraduate non-traditional students in an adult education program; the

TABLE 1: MULTIPLE INTELLINGENCE STRENGTHS* OF THIRD YEAR STUDENTS IN A TEACHER EDUCATION PROGRAM
N=100

MI	REPORTED AS PRIMARY STRENGTH	REPORTED AS LOWEST SCORE
Musical	8%	10%
Logical/Mathematical	12%	13%
Interpersonal	50%	0%
Bodily Kinesthetic	50%	0%
Visual/Spacial	10%	8%
Intrapersonal	8%	48%
Verbal Linguistic	10%	7%

*At the time the survey was administered, only seven intellingces had been identified.

TABLE 2: ANALYSIS OF GROUP RESULTS

GROUP	AUDIENCE	STRENGTH 1	STRENGTH 2
Non-traditional Undergraduate Students (30)	Adult Majors	Interpersonal	Logical/ Mathematical Musical
Traditional Undergraduate Students (24)	Elementary Education Majors	Interpersonal	Bodily–Kinesthetic
Graduate Students (24)	In-service Teachers in a Curriculum Course	Verbal–Linguistic	Interpersonal

second class was composed of undergraduate elementary education majors, and the third class were students in a graduate course in education. The purpose in completing this exercise at the beginning of a semester was to introduce education majors to the concept of MI Theory and to illustrate how the identification of the strength intelligences of the group could be enhanced by the selection of teaching strategies that would promote success. Conversely, it was hypothesized that the use of strategies that were not strengths would provide learning experiences that would expand their repertoire of learning skills, and students were cautioned that these learning experiences may or may not be comfortable for them.

As indicated by Table 2, undergraduate students in this study, whether traditional or non-traditional, scored highest in the Intrapersonal category. Graduate students scored

TABLE 3: TEACHING STRATEGIES TO ENHANCE/EXPAND
GROUP INTELLIGENCE

GROUP	STRATEGIES TO ENHANCE	STRATEGIES TO EXPAND
Non-traditional Undergraduate	Cooperative groups Collaborative groups Interviews Role playing	Reflection journaling Independent assignments Creating things
Traditional Undergraduate Students	Cooperative groups Collaborative groups Videos, computers	Reflection journaling Making manipulatives Electronic mail messaging Venn diagrams Create and use songes to teach/learn
Graduate Students	Reflection journaling Designing self-evaluation tools Independent assignments	Cooperative groups Interviews Computer presentations

higher in Verbal-Linguistic with Interpersonal as a close second strength which might indicate a more reflective posture toward teaching and learning.

Both the non-traditional undergraduate students and the graduate students were chronologically more mature than the traditional undergraduate students and had life experiences including work, family, and community responsibilities, to name a few, that most of the traditional students did not. The need to use time more efficiently and effectively, the need to see practical applications of what is learned in the classroom, and the time constraints often

involved in traditional group work, are embedded in andragogical principles of learning and were evident in the dichotomy between traditional undergraduate students and the non-traditional undergraduate and graduate students.

IDENTIFICATION OF IN-SERVICE TEACHERS' MULTIPLE INTELLIGENCES

The purpose of this study was to investigate if there was a correlation between a teacher's preferred MI and the strategies used in their respective classrooms. The results of the data analysis indicated that the teachers knew very little about the theory of MI, yet they developed teaching strategies based on their respective teacher education programs and observations and through trial and error procedures in an effort to meet the needs of a diverse student population. The research question in this study was:

Is there a correlation between a teacher's preferred multiple intelligences and the strategies used in the teacher's respective classroom? The question is relevant based on a review of the literature and current practices in the application of the theory of MI. The question relates to the application of MI to an adult population of teachers and contributes to that body of research that relates to MI Theory applied to adults.

All participants who volunteered for the in-service teacher study completed a survey of multiple intelligences, participated in an individual interview with the researcher and/or participated in a focus group interview. Participants in the survey and individual interview included a vocational teacher of shop subjects, one academic teacher whose area of teaching responsibility is English, and one teacher of social studies, science, and health. All are certified special education teachers at the high school level. The focus group interview involved four teachers. Their primary teaching responsibilities are mathematics, a course in school-to-work, and health.

An initial survey was administered to determine the teachers' MI strength as described in the MI theory. The *Multiple Intelligences Survey* was designed by McKenzie (2000) to include accurate descriptions of activities the survey completers did or did not enjoy, as described by Denzin & Lincoln (1998). The self-scoring survey was used as a preliminary assessment investigating the teachers' level of understanding of the MI Theory by reflecting on themselves as students as well as teachers. Further, in a pilot test of the survey instrument with three colleagues in the field of education, all reported that the results were accurate reflections of their preferred styles. The tables below illustrate the results of this survey.

It was interesting to note that one of the participants did not register above 70% in any category and five participants scored weakness levels (score of 30% or lower) in naturalist,

TABLE 4: MULTIPLE INTELLINGENCES SURVEY RESULTS

SUBJECTS TAUGHT	STRENGTHS
School to Work	Musical, kinesthetic, intrapersonal
English	Musical, interpersonal, kinesthetic
Generalist 1	Logical, existential, interpersonal
Carpentry	Naturalist, musical, kinesthetic
Generalist 2	Interpersonal, interpersonal visual
Science/Health	Kinesthetic, intrapersonal

TABLE 5: MULTIPLE INTELLINGENCE STRENGTHS BY GENDER

MI	MALE	FEMALE
Naturalist	1	0
Musical	1	2
Linguist	0	1
Existential	0	1
Interpersonal	0	3
Kinesthetic	3	2
Verbal	0	1
Intrapersonal	2	2
Visual	1	2

musical, logical, existential, interpersonal and verbal.

Individual interview questions related to (1) varied teaching strategies, (2) the teachers' preferences, and (3) their knowledge of those strategies were posed to the interviewee. All teachers reported that they used interdisciplinary approaches to teaching, hands-on activities, and alternative strategies for individual students. When given a scenario about a musically and artistically gifted student who found it difficult to read, teachers were asked how they would address the issue. The English teacher responded that she would "almost do an independent study or an indepen-dent project…would have that student maybe create a musical score…or do backdrops if the play were actually being performed". The science teacher responded that it would "provide a perfect opportunity for a teacher to experiment with interdisciplinary approaches" but offered no concrete example. The shop teacher stated that he would "try to let the student express his/her artistic and musical talents" but offered no concrete example.

When queried about the level of knowledge of Gardner's theory of MI, responses focused on different learning styles. Teachers were vague about any other knowledge and admitted they had not heard of MI in teacher education programs. One teacher was interested in learning more about it. The English teacher stated that she "was not versed in this area" and that she "understood it to state that students learn different ways." The science teacher stated he was "familiar with it only as I have heard bits and pieces of it from you…understood that there are several categories of learning into different types…to make sense of the world". The shop teacher stated that "there are auditory and visual learners while others have kinesthetic, musical, rhythmic, and mathematical intelligences."

SUMMARY

Clearly, the possibilities of exploring individual and group multiple intelligences in higher education are unlimited. Developing an understanding of MI, applying the theory in practice, and evaluating the results of teaching to the intelligences are but a few of the ways MI Theory was utilized in this paper. Pre-service teachers demon-strated in surveys that they did in fact have an intelligence strength that was supported by their testimony on how they learned best and the types of assessments they preferred. College teachers can use MI Theory to design strategies and assessments to enhance and expand on students' group intelligences. Equally important, students who participated in these studies had breadth and scope in learning the theory and applying it to not only themselves, but to the children they observed and worked with in early field experiences in teacher education. And finally, it should be noted that while in-service teachers in the research study reported in this paper did not know about Gardner's theory of multiple intelligences, they were practicing those varied strategies in their classrooms in an effort to meet the needs of diverse student populations.

REFERENCES

Campbell, L. (1994). *The MultipleIintelligences Handbook: Lesson Plans and More*. Stanwood, Washington: Campbell and Associates, Inc.

Denzin, N. & Lincoln, Y. (1998). *Collecting and Interpreting Qualitative Materials.* Thousand Oaks, CA: Sage Publications.

Gardner, H. (1983). *Frames of Mind: The Theory of Multiple Intelligences.* New York, NY: Basic Books.

Gardner, H. (1993). *Multiple Intelligences: The Theory in Practice.* New York, NY: Basic Books.

Gardner, H. (1999). *The Disciplined Mind: What All Students Should Understand.* New York, NY: Simon & Schuster.

Glesne, C. (1999). *Becoming Qualitative Researchers: An Introduction, 2nd ed.* Addison Wesley Longman: New York, NY.

Gutloff, K. (1996). *Multiple Intelligences.* Teacher-to-Teacher Books.

Marzano, R. (1992). *A different Kind of Classroom: Dimensions of Learning.*

McKenzie, W. (2000). *Creative Classroom Consulting.* As found on the Internet site: http://surfaquarium.com/ Miinvent.htm.

If individuals are to understand things that are meaningful to their lives, they need to be exploring topics that are consequential to what is important in the culture.

(Dobry, 1999, p. 8)

College classrooms are changing. Professors are greeted with a more diverse population of students and are seeing many different types of learners. This trend in university settings is even more profound in elementary and secondary schools.

Recent census data confirm that the United States population is becoming more multi-cultural and that this diversity will continue to increase. As professors of education, a core part of our curriculum in teacher preparation is to help our students understand issues of multiculturalism and diversity and apply that knowledge in their work. As our world is becoming more diverse, we believe that students in all domains of university study can benefit from developing an appreciation and understanding of issues of diversity.

The changing makeup of our nation's population demands that we seek ways to ensure that "valuing diversity" becomes more than a catch-phrase. This knowledge is beneficial not only for professors and college students, but also for all individuals, as we work towards a more peaceful society. Clearly, Gardner's work, although not specifically related to cultural differences, has implications for understanding diversity and multiculturalism. *Intelligence* is defined by Gardner as the ability to solve problems or develop products that are valued in a particular cultural setting (Nieto, 2000, p. 144).

Four Levels of Understanding

We define multicultural education in a sociopolitical context as a process of basic education that challenges and rejects racism and other forms of discrimination and accepts and affirms the pluralism (ethnic, racial, linguistic, religious, economic, and gender, among others) that students, their communities and teachers reflect (Nieto, 2000). Nieto (1994, 2000) proposes four levels of understanding diversity:

- Tolerance
- Acceptance
- Respect
- Affirmation/Solidarity/Critique

Tolerance, the lowest level, implies that differences are acknowledged and, perhaps, accepted. This level is sometimes targeted through workshops, readings and seminars that focus on diversity issues. However, in order to achieve the highest level (Affirmation/Solidarity/Critique), *many* opportunities for regular exploration of values as an integral part of the curriculum are necessary. According to Nieto, true multicultural education includes instructional strategies and interactions among teachers, students, and families. Additionally, multicultural education is a *process*, continually changing and never finished. Given that multicultural education is critical pedagogy, it is necessarily dynamic (Nieto, 2000, p. 337).

UNDERSTANDING DIVERSITY THROUGH INTERPERSONAL AND INTRAPERSONAL INTELLIGENCES

HOLLY SEPLOCHA AND JANIS STRASSER

OUR OWN RACIST ASSUMPTIONS

Finally, by engaging in constant self-reflection, we, as educators must become aware of our own unconscious racist assumptions (Wynne, 2000). Do we have high expectations for all students? Do we model fairness and understanding through what we say and do? Do we use books and materials that are free of bias? How do we define bias and freedom from bias? Adults bring to the classroom a complex web of experiences, knowledge, skills, and dispositions regarding themselves and the topic at hand. College students lead busy and frenetic lives. They often have fixed viewpoints and entrenched habits. Many have a problem-solving orientation and can be a valuable resource for one another. Some have a need to be self-directing. They almost always represent a diverse group of learners who have strengths in one or more of the various Multiple Intelligences.

USING GARDNER'S THEORIES

In helping college students understand multicultural perspectives and diversity issues, we have found it useful to approach the study using strategies to support Interpersonal and Intrapersonal Intelligences. Typically, students who operate well in the Interpersonal Intelligence tend to understand other people well, can mediate conflicts, understand and recognize stereotypes and prejudice, enjoy cooperative learning strategies, group projects, give feedback, and display empathy. While those who feel comfortable in the Intrapersonal Intelligence understand themselves, focus and concentrate well, know their strengths and weaknesses, are intuitive, and excel at emotional processing and metacognition techniques. Both of these Intelligences are critical to consider when exploring issues of prejudice, diversity and multicultural perspectives (racism, gender bias, ageism, etc.).

INTERPERSONAL INTELLIGENCE

Interpersonal Intelligence denotes a person's capacity to understand the intentions, motivations, and desires of other people and, consequently, to work effectively with others. "Interpersonal intelligence allows one to understand and work with others" (Gardner, 1993, p. 25). In *Creating Minds* (Gardner, 1993), Gardner describes seven creative geniuses that lived during the 20th century (each of whom was born before the turn of the century). Each of the seven represents one of the multiple intelligences. In the book, Gardener chooses Mahatma Gandhi to embody the Interpersonal Intelligence. Other examples of famous people who reflect strong Interpersonal skills include Eleanor Roosevelt, Winston Churchill, Lee Iacocca and Mother Teresa. College classrooms that are rich in cooperative learning support the development of this intelligence. Individuals with strengths in Interpersonal Intelligence are capable of understanding others and excel at relating to other people. They are usually quite social and often exhibit leadership. They learn best by sharing, comparing, relating and cooperating.

Interpersonal learners get along well with others and can motivate others toward a common goal. They enjoy collaborating with others, discussions, small-group projects and solving problems together. They respond appropriately to the moods, feelings, temperaments, motivations, and intentions of others. They can recognize prejudice and stereotypes. General instructional strategies that support Interpersonal Intelligence include the following: Discussing; Presenting; Cooperative Learning Groups; Role-Playing; Group Projects; Sharing Ideas in Whole Group and Small Group Formats; Literature Circles and Book Groups; and Collaborative Problem Solving.

INTRAPERSONAL INTELLIGENCE

Intrapersonal Intelligence involves the capacity to understand oneself, to have an effective working model of oneself—including one's own desires, fears, and capacities—and to use such information effectively in regulating one's own life. "Intrapersonal intelligence allows one to understand and work with one's self" (Gardner, 1993, p.25). In *Creating Minds* (Gardner, 1993) Gardner chooses Sigmund Freud as the example of a creative genius in Intrapersonal

domain. Other examples of famous individuals who exhibit strong Intrapersonal skills are Marva Collins, Marie Montessori, Malcolm X, Aristotle, and Helen Keller.

Opportunities to reflect and explore inner feelings and thought support the development of this intelligence. Students with strengths in Intrapersonal Intelligence have an understanding of themselves and are aware of what they can and cannot accomplish. They learn best through working alone, individualized projects, self-paced instruction and having their own space to pursue interests.

Intrapersonal learners are reflective and intuitive. They identify and understand their own feelings and can use them to guide behavior. They understand their own strengths, weaknesses, and desires. The Intrapersonal learner enjoys working alone, individual projects, self-study, self-evaluation, and independent research. General instructional strategies that support Intrapersonal Intelligence include these techniques: Journalizing; Autobiographies; Self-study; Self-Assessment; Divergent Questions; Analogies; Visualization; Metacognition (thinking about thinking); Reflection; and Connections to Personal Life.

SUPPORTING THE INTERPERSONAL AND INTRAPERSONAL LEARNER

College coursework and assignments in the Interpersonal domain give students the opportunity to dialogue and share opinions. While coursework and assignments in the Intrapersonal domain encourage students to reflect and make individual meaning. As we looked to improve our teaching, we asked ourselves the following questions. We encourage you to take a moment to reflect on your own teaching.

INTERPERSONAL QUESTIONS FOR THE PROFESSOR

Am I, as professor, supporting the Interpersonal Intelligence in my courses?

- Do I have opportunities for questioning, sharing of experiences, and feedback?
- Have I created opportunities for students to get to know one another?
- Do my assignments include group work?
- Do I encourage collaboration?
- Have I fostered a community of learners?

INTRAPERSONAL QUESTIONS FOR THE PROFESSOR

Am I, as professor, supporting the Intrapersonal Intelligence in my courses?

- Do I relate material directly yet at the proper distance from students' lives, loves, and experiences?
- Am I teaching from life experience?
- Do my assignments include individual projects, journal-

izing, reports, students' opinions and reflections?
- Do I encourage the exploration of feelings?
- Do I provide time and opportunities for introspection?

CRITICAL FACTORS

It is important for college professors to understand and include *both* the Interpersonal and Intrapersonal Intelligences in planning coursework intended to broaden awareness of multicultural perspectives and diversity. "Under multiple intelligence theory, an intelligence can serve both as the content of instruction and the means or medium for communicating that content" (Gardner, 1993, p. 32).

Understanding what diversity and multiculturalism involves is both internal reflection (Intrapersonal) as well as getting along (Interpersonal). Derman-Sparks reminds us of some of the Intrapersonal goals for children (which we apply to college students, as well): to construct a knowledgeable, confident self-identity; to develop comfortable, empathetic, and just interaction with diversity; and to develop critical thinking and the skills for standing up for oneself and others in the face of injustice (1989, p. ix). Tiedt & Tiedt (1990) include many outcomes for multicultural education that are Interpersonal. Among these are discussions of literature by and about members of diverse cultures, discussions of age-related and gender related concerns, participation in community and school affairs, and discussions of real life scenarios where stereotyped thinking and prejudice have occurred.

SPECIFIC EXAMPLES

Specific examples of strategies and assignments that have been successful in helping students in our college classes understand multicultural perspectives and diversity issues through the Interpersonal and Intrapersonal domains include:

1. *Exploring and sharing one's own values*: Make a list of instrumental values including as many as you can think of (e.g. honest, clean, open-minded, ambitious, courageous, forgiving, helpful, independent, intellectual, logical, loving, obedient, polite, responsible, cheerful, capable) and ask students to rank order the values with one being most valuable. Share as a group and discuss the diversity in the class and how we learn our values (There are several published surveys for this activity. The U.S. Postal Service has one that we have adapted.)

2. *Using a quilt as a method of sharing:* Following a read-aloud of the children's book *Tar Beach* by Faith Ringgold, our college students were given a 10" x 10" piece of oak tag, asked to depict their dream and return with it the following week. Some students made

collages; some wrote poetry; some drew a picture; some made a web; some wrote a paragraph. After sharing their "dream" with each other during class, the pieces were quilted together using a hole punch and pipe cleaners. This was hung in our class and referred to during later class discussions on the diversity of our dreams and values. A similar assignment could be given to depict why they want to teach or to depict themselves based on their ethnicity.

3. *Evaluating children's books for stereotyping and bias:* An excellent checklist for this is *Ten Quick Ways to Analyze Children's Books for Sexism and Racism* (Derman-Sparks, 1989 pp. 143-145).

4. *Author presentations of why and how diversity picture books are written:* We have worked with author Ann Morris (*Teamwork*, *Bread Bread Bread*, *Families*, and other multicultural picture books).

5. *Viewing and discussing videotapes on diversity:* Some of our favorites are *Starting Small* (Southern Poverty Law Center, 1997); *Anti-bias Curriculum* (Pacific Oaks College, 1988), *It's Elementary: Talking about Gay Issues in School* (New Day Films, 1996), and *Start Seeing Diversity: The Basic Guide to an Anti-Bias Classroom* (Redleaf Press, 1999).

6. *Reading and discussing research and journal articles about tolerance and multiculturalism:* The National Association for Multicultural Education (NAME) publishes the journal *Multicultural Perspectives*. This is an excellent source for such articles.

7. *Sharing personal experiences of prejudice and bias:* Informal narratives by students and teachers

8. *Reading and discussing personal perspectives of diversity and bias issues:* Some good examples include: *Maggie's American Dream* (Comer, 1988), *White Teacher* (Paley, 1979), *Kwanzaa and Me*, Paley, (1995), *Among Schoolchildren* (Kidder, 1989), *The Water is Wide* (Conroy, 1987), *The Dreamkeepers: Successful Teachers of African-American Children* (Ladson-Billings, 1984) and *The Color of Dirt* (Northington, 2000).

9. *Developing curriculum for children that supports diversity/multiculturalism:* Curriculum models include Kendall (1983), York (1992), and Williams & Gaetano (1985) and Derman-Sparks (1989). Beaty (1997) references multicultural picture books and presents related activities for young children.

10. *Concept Maps:* This assignment asks the student to take a word such as diversity, anti-bias, multicultural education, or curriculum and develop a weblike organizer expressing their understanding of the concept. In the

center of the paper, the student writes "diversity is" and then adds phases or words to depict their understanding. Usually a concept map is completed prior to classroom coverage of the topic and then again repeated later in the semester after instruction, readings and discussion. By viewing the two concept maps together, the instructor can assess the student's prior knowledge and then growing knowledge of the concept at-hand. This assignment provides an opportunity for individual expression and reflection.

11. *Aha! Slips:* Students are given blank "Aha!" Slips prior to the end of each class meeting, and asked to reflect on a new learning or knowing they had during the class or as a result of readings.

12. *Journalizing:* Time is provided in class or assigned outside of class for students to process and reflect on class discussions and readings. Journals are usually collected midway and again at the end of the semester. This vehicle provides the student the opportunity to process and reflect on class discussion and learnings - and provides the instructor the opportunity to dialog individually with students.

13. ***Using a children's book as a springboard for discussion:*** One of our favorites is *The Other Side* (Woodson, 2001), a story about an African American child and a white child who live next door to each other with a fence between their yards. After watching and guessing about the other, they eventually decide to sit on the fence together. This book easily lends itself to a discussion of the barriers or "fences" in our life and how we could overcome them. Other good books include *All the Colors of the Earth,* (Hamanaka, 1994), *Whoever You Are* (Fox, 1997), *Amazing Grace* (Hoffman, 1991) and *We are All Alike…We are All Different* (Cheltenham Elementary School Kindergartners, 1991).

- After reading a picture book describing the various shades of brown skin color, another student shared her negative experiences within the black community, growing up as a light skinned African American child. This type of prejudice was very unfamiliar to the white students in the class.
- When a Jewish professor shared an experience of bias that she encountered while she was a college student in the South, many of the students responded with their own personal experiences of discrimination.

The exploration of diversity and multiculturalism is an exciting and often frightening challenge! As we open our college classrooms to discussions of issues that involve honesty, controversy and self-examination, often, there is disagreement, discomfort, and initial hostility. However, only through these opportunities can we all reach higher degrees of self-awareness and understanding for ourstudents and ourselves.

REFERENCES

Armstrong, T. (1994). *Multiple Intelligences in the Classroom..* Alexandria, VA: ASCD.

Beaty, J.J. (1997). *Building Bridges with Multicultural Picture Books: For Children 3-5.* Upper Saddle River, NJ: Prentice Hall.

Cheltenham Elementary School Kindergartners. (1991). *We are all alike…We are all different.* New York: Scholastic.

Conroy, P. (1987). *The Water is Wide.* New York: Bantam Books.

Comer, J. (1988). *Maggie's American Dream.* New York: Penguin Books.

Derman-Sparks, L. (1989). *Anti-bias Curriculum: Tools for Empowering Young Children.* Washington, DC: National Association for the Education of Young Children.

Dobry, D. (1999). *It's Not What You Know, It's How You Use It That Matters.* TC Today: Teachers College: NY. Spring 1999, **Vol. 24** No. 1, pp. 7-9.

Fox, M. (1997). *Whoever You Are.* New York: Harcourt Brace & Company.

Gardner, H. (1983). *Frames of Mind: The Theory of Multiple Intelligences.* New York: Basic Books.

—. (1993). *Multiple Intelligences: The Theory in Practice.* New York: Basic Books.

—. (1993). *Creating Minds. An Anatomy of Creativity Seen Through The Lives of Freud, Einstein, Picasso, Stravinsky, Eliot, Graham, and Gandhi.* New York: Basic Books.

Hamanaka, S. (1994). *All the Colors of The Earth.* New York: Morrow Junior Books.

Hoffman, M. (1991). *Amazing Grace.* New York: Dial Books for Young Readers.

Jones, E. (1986). *Teaching Adults: An Active Learning Approach.* Washington, DC: National Association for the Education of Young Children.

Kendall, F.E. (1983). *Diversity in the Classroom: A Multicultural Approach to the Education of Young Children.* New York: Teachers College Press.

Kidder, Tracy. (1989). *Among Schoolchildren.* New York: Avon Books.

Ladson-Billings, G. (1984). *The Dreamkeepers: Successful Teachers of African-American Children.* San Francisco: Jossey-Bass Publishers.

Lazaer, D. (1991). *Seven Ways of Knowing.* Palatine, IL.

—. (1994). *Seven Pathways of Learning: Teaching Students and Parents About Multiple Intelligences.* Tucson, AZ: Zephyr Press.

Morris, A. (1999). *Teamwork.* New York: Lothrup, Lee & Shepard.

Neugebauer, Bonnie. (1992). *Alike and Different.* Washington, DC: National Association for the Education of Young Children.

Nieto, S. (2000). *Affirming Diversity: The Sociopolitical Context of Multicultural Education, 3rd Ed.* White Plains, NY: Addison Wesley Longman Publishers.

—. (1994). "Affirmation, Solidarity, and Critique: Moving Beyond Tolerance in Multicultural Education" in *Multicultural Education,* Spring 1994, pp. 9-12 & 35-38.

Northington, C. (2000). "The Color of Dirt" in *Multicultural Perspectives.* **2** (3), pp. 32-33.

Paley, V. G. (1995). *Kwanzaa and Me.* Cambridge, MA: Harvard University Press.

—. (1989). *White Teacher.* Cambridge, MA: Harvard University Press.

Ringgold, F. (1996). *Tar Beach.* New York: Crown Publishers.

The Teaching Tolerance Project. (1997). *Starting Small: Teaching Tolerance in Preschool and the Early Grades.* Montgomery, AL: Southern Poverty Law Center.

Tiedt, P.L. & Tiedt, I.M. (1990). *Multicultural Teaching: A Handbook of Activities, Information, and Resources* (3rd Ed.). MA: Allyn & Bacon.

Williams, L. R. & De Gaetano, Y. (1985). *ALERTA: A Multicultural, Bilingual Approach to Teaching Young Children.* Menlo Park, CA: Addison-Wesley Publishing Company.

Woodson, J. (2001). *The Other Side.* New York: GP Putnam's Sons.

Wynne, J. T. (2000). *The Elephant in the Living Room: Racism Is School Reform.* Paper presented at the annual conference of the American Association of Colleges and Universities. Washington, DC.

York, S. (1992). *Developing Roots and Wings: A Trainer's Guide to Affirming Culture in Early Childhood Programs.* St. Paul, MN: Redleaf Press.

VIDEOS:

Starting Small. (1997). Southern Poverty Law Center.

Anti-Bias Curriculum. (1988). Pacific Oaks College.

It's Elementary: Talking about Gay Issues in School. (1996). New Day Films.

Start Seeing Diversity: The Basic Guide to an Anti-Bias Classroom. (1999). Redleaf Press.

*T*he chords of piano music that waft into the conference room are unmistakably Scott Joplin; his lively cross-rhythms ragtime sounds greet the conference participants much the same way that they do my students. Later excerpts from "The Poor Soul Sat Sighing (The Willow Song)" from Shakespeare's Othello follow as I relate how music and images stimulate the students' imaginations and then are transposed into the writing process. The following text remarks on the exercises that are utilized in my classes and highlights the why's and how's of my approach.

A PERSONAL ODYSSEY

My odyssey as a teacher and journalist brought me into many new places in my thinking and actions; however, it was a mid-life BFA in studio arts that helped stir up my world, giving me a fresh eye. The visual worked in tandem with my writing, making me feel more integrated as a person, and a return to teaching in an urban university gave me an opportunity to share my new perspectives. Our forty-six acre campus is an oasis in the midst of a congested, changing urban city where at least 43% of its households speak a foreign language. Jersey City, located on New Jersey's "Gold Coast," is across the Hudson River from Manhattan and is situated in one of the world's most populated and heavily traveled corridors, therefore providing abundant resources for research and job opportunities. Most of our 9,600 students commute and work at least 20 hours per week; only 275 of them live in residential dormitories.

The area's diversity is reflected in our student population: 42% White; 25% Hispanic; 19% Black; 10% Asian and 4% students who join us from 50 foreign countries. New Jersey City University is also designated as a Hispanic Serving Institute, making us one of 160 such institutes in the United States and the only designated four-year college in New Jersey.

This year's fall college entrance testing revealed that 90% of our incoming freshman needed remedial courses in one or more skills, 64% needed college remedial courses in writing, while 90% required remedial courses in reading. These statistics do not include a one-credit Open Writing Lab course that most of our English Composition I students must register for. Many of our students are first generation Americans or immigrants who divide their days between school and work. Many are strangers to leisure reading.

TAPPING INNER RESOURCES

Faced with a wide range of student writing skills, my focus as a professor was to explore approaches that would touch a student's inner resources and relate that discovery to their writing voices. This process expanded into interactive learning approaches, integrating the creative arts into the writing process by utilizing images, music, and creative drama. For me, using the arts as a base appeared more equitable because inner city students tend to have poor verbal skills but often excel in expressive arts like music, fine

VAN GOGH, CHOPIN AND BATES: USING IMAGES, MUSIC, AND CREATIVE DRAMA AS CATALYSTS IN THE WRITING PROCESS

CONSTANCE SICA

arts, filmmaking, performing arts and dance. I wanted to create an integrated dance, interlocking the processes of thought, image, and the word.

Initially, several assumptions fueled my classroom research. America is a visual nation. In a series of research studies by Robert Kubey and Mihaly Csikszentmikhaly, viewing television "is by far the single most time-consuming home activity" (p. 71). Today's students are more visually oriented. Most rise and go to sleep with television and in between slip in Internet time. They are most at home with images. Realizing this makes it is easier to enter their world.

Secondly, multidimensional approaches could be used in releasing students' creativity, thus opening the gateway to their personal voices. Therefore, the arts, particularly images, music and creative drama, would be a comfortable vehicle in helping students explore their creative process and then transpose the process to finding their own writing voices. "Engagements with the several arts," says educator Maxine Green, "would be the most likely way to release the imaginative capacity and give it play" (p. 379).

In the past thirty years, creativity and its impact upon

109

learning has been greatly championed by Howard Gardner's multiple intelligences theory. His notion that each kind of intelligence should be approached in its own terms, "rather than through the language-logic lens" (p. 16) certainly helps support my diverse pedagogical activity. One cannot also discuss creative learning and multiple intelligence theories without commenting about the work in recent years of behavioral scientist Dr. Daniel Goleman and neurologist Dr. Antonio Damasio. The results of their research have elevated emotions and feelings to the loftier position generally held by reason.

CLASSROOM RESEARCH

In teaching, the classroom is the hub: all roads lead to and from this point. For me, learning becomes a real partnership. The teacher becomes the student, and the student becomes the teacher for it is in the classroom that the art of teaching develops. Teaching is a circular process with a constant dynamic flow into its twin—learning. Therefore, a classroom should have no borders to separate teaching, learning, student, and teacher because it is an organic structure, like a spider's web, growing out of the mind, body, and spirit of the students and teacher. Its lace pattern is frail, yet strong and temporary for perceptions are constantly being stretched and challenged. Teachers and students are constantly weaving beginnings.

My strategies for teaching writing are evolutionary rather than revolutionary. From the moment my students step into my classroom, there is a deliberate effort on my part to foster a spontaneous atmosphere. It isn't easy; it takes time, sometimes the better part of the semester. Sometimes we never make it! Every class is different and has its own transformational characteristics. Some strategies are aborted while others are born.

For me the classroom is like water always in motion, and I have always been teacher, researcher and observer in it. Initially, my study was limited to my *Creative Writing* classes, a general studies course for sophomores, juniors, and seniors with a maximum of 15 students per class. A few semesters later, I incorporated some visual, musical and creative drama exercises from it into *English Composition II*, a required course which is basically an introduction to the literary genres with a required writing component.

RESULT OF MY INITIAL STUDY

A total of 50 students were involved in a study over two years: two *Creative Writing* classes of 24 students, one *English Composition II* with 12 students and seven in-depth interviews with selected students. The springboard for my study was the design of specific exercises utilizing images, music and creative drama and then interpreting these classroom activities through students' reactions, interaction, work, and questionnaires. Two separate questionnaires totaling 19 queries were developed, and tailored to the specific courses. The results overwhelmingly supported the effectiveness of using the creative arts as catalysts in the student's writing process. For example, in the question, "Did you find that looking at a visual image stimulated your thoughts?" Nineteen responses were definitely positive; three felt that it was sometimes effective, and one was undecided. Another question asked, "Did images promote more detail to your writing?" Nineteen students made favorable remarks. There were five "no's".

Music, my classroom research revealed, was a major influence in setting a mood or creating an atmosphere for most students' writing. Twenty students definitely liked its effect. One student did not answer; one said both yes and no; and another stated that music was not as effective as visuals. Most of my students also reacted positively to dramatization. Twenty-one of 24 felt that re-enacting their work (such as casting classmates for their characters in their one-act plays) aided their writing.

VISUAL CLASSROOM ACTIVITIES

In my *Creative Writing* class, visual work is a raft, a dock to start from. The introduction of images is part of the initial greeting. In one exercise during the first meeting, I asked them to select a pictorial image that would help to describe themselves from among dozens of magazines. Most of the time this leads us farther into a warm, informal introduction of ourselves. When I think they're ready, I quickly flash a series of colored-and-black and white images before them. Uncensored and spontaneous responses are encouraged. Eventually, we move the exercise into small groups to facilitate a comfort zone for storytelling. Each group receives the same image and is asked to create a story from it. The class circle then reunites, and each group shares their creation. We usually stay with the oral tradition of storytelling for awhile. Simple story lines are embellished, and characters gain dimension.

Students encounter fewer difficulties as they create additional stories, and they seem to be having a good time interacting with peers. Laughter is part of the process and is so important in a commuting urban university. There is little time for socialization, and the exercises serve as social ice breakers. At this point, some classes are ready to move some parts of oral stories into writing, especially with dialogue. They continue to write as a group. At the end of the class, new images are placed on a long table near the door, and each student is asked to select one that she/he is immediately drawn to as they leave the class. They can do anything that they wish with the image for the next class. However, their stories must be written. For part of the next few sessions, we continue to work with images for ideas, description, setting, character, dialogue development, etc. Each class period builds upon the previous one.

Sometimes there are unexplainable coincidences in their stories. Two different groups in two different *Creative Writing* classes in two different semesters created a similar story from the image of an Indian guru sitting in the lotus position upon a cushion. His face is illuminated; his eyes are wide with surprise; his smile is generous with delight. "He just heard that he won the lottery," exclaimed both groups as they wove a loose plot about that event. To one group, he was a *holy man*; to the other, just a lucky man. However, to both groups, his way of dress suggested poverty, thus indicating a difficult life. Then the stories went their own ways until the end. Both groups then placed the man in a mansion living with all the accoutrements of the rich. He and the members of his family never had to work again. To most inner city students who have had to work from an early age or whose parents work long hours, having money means buying things and being free from work. It's one guarantee of happiness.

CLASSROOM ACTIVITIES/MUSIC

Almost from the onset of the first class, music greets the students as they enter the class. Listening to music from classical to disco seems to unleash their creativity and stir their fantasies. What images does the music suggest to them? What characters fit best in their scenes? What atmosphere is created? What scenery does the music suggest to them? Does the image move into other actions? Each week the exercise becomes more sophisticated as their thoughts are woven into deeper plots while we wrestle with ideas about credibility, subtleties or the obvious. At first, this storytelling exercise does not reach the written word, and rarely takes more than 10 or 15 minutes. However, a second music selection has to be written in class. Initially, the class works in threes. Later, they can decide to go solo or pair up. Fortunately, our classroom is equipped with computers for each person, and long working tables. Often a student will utilize some concept of her/his classroom work as a jumping off point for a future story.

CREATIVE DRAMA

Another learning modality is kinesthetic. Drama can become a bridge to understanding foreign or controversial issues or situations. Improvisation is a tool for enchancing insight. Often it can be used for promoting description, refining a gesture, suggesting an attitude or trying to move the story forward. Role playing adds dimension to the students' characters and takes them in unexpected directions. It helps enormously with writing credible dialogue.

By using creative drama, students are helped in developing and refining their one act plays. When the plays are presented, the student authors first cast their characters from classmates. The group then adjourns to other rooms or a nearby student lounge for a brief rehearsal. Finally, the class rejoins for the reading from a written script. Using drama, in a sense, extends the author's role and involvement: the student is now the producer, director, and casting director—and sometimes stage manager. These mini productions enable the students to see what is or isn't working in their plays. The rest of the class also becomes involved and offers suggestions in a non-threatening way. It is a successful segment of the course.

The atmosphere in the classroom is lively and warm, and I have found that drama fosters group involvement and is a cultural bridge for greater understanding. "Drama can become a vehicle for students' interaction with conceptual material and content as the play unfolds" (Bonwell and Eison 46). Larger political and social issues are often exposed in the student's work. The entry of these issues is then at the level that the students are able to grasp. Topics, involving sexuality, racism, and sexism are inherent not only in the material, but are approached throughout students' participation. Sometimes heterosexuals play homosexuals and vice versa; females play males; males play females; Caucasians play African-Americans; African-Americans play Caucasians; young play old, and old play young. Students are able to step outside of themselves.

SELECTED STUDENT FEEDBACK

Student feedback is invaluable; these are a few comments.

Visual: "Visual images promote more detail because you are able to describe and portray a vivid representation of the event." (Curtis)

"Images brought peculiar yet simple thoughts to my mind. It focused my concentration on one particular image and then my mind produced explanations and thoughts." (Hoda)

"They inspired writing in both big and small ways—sometimes setting a tone, supplying a phrase, or weaving an *entire plot*." (Cara)

Music: "The music helps to create settings for many stories." (Diana)

"I can't write without music because it also helps to set my mood in situations or scenes." (Mauricio)

"It brought a picture in your mind which helped to create the writing." (P)

Creative Drama: "Peer feedback was very instrumental in my gaining confidence in my work. Class discussion, plays and other small group-orientated exercises were useful, not only in gaining a friendship, so as not be embarrassed by reading aloud out and also in gaining insight into others' mind sets." (Hernadez)

"At first, I was really nervous, but acting out my work helped me see where my mistakes were. It also made me want to add more to the story." (Jessica)

"I'm not very confident in my stories, and hearing someone else read it with feeling made me feel a little better about my work." (R)

Summary

My classroom research is far from definitive. As a researcher, I was fortunate to have a strong foundation and involvement with a multi-racial and multi-enthic college population. I'm also a writing teacher engaged in the subject matter, not an outsider from afar, for no epistemological framework has yet served adequately to assess the writing process, and I don't profess to have one. A finding is a new beginning.

As a teacher, I allowed the student in me to surface and encouraged the students to find teachers in themselves. In the process, we became flexible, open, and more considerate. We took risks, turned failures into learning and enjoyed our successes. I became more observant, less concerned with a goal, and more involved in the process. As an interviewer, I learned to share experiences as well, and when necessary, as Maya Angelou suggests, to "close my mouth and become an ear." The process also became a journey into myself. Currently, student exercises are becoming more integrated as they combine computer or hand-drawn images, and recorded or live music to their writings.

Limitations

There are, of course, limitations to my original findings. Complete objectivity does not exist. Inherently, the wording and selection of any questionnaire is biased. There may have been an unconscious tendency to teach to the questions or arrange the questions to the teaching. The research was exclusively conducted by me, as was the selection of comments, and classes. However, the enthusiasm, motivation and respect that both the students and I have for inclusion of these alternative ways of enriching one's writing outweighs the negative variables.

Priceless Rewards

On the last day of an *English Composition II*, the class was discussing some of their reactions to the course. Suddenly, blonde, brown-eyed Tracy slowly pushed her chair away from the table, stood up, looked around at her classmates and said in a confident tone. "I've gone beyond what my parents think. I don't want to be limited. They talk about races and religions. I learned that I will be different with my children." Tracy's comment is a wonderful beginning, for what really lies at the core in the classroom is the world of the students, expressed in their own voices.

References

Csikszentmihalyi, M. and Kubey R. (1990). *Television and the Quality of Life: How Viewing Shapes Everyday Experiences.* Hilldale, NJ: Lawrence Eribaum Associates.

Bonwell, C. and Eison J. (1991) "Active Learning: Creating Excitement in the Classroom" in *ASHE-ERIC Higher Education Report.* No. 1. Washington D.C.: George Washington University.

Gardner, H. (1995) *Multiple Intelligences as a Catalyst.* New York: Bantam Books.

Green, M. (1995) "Art and Imagination" in *Phi Delta Kappan* **76**: 378-82.

Students who are sophisticated in spoken languages are usually fluent in a variety of oral traditions such as verbal games, rhyming, and extemporized poetry. In the voices they have developed and are familiar with, these students are usually powerful and dynamic. In relatively formal written English, however, they often lack proficiency. Some of them have heard and dimly recall a higher register, which they try to imitate—without really knowing the fixed phrases, grammatical locutions, or argument structure that characterize what we consider acceptable writing.

As an African American I have pride in my ability to segue from a formal, crisp, academic English to the relaxed, inner city vernacular that I share with friends and neighbors in Brooklyn, where I live. Yet a major challenge is how to help my present students at New Jersey City University to write simply and directly in a voice that sounds natural to them—and to their audience. For that purpose, I highly recommend two techniques that I learned while working with corporate writers and with students in law school. (From 1990 to 1993, I assessed corporate documents at SWG Consulting Resources in New York City and used the company's manuals to design courses to facilitate training in business writing. That experience was significant in my development as a teacher of writing.)

The first technique, *Interpretive Paraphrase*, was created by semanticist Ann E. Berthoff (*The Making of Meaning* 71-72). SWG Consulting Resources' trainers assigned Interpretive Paraphrase exercises to emphasize that if we listen acutely to the words we choose, we bring to bear great powers of discernment and analysis—powers that we can learn to transfer to writing. When refining a sentence or passage through a sequence of rewrites, clients were encouraged to draw upon that aural power. They were reminded that to revise and edit, they should read the writing aloud, as if it were a script to be performed.

We will examine interpretive paraphrase in the paragraphs that follow. Then I will present a technique that I developed and call *A Companion Audience*. In this method, we set aside ego, prestige, and public persona, and imagine that we are talking to someone we know very well and really want them to understand what we are saying—or writing. Both of these strategies honor the strength of students' ability in spoken language and enable them to decide what it is that they wish to express.

INTERPRETIVE PARAPHRASE

Interpretive paraphrase emphasizes two dynamics: "To explain or tell the meaning of; to present in understandable terms" (interpretation) and "To restate the same essential meaning using new words and a new word order" (paraphrasing) (*Webster's Collegiate Dictionary,* tenth edition, 1994). Corporate clients practiced interpretive paraphrase to rid sentences of big words, awkward syntax, and bureaucratic jargon, such as the following:

USING "INTERPRETIVE PARAPHRASE" AND "A COMPANION AUDIENCE" TO CLARIFY STUDENTS' PROSE

CHARLES H. LYNCH

We really are pleased that you all believe that the expected savings from group insurance consolidation are worth pursuing

would become

We are pleased that you will set up a group insurance plan to save more.

Likewise, the wordy

It is clear that this information is critical to assess where further efforts for the development of new business opportunities would be economically in our favor

became

We must use this information to assess which business opportunities will be profitable (SWG "Interpretive Paraphrase Exercise," 041+, p. 30).

From September 1990 until June 1996, I was a Writing Specialist at Seton Hall University School of Law in Newark, New Jersey. I had a doctorate in English. Other Writing Specialists, who were attorneys, coached me in the rudiments of the set organizational formats and phrasing of legal memorandums and persuasive briefs. Then I could tutor individual students. First-semester students struggled to satisfy legal writing's demands. Many were excellent stylists (even award-winning journalists and accomplished technical writers), but they had to develop a new "ear" and "voice." As attorneys-in-training, they had to learn to think and write within a rhetorical format that was not thesis-oriented (which, of course, previous education emphasized). They had to consistently weigh and balance facts, assert ideas and rebut them, qualify their nouns and verbs, and not rush to conclusions. Haphazard paraphrases and awkwardly inserted quotations blared at me (especially when I was ignorant of the law and the cases under scrutiny). Dependent upon the students' knowledge of the law in order to help them write well, I learned to listen intently to the quality of their voices.

Legal writing courses promoted plain English, but students taking notes on cases still had to wrestle archaic, stale statements such as

Unilateral nullification of the terms and conditions of the expiring agreement absent bona fide impasse is prohibited

into sprightly, fresh

One party cannot leave the contract early without good reason (Odum B8).

Attempting to sound "lawyerly," many first-semester students became stilted and pompous. After reciting their prose, they were befuddled. "Damn! What gibberish! That doesn't sound at all like me!" One obvious reason was because of their clumsy attempts to imitate and integrate unfamiliar phrasing from case law, statutes, and appellate briefs.

Imagine how daunting the authoritative, erudite, elevated voice emerging from legal precedent can be to an amateur. Rules and regulations and interruptive citations abound. Consider this paragraph from a sample appellate brief printed in a legal writing textbook. The essential issue is custodial interference and potential physical harm to the child.

In deferring to the legislature on the advisability of civil actions for interference with familial rights to society and companionship, the First and Fourth Appellate Districts have implicitly recognized the potentially detrimental effects such actions may have on the parent and child involved. *Koskela v. Martin,* 91 Ill. App. 3d 508, 414 N.E.2d 1148; *Whitehorse v. Critchfield,* 144 Ill. App. 3d 192, 494 N.E.2d 743. In the *Politte* case, a Missouri appellate court addressed these detrimental effects directly. In dismissing an action for custodial interference, the court reasoned that the primary goal of this tort was "the vindication of one parent against the other" to the potential detriment of the child involved. *Politte v. Politte*, 727 S.W.2d at 200. "Disarmament is needed to limit post-marital warfare," the *Politte* court declared, "not additional armament to increase it." *Id.* at 201. (Shapo 399)

For some advanced law students who are paraphrasing documents similar to the one above, a face-saving opener when they entered the Writing Specialists' chambers was tedious and tired: "I know what I want to say, but I just don't know how to say it." Resorting to interpretive paraphrase quickly reminded them they cannot merely *think* about what they wish to express. They had to write it down in words that made sense. That transcription would release them to mull over an idea and details, and refine them into more clear, concise language.

USING A COMPANION AUDIENCE

In my second year as a Writing Specialist, however, I realized that some law students had lost an assured sense of audience. My reliance on interpretive paraphrase was not enough. I developed a strategy I tagged "Using a Companion Audience" to charm the hydra-heads who distracted the writer: the course's professor and other competitive students—and hypothetical audiences. These may be judges, partners in the law firm, clients, counsel on the writer's side and those opposing, even a jury that the writer hopes to help to convince.

Writing in undergraduate courses, unlike that in law courses, usually has a primary audience of one professor who grades the essay or term paper and/or student peers. Like first-year law students, undergrads may lack the conviction that their words carry authority. Insecurity about generating formal, academically sound prose and about interpreting established writers' words accurately may cause them to become defensive or self-protective. They may try to mimic a verbal style. They posture as a persona on the page who they feel will be admired and acceptable. Listen to one of my English Composition student's paragraphs responding to this assigned essay subject: " '*Life would be better if humans were the same color and spoke the same language.' Agree or disagree, and explain your opinion using reasons and examples.*"

The other topic, language, would be a monumental loss toward the betterment of our society as a whole. While viewing this issue from the standpoint of convenience one might think that a single language would be helpful, however the issues of individuality and diversity as well as the expression of our cultural differences. Consider the dullness of this world. There would be no new languages to learn and thus the culture involved with that language would be lessened. So these changes would be a great loss for this earth.

VIVID, PROVOCATIVE DETAILS

When we discussed his essay, he admitted that his priority is to "sound smart." He was surprised that I felt he made no definite, compelling points (even though he clearly did not develop or support his ideas). His perspective is broad; his diction, too general. Above all, he needed a more assured sense of audience, which I provided as an interested listener. His rather detached perspective on the topic was due, in part, to diminishing the importance of specific instances he knew well. We isolated one idea from the paragraph. I asked him to support it by talking it through. He smoothly contrasted how language bonded and alienated people that he knew personally. Vivid, provocative details! Convincing point! His writing improved wonderfully during the semester as he gained confidence in revising and editing his drafts to generate concrete diction and to be more simple and direct.

To an undergraduate, an instructor grading a paper may be a harsh critic or a looming presence with unfathomable depths of expertise about the student writer's subject or theme. Therefore, students may write merely to compile information, not to communicate. Also, to lessen the anxiety of being D-graded or not meeting the instructor's standards, the student writer may project the audience as "everybody" or "just anyone," anonymous entities that betray the writer's voice, obfuscating it with vague diction and generalizations.

In another student's paragraph below, organizational and grammatical weaknesses are obvious. The essay question was "*Some people readily identify themselves as 'slackers.' What do they have in common? How can they be encouraged to challenge themselves more?*" Her introduction reads as follows:

I would like to discuss some ways or how slackers are different from other slackers. Are all slackers exactly the same? I would say no because not all people consider themselves to be slackers. Slackers are people who generally don't do anything or don't care. Some reasons that slackers have in common with other slackers are they are different in some ways. I would say that some slackers not all are lazy. There are slackers that do work but are lazy in their own way. Most people that are slackers generally do nothing and don't care. Also, some slackers are messy but not all. So not all people are slackers.

First of all, the writer evaded the questions' demands, which were not only that she categorize slackers but distinguish them enough to suggest how they can be encouraged to be industrious. "Slackers" echoes, initiating parallelism and reinforcing (at least for the writer) the general topic. Repetition also demonstrates that she is "stuck" and unsure of how to proceed with a specific argument. When I pointed these features out, a primary audience surfaced whom the student had confidence in. As an emergency medical technician, she regularly perused manuals and jotted brief reports and checklist memos. For her audience, supervisory and hospital personnel, terse phrasing and repetition of key words were useful to make major points and concrete details interrelate. So, to my surprise I discerned that the paragraph above is informed by a voice she habitually uses to get results.

FINDING ONE'S TRUE VOICE

Using "A Companion Audience" helped the medical technician to distinguish between the requirements of her job and of an essay assignment. I introduce a writer to this strategy for generating clear, concise prose through five simple steps.

1. I begin with "Let's look at this passage. Read it for me." After she or he finishes, I state, "What you would never speak aloud over the dinner table to a family member or friend—or even to a courtroom audience—is here on paper. This is not your true voice, right? Let's see if we can find it."

2. To give the writer confidence in confronting this problem, I ask, "Who is someone you feel close to, are 'sympatico' with, who you easily converse with? Someone you trust will listen carefully and respond honestly. It may also help to pick someone who has less education than you." (That may simplify intimate self-expression and thus clarify one's exact meaning.) "Let's take two or three minutes to think about the person you'll choose for your companion audience."

3. After the writer identifies someone, and briefly explains the relationship, I usually reveal my companion audience is my maternal grandmother, Agnes May Thomas, who passed away in 1981 at ninety-nine-years old. She only finished the eighth grade, but as devoted friends we "conversated" about all kinds of subjects. I often had to cast my words so that she would understand me and be comfortable with knowledge she lacked.

4. Then, I remind the student "When you feel stuck or the words don't flow, *see* your special audience very specifically. Imagine he or she is there with you. At any moment—when prewriting, revising, or after you feel you've finished—perform your writing slowly and dramatically aloud. Practice hearing your natural-

sounding, direct, clear voice as you project it toward your companion audience."

5. "If you sense your companion audience has trouble grasping your meaning, what would she or he tell you about why there's a problem? Did you stumble when speaking or sound strange? Is there something you need to explain? Does a term need to be defined? If so, rephrase those ideas or sequences ALOUD until you're comfortable with your voice and know your companion audience will comprehend your intended meaning. Once you're confident you're clear, you can always revise the sequence to make it more formal or appropriate for academic discourse."

REFERENCES

Berthoff, Ann E. and James Stephens. (1988). *Forming, Thinking, Writing (The Composing Imagination)*. 2nd ed. Portsmouth, New Hampshire: Boynton/ Cook.

Berthoff, A. E. (1981). *The Making of Meaning (Metaphors, Models, and Maxims for Writing)*. Montclair, New Jersey: Boynton/Cook.

Odum, M. (1992). "Some Hereby Resolve: Let Plain English Prevail" in *The New York Times* 5 June: B8.

Shapo, H. S., Walter, M., and Fajans, E. (1995). *Writing and Analysis in the Law*. 3rd ed. Westbury, New York: The Foundation Press.

SWG Consulting Resources. (1991). "Interpretive Para-phrase Exercise." O41+, p. 30, in *The Successful Writing Process* Workshop Manual. New York City.

Most formal teaching and learning unfold through what Howard Gardner has termed the linguistic intelligence: the capacity to use words effectively, whether orally or in writing. Yet other forms of intelligence can be as, if not more, effective in the classroom. One form that is rarely included or even acknowledged as relevant to teaching and learning is Gardner's Bodily-Kinesthetic Intelligence: expertise in using one's whole body to express ideas and feelings. In this essay, we describe two educational opportunities through which linguistic and bodily-kinesthetic modes of experience and expression informed one another and deepened our understanding of one of the most complicated aspects of education—evaluation—and how evaluation informs the education that precedes and follows it.

The first educational opportunity was a professional development workshop designed and facilitated for us by five Haverford College students. The workshop employed interactive, improvisational theatre techniques followed by discussion to help us as teachers explore our struggles and concerns with evaluation of student work. The second educational opportunity was a mid-term assignment for the introductory, undergraduate education course we all teach. For this midterm assignment, students had the option of using the bodily-kinesthetic intelligence, alone or in combination with other intelligences, to demonstrate their understanding of the course material.

EMBODIED PARTICIPATION

These two educational opportunities and our reflections on them illustrate for us the educative power of combining varieties of what we have come to call "embodied participation with verbal analysis." By "embodied participation" we mean forms of engagement and communication that foreground the body as medium—through movement, physical interaction, and particular kinds of performance. Embodied participation, as we discuss it here, also implies involvement in learning situations that are not fully defined in advance, predictable, or even familiar to learners. And finally, with the word "participation" we mean to emphasize that these forms of embodied experience require participants to engage actively and responsively within these learning situations. Throughout this essay, we use vignettes to evoke experiences of embodied participation and critical reflection to analyze those experiences. In writing about the experiences for this essay, we help our minds recall what our bodies remember. It was this integration—as contrasted with higher education that is premised

"MY BODY WILL REMEMBER EVEN IF MY MIND DOESN'T": A NEW APPROACH TO EVALUATION

ALISON COOK-SATHER, ALICE LESNICK, AND JODY COHEN

EDITOR'S NOTE: *The following, a close analysis of diversity in assessment pedagogy, may well become required reading for anyone interested in dynamic teaching. It is somewhat long and at times complex, but the ultimate effect of the article is compelling and convincing.*

on a separation of mind and body and a privileging of the conscious and linguistic over the unconscious and bodily—that made these experiences particularly powerful for us.

INTEGRATING EMBODIED AND ARTICULATED UNDERSTANDINGS

To contextualize our exploration of embodied participation in teaching and learning, we synthesize aspects of three intellectual and practice-based frameworks: improvisational theatre, Multiple Intelligence (MI) Theory, and feminist theory and pedagogy. Each of these frameworks argues from a different tradition and perspective for embodied experience—juxtaposed against more disembodied and purely abstract, linguistic knowledge—as an essential form of understanding. Synthesizing and extending these arguments, we explore and aim to effect the integration of embodied experience and intellectual analysis. We create an intellectual and practice-based framework that does three things. First, it conceptualizes performance as experience rather than as representation. Second, it combines bodily-

This essay was inspired in part by the work and words of Sara Narva, who graduated from Haverford College in 1999. We are deeply grateful to her for her contribution to our experience and evolving understanding of embodied participation and for her multiple critical readings of this essay. We are also grateful to Paul Grobstein, Elliott Shore, Jeffrey Shultz, Cheryl Kaplan, Scott Cook-Sather, and Linda Caruso-Haviland for their thoughtful critiques and to Eula Jackson and Evan Bananti for their careful research.

kinesthetic and linguistic forms of expression to have and name that experience. Third, it recognizes that the knowledge produced and shared through such experience is always situated and multiple.

IMPROVISATIONAL THEATRE

Improvisational theatre is the first tradition upon which we draw. The interactive, improvisational theatre techniques that the Haverford College students used to design our professional development workshop were *Hope is Vital* techniques. The purpose of these techniques is to help people envision choices in situations of struggle. Conceptualized by Michael Rohd (1998), *Hope Is Vital* draws on and shares in the premises of other participatory forms of theater that seek to contribute to social change by challenging the dichotomy between audience and actor. Most relevant to our exploration here is improvisational theatre's emphasis on performance as experience rather than representation. Through embodied participation and the blurring of roles of actor and audience—analogous to teacher and learner—participants work together toward deeper felt understanding, greater ability to articulate that understanding, and application of that understanding to life outside the immediate learning context.

Rohd's intellectual tradition draws on Augusto Boal's (1979) *Theatre of the Oppressed* and Bertolt Brecht's (1964) Marxist poetics, among other traditions. These viewpoints make problematic the Aristotelian view of theater as imposed on spectators "who passively delegate power to the characters to think and act in their place" (Boal, 1979, p. 155). For Boal, traditional Aristotelian theater robs spectators of the will and agency necessary to change their lives and worlds, rendering them complacent in their witnessing of others' transformations, others' resolutions. Rohd's techniques also draw on Jacob Levy Moreno's (1987) concept of psychodrama and Patricia Sternberg and Antonina Garcia's (1989) work on sociodrama. Psychodrama is a therapeutic technique in which a client tells a story, and a group of enactors act out what he/she has told. This offers the promise, for the client, of being able to interact with his/her characters, replay the drama, change the ending, etc. Sociodrama takes some techniques from psychodrama, but as a group learning approach, is not as psychologically personal.

MULTIPLE INTELLIGENCE THEORY

We employ MI Theory as another framework for our analysis of embodied participation and understanding. Most relevant to the present exploration is how what Gardner calls the Bodily-Kinesthetic Intelligence, in conjunction with the Linguistic, can encourage students to explore and

learn in greater depth and complexity. Gardner (1999, 1995, 1993) argues that there are eight intelligences that everyone possesses, although each is developed to different levels in different people. Gardner deliberately calls these "intelligences" and not aptitudes or talents because he believes they deserve the recognition that the dominant intelligences receive. Gardner argues (1) that everyone possess all eight intelligences, (2) that most people can develop each intelligence to an adequate level of competency, (3) that the intelligences work together in complex ways—and are always interacting, and (4) that there are many ways to be intelligent in each category. He counters the notions in schools that only two of those eight—the linguistic and the mathematical—are important. Gardner contends that: "We know people truly understand something when they can represent the knowledge in more than one way" (quoted in Checkley, 1997, p. 11). The table on the facing page maps the eight intelligences Gardner has identified.

Hatch focuses on the ways children demonstrate intelligence rather than on how much intelligence they have, while Greenhawk gives students choices in their approaches to research (Greenhawk, 1997). Hatch (1997) and Greenhawk (1997) offer two dramatic contrasts to traditional, standardized forms of teaching and assessment in which the teacher makes the choices regarding those forms, and evaluation is based on students regurgitating what the teacher has taught.

Most of the research and writing on multiple intelligences in teaching focuses on pre-college populations, particularly elementary school age children. But the findings and questions raised in this research have implications for education at all levels. In a number of arenas—including the corporate world—facilitators are increasingly drawing on this theoretical framework in conceptualizing approaches to learning and professional development. Integrating MI Theory into educational contexts beyond the elementary years works against the gradual narrowing of people's expression into the linguistic and mathematical grooves.

WORKING AGAINST THE FACTORY MODEL OF EDUCATION

We consider three classroom contexts in this essay: (1) the educational space created for us by five students in the form of a professional development workshop; (2) the classrooms in which we teach our students; and (3) both the classrooms in which our students currently learn, and the classrooms for which our students are preparing to be teachers. Historically, the classroom has been a confined and confining space. As a result of the industrial revolution and the shift in economy in the United States in the early part

TABLE 1: MULTIPLE INTELLINGENCES

Adapted from Armstrong, 1994, and Checkley, 1998.

INTELLIGENCE	DEFINITION	EXAMPLE
Linguistic	The capacity to use words effectively, whether orally or in writing	Story-telling, oral histories, poetry, essays
Logical-Mathematical	The capacity to use numbers effectively and reason well	Scientific discoveries, mathematical theories, classification systems
Spatial	The ability to perceive the visual/spatial world accurately and perform transformations on those perceptions	Artistic works, navigational systems, architectural designs, inventions
Bodily-Kinesthetic	Expertise in using one's whole body to express ideas and feelings and facility in using hands to produce and transform things	Crafts, athletics, dramatic works, dance forms, sculpture, mechanical manipulations, operations
Musical	The capacity to perceive, discriminate, transform and express musical forms	Composing, recording, and performing songs and other music
Interpersonal	The ability to perceive and make distinctions in mood, intentions, motivations, and feelings of other people	Social and political facility and interactions
Intrapersonal	Self-knowledge and the ability to act adaptively on the basis of that knowledge	Rituals, rites of passage, religious systems, psychological theories and expressions of self-awareness and understanding
Naturalist	The ability to recognize and classify natural (and perhaps cultural artifacts)	Recognizing and classifying plants, minerals, and animals, including rocks and grass and all variety of flora and fauna; perhaps cars or sneakers or other cultural artifacts as well

of the 20th century, what is often called the factory model of education arose. According to this model, schools (the factories) are responsible for producing products (students) that will best contribute to the economy. With the factory as the model, the student's body is forced to be isolated and still; only the mind, located literally in the head, may move. Physical confinement in bolted down chairs and through the regulation of all forms of movement was and remains a deeply ingrained feature of classroom life. Our work with bodily forms of knowing has shown us a means of challenging this physical and social confinement.

The question we address to guide our analysis in this essay is the following: What happens when pedagogy deliberately invites the integration of embodied participation and linguistic expression? We address the question first from our perspective as teacher-learners in the context of the professional development workshop. We then turn to our analysis as learner-teachers of an instance in our own practice: the midterm assignment in *Critical Issues in Education*.

RE-MEMBERING THE BODY IN OUR LEARNING AS TEACHERS

Last spring, inspired by a demonstration a student had given in her class, Alice Lesnick, [an author of this article] asked the student, Sara, to design a professional development workshop that would teach us about the *Hope Is Vital* techniques she drew upon in her demonstration. Sara and her four co-facilitators invited us to choose the focus of the workshop, and we agreed that we wanted to explore what we experience as charged and challenging issues associated with the evaluation of student work, specifically the midterm assignment in *Critical Issues in Education*.[1]

Assigning grades to these projects is for us invariably difficult because traditional standards for judging and ranking student work are neither complex nor responsive enough to the alternative forms of presentation created by students. Below is a description of the workshop followed by a vignette that re-renders our embodied experience.

The workshop opened with some warm-up exercises through which we got comfortable in our bodies and with one another. In one, we stood face-to-face in pairs and grasped one another's right hands, then closed our eyes, then stepped away from one another, and then tried to step back into the handshake. In

[1] This is a course offered each semester through the Bryn Mawr/Haverford Education Program, which is taught by all three of us, and for which students complete midterm projects using a variety of modes of expression. As it happens, four of the five student-facilitators of the workshop had taken *Critical Issues in Education*.

another, working with words we associate with evaluation—such as "judgment," "vulnerable," and "standards"—we broke into pairs or triads and rendered these words in bodily shapes. These exercises prepared us for one of the most powerful activities in the *Hope Is Vital* repertoire: "The Machine." A machine is built around a central idea or dynamic. The group selects an idea to be embodied, and with the central idea in mind, one person after another takes up a position in relation to the other people composing the machine, executes a simple movement accompanied by a word or a short phrase, and repeats this movement and phrase. Each body contributes to the larger body that is the machine.

THE MACHINE

We agree that we will create a machine that attempts to capture the conflicting allegiances and responsibilities a professor might feel to herself, to students, and to colleagues regarding evaluation. One student-facilitator, Debra, volunteers to embody and represent a professor teaching Critical Issues. *Debra stands in the middle of the room and opens her arms, elbows bent and angled out from her ribcage, palms facing upward. Each half-extended arm extends toward a realm of relationships: one set is her colleagues and one set is her students. Slowly, one after another, the teacher-learners and student-facilitators in the workshop arrange ourselves around Debra, some assuming the role of student and some assuming the role of fellow professor or administrator. Each of us repeats a simple movement and a short, spoken phrase, which together articulate, with body and voice, our perspective.*

Alison Cook-Sather [another author] chooses to embody a student who feels the grade assigned to her midterm does not reflect accurately her investment in it—something students have, on occasion, expressed. She kneels in front of Debra and extends her arms toward Debra's face, unfolding them from her chest until they are stretched out fully. Over and over, she extends arms and repeats the words, "But I put my whole self into my painting"—the project she imagines she has completed for her midterm in Critical Issues.

Alison continues:

> *Each time I extend my arms and repeat the words, I feel more and more exposed, more and more hopeless in the face of inevitable judgment. I feel in my extensions and retractions the paradoxical swirl of fear and hope, of satisfaction of work that is well done and uncertainty of accomplishment that may not be perceived.*

> *Alice chooses to explore her fears about the status of the midterm project within a broader institutional context wary of student work that is not primarily or exclusively linguistic and linear. She assumes the stance of a colleague skeptical*

about the validity of the midterm assignment. She stands confidently, serene in the legitimacy of her position, leaning back a bit, like one accustomed to big meals, and says, over and over, hands out as if all is obvious, open, clear: "He's usually a B student."

> *As I repeat these words and gestures, I feel, within my body, the power conferred by fidelity to externally legitimate standards, and inhabit, for a time, the certainty and clarity that seem to flow from such a position.*

Jody Cohen [an author] hangs back as Debra, Alison, then Alice, and Jill take up positions. A student in her Critical Issues class last semester and one of the facilitators for the day's workshop, Jill had created as her midterm a series of posters that had left Jody confused. While they'd exchanged emails and through her words Jody had come to understand Jill's intentions, Jody feels now as if she and Jill share a dark knowledge about representation/communication and evaluation.

Jody says:

> *I rise, position myself in relation to Debra as professor and behind Alison as another student. "But you didn't explain the criteria," I say, hands opening to gesture no reins. I am in this instant my students, habituated to giving up control. I am also myself in the person of Debra, who responds to each of us, compassionately and firmly, acknowledging both effort and humanness.*

> *After we have completed the machine and let it run for a few minutes, we sit together in a circle on the floor and discuss the power of what we experienced and observed.*

Although each of us had a different experience of this "machine" and other workshop activities, all of us felt and observed in each other a quality of understanding we would not have been able to experience through a solely intellectual exploration. Embodying, or seeing embodied, the dynamics—of the complex teacher-student relationships, of the challenge of evaluating alternative forms of work, of how these alternative forms are judged by others in the educational community—yielded a different kind of understanding.

WHAT WE RE-MEMBERED IN OUR EMBODIED LEARNING

The professional development opportunity Sara and her co-facilitators offered us was unlike any other we had experienced. Often professional development, like much formal education, is based on what is variously called the delivery or transmission or banking (Freire, 1990) model, according to which prescribed knowledge is presented to learners (in this case, teachers) who sit, listen, and record. There is no question, according to this model, about who has knowledge and who needs it. This approach does not take into account who the learners are in relation to their educational contexts, and it keeps them basically isolated from one another, each left alone to receive the same information.

The professional development workshop challenged the traditional transmission model of education through inviting us not only to choose but also to embody the focus of our exploration—evaluation—and to work interactively through unpremeditated themes toward a deeper, more multifaceted understanding of the issues that surround evaluation. Because we have lived the experiences invoked in the workshop—including grading alternative forms of expression, talking with students about their graded work, and explaining our unconventional pedagogical approaches to colleagues—we carry viscerally our knowledge of these dynamics and discourses. For example, we are cognizant that we have power over students for a variety of institutional reasons. However, it is a qualitatively different experience to feel and observe these power dynamics embodied as each of us assumes a physical position in relation to the others, particularly when we embody unaccustomed roles (i.e., Debra as standing teacher, Alison as kneeling student). The positions we assumed in relation to one another made palpable the power dynamics and traditional structures for interaction that channel people's interactions into pre-defined roles, such as "teacher" and "student." The opportunity to communicate using embodied forms of participation enabled us to have an intimate recognition of the standard, hierarchical arrangements we both live and struggle against, as well as a critical perspective of those arrangements.

PARTICIPATORY THEATRE

The professional development workshop exposed us to a particular form of embodied participation—participatory, improvisational theatre. The *Hope Is Vital* techniques we experienced in the workshop reflect a project Rohd (1998) shares with others: to construct participatory, lived experiences through theater in which the participants (no longer "audience" in the traditional sense) may reclaim and be re-energized by their agency to think, feel, act, and create an impact on the social order. As we embodied different perspectives on evaluation, we both revisited old and created new understandings of them. We both stepped outside of and experienced more deeply our accustomed roles; we understood more fully both our own and others' feelings; we were challenged and inspired to learn from the interplay among us; and our thorough engagement prompted insights into the dynamics of inviting and evaluating alternative forms of student work.

NEW ROLES IN A DIFFERENT MEDIUM

Working together in these new ways let us see one another taking on new roles in a medium different from our usual repertoire. We experienced the exhilaration of interacting in various dimensions (movement, touch, words, taking turns observing and participating). We had to "listen" to one another differently: paying attention means something different when someone moves one of your limbs. This fuller, wider kind of attention worked against the split between mind and body that has characterized much of our learning. Similarly, the workshop expanded our understanding of what it means to respond. Instead of meaning to frame verbal replies, responding could mean getting up and adding one's self to a moving representation; silently observing a theater activity then commenting afterwards; and discussing where the workshop would go next. At no point was anyone passive: the experience was a multi-faceted form of co-construction of understanding using and in response to bodily expression.

MULTIPLE MEANINGS

Finally, the opportunity to express ideas physically seemed to allow for more multi-layered explorations of concepts, letting in ambivalences and multiple meanings rather than insisting on a single stance. We did not have preconceived notions about "right"—pre-articulated, accepted—ways of representing with our bodies our understanding of evaluation. As a result of this, trust emerged as an important feature of embodied participation in this workshop. We seemed more inclined to trust and respect the choices we each made about our understanding, as opposed to taking the skeptical, doubting stance of the academic. We recognized and accepted one another as teachers and learners engaged in unprescribed, unfolding negotiations of meaning.

THE PHYSICAL JOLT OF COMPREHENSION

What was so powerful about this experience was that it allowed us to step outside of our own familiar roles and experience more deeply the feelings of others. Relying on and inspiring interplay between and among us, it prompted insights into the dynamics of inviting and evaluating alternative forms of student work. The openness of this context to multiple, divergent, and to some degree conflicting perspectives on evaluation helped us understand our decisions as in dialogue with many voices, actual and imagined. Learning from students and exploring this complex issue with them, we experienced a blurring of roles that enhanced our understanding of past experiences and, we hope, reinforced our commitment to being open to future negotiations of meaning concerning evaluation. We have found these words to express and extend our understanding, but there is also an understanding that stays with us viscerally. When we remember our experience of the workshop, part of what we remember is the physical jolt of comprehension as we felt, in our own bodies, the power dynamics and the complexities of relationship and responsibility they imply. Our bodies remember the positions we assumed and observed, and remind us, differently than words, of what we learned.

AN UNDERSTANDING OF MI THEORY

Turning from what we learned through our embodied participation as teacher-learners in a professional development context, we now address our question regarding an instance in our practice as teachers—the midterm assignment in *Critical Issues in Education*. What happens when pedagogy deliberately invites embodied participation as a primary mode of experience and expression? The midterm assignment invites students to select one or more of Howard Gardner's multiple intelligences and demonstrate their understanding of the course content through those. Rather than the teacher identifying the critical issues in the course and designing a test to measure student mastery of those, students select what they consider to be the critical issues in education and construct their own interpretation of them. Specifically, students must: (1) Demonstrate that they have engaged with the materials and activities offered thus far in this class; (2) Demonstrate that through deep critical reflection and analysis, they have made coherent sense of that material and those activities; and (3) Submit a representation, and when necessary, a written, analytic explication, which captures the sense they have made.

Below we offer three descriptions of students' midterm presentations that drew on the bodily-kinesthetic, as well as other intelligences. Rather than removing ourselves as the "perceiving eye/I" (c.f. Kondo, 1990; Haraway, 1988), each of us articulates her respective experience as integral to the meaning of the learning experiences that the students both enacted and invited. The three instances are intriguingly different, and thus they raise provocative questions about what constitutes embodied participation. Our analysis of these midterm presentations examines (1) the degree to which students themselves engaged in embodied participation and (2) the extent to which the midterm actively engaged the audience in embodied participation.

ALTERATION OF THE SELF THROUGH MUSIC

In this first vignette, a student in Alice's *Critical Issues* course recasts the classroom as an intimate musical setting and deliberately integrates words with music. The student inhabits and uses his body to become the musician and thus to take on a persona that amplifies an aspect of himself and alters his customary "classroom self." His presentation features a degree of immediacy as well as vulnerability and risk through which he incites the audience to experience themselves differently than we usually do in the classroom. Alice tells the story and offers an analysis of the experience:

STORY AND ANALYSIS

Last fall we were enjoying the class presentations of students' midterms. I remember keenly and with pleasure the way one young man, guitar in hand, took the floor, ambling to the front of the room and hitching himself up onto a corner of the table I usually used to hold papers awaiting distribution. He proceeded to perform, coffee house style, a ballad he had written, a narrative expressing course themes and questions. He took on a singing performer's persona—different from the classroom persona (as an intense analytic and social thinker, a senior math major with a commitment to kids) we'd known. There was great humor and fun, and also vulnerability, in this performance, I thought. It carried us into a different relationship to this student, his work, his life outside of our class (in which he had learned to write, sing, and play songs on the guitar), and to one another (as people who might go out to hear music, or might ourselves make it in other spaces than this). I was struck by the risk he had taken in sharing this facet of himself with us, and the invitation his performance made to us to experience him and ourselves, one another, in a different key.

In other sections of *Critical Issues*, students have also composed and shared original songs, but in both cases (the first a solo act and the second created by two people working together) chose to share them with the class using tapes. In their midterm performances, technological mediation played a key role, especially in the solo student's performance, where part of his accomplishment lay in his having manipulated digital technology so as to allow him to perform multiple parts simultaneously. His making a point of this in class seemed to position his voice and hands—and, in some way, those listening to the tape—at an even further distance. Alice wondered if this were a way of dealing with the vulnerability occasioned by more immediately embodied work.

VIGNETTE NUMBER TWO

The second vignette illustrates embodiment enacted as role-playing for a midterm for Alison's *Critical Issues* class. This student takes on a persona not his own, acting as a teacher through his body language as well as his words. In his creation of a shaped but also open-ended classroom scenario, Tim highlights how an embodied presentation can be interactive and non-determined. By role-playing the teacher and asking students to role-play the students, Tim uses the shared, familiar script of the classroom to demand that students participate. Furthermore, Tim asks that members of the class attempt to express themselves through intelligences not generally privileged in school. As a bounded context for collective improvisation, Tim's midterm cuts against the grain of both conventional completion of a midterm assignment and conventional pedagogy. Alison tells the story of one portion of Tim's midterm presentation and offers a critical reflection on it:

TIM'S MIDTERM EXAMINATION

Desks are ranged in an uneven circle around the wood-floored and windowed classroom. Tim, a tall, lanky, energetic sophomore with tousled blond hair, leaps about the front of the room, setting up speakers, a small electronic keyboard, and a cassette player. The rest of us watch with interest.

With his equipment in place, Tim gathers himself together by clearing his throat and straightening his disheveled clothes, and then with a sudden call to order— "OK, class!"—he assumes the persona of teacher. The other students enrolled the class and I respond by sitting up straighter and turning our attention toward Tim. He proceeds: "We're going to explore today how we're all feeling. How we feel affects how we think and how we interact with others and just about everything, so it's important to pay attention to how we feel. It's also important to think about how we express how we feel. I've brought a short recording to share with you that captures how I was feeling this morning." At this point, Tim turns on the cassette player he has set up and begins playing an accompaniment on his keyboard to his recorded screaming, which sounds as though it is issuing from an echoing chamber.

Tim switches off the cassette player, we sit for a moment in stunned silence, and then he says to us: "Now, you take a few minutes and think about how you're feeling." We follow Tim's instructions, dutifully turning our attention inward. After a few more minutes, Tim turns to the blackboard, makes some swift strokes, and says to us: "Now, represent how you are feeling using these symbols." He has drawn a musical staff on the board filled with a variety of musical notes. Most of us are paralyzed by these instructions, unable to read let alone compose music. Tim is silent, emanating the sense that we should be composing.

After a few minutes, Tim asks for volunteers to share their compositions. One student raises her hand. Tim calls on her and she hums her notes. Tim praises this effort and asks us all to think about this form of expression and how well it does or does not capture how we are feeling.

AN ANALYSIS OF TIM'S PRESENTATION

As Tim explained later, his midterm had a number of purposes. By assuming this role and commanding our attention, Tim also assumed the authority that generally attends the role of teacher—the authority to dictate both content and form of expression. By choosing "how we are feeling" as the content of the lesson, he introduced an intelligence—intrapersonal intelligence—not generally invited or expressed in the classroom. Furthermore, by choosing a medium of nonverbal expression that draws on an intelligence also not privileged in most classrooms—musical—he highlighted our reliance on linguistic communication and conjured for us the discomfort of being asked to express ourselves in a medium with which we may not be fluent, comfortable, or even familiar. Tim involved us all, asking us to accept him as teacher and to look inwardly and express ourselves in unanticipated ways. His questions directed us to focus on our experiences, first in whatever ways made sense to us, and then in a prescribed medium. When Tim instructed us to express ourselves using musical notation, I, and I imagine others, felt a wave of fear prompted by the realization that we could not do what he asked. Tim embodied himself as teacher and caused us to have the embodied experience of, in my case, fear and inability, and, in the case of the student who volunteered to hum, perhaps an unusual sense of ability and accomplishment. This was a powerful experience.

COMMUNICATION THROUGH PHYSICAL MOVEMENT

In the third vignette, drawn from Jody's *Critical Issues* class, the performers enact a fully and literally embodied process, which involves, as the student presenters explained, "thinking [about the course material] in dance" as well as their effort to communicate their understandings through reliance on the medium of movement. An almost purely physical experience and expression, this dance both embraces and invites full attention to embodied participation. Jody tells the story and analyzes its significance:

A VISUAL UNDERSTANDING

It is a cool spring evening. We sit in a large room with windows thrown open. Jen and Pilar, dancers and students in Critical Issues, *have arranged us in a semicircle around the perimeter of the room. Then they darken the room and leave us to wait. I am worrying: What if this midterm performance is vague, fluffy, incoherent? What if I have misled them? How can movement demonstrate comprehension of this kind of content? What if I don't understand what I am seeing in this foreign language of dance? Students stay in their seats and talk softly, perhaps uneasy as well.*

Pilar enters first: tall, muscled with strong features, her initial sweep rivets us as she takes center stage in the classroom. Jen, younger and also smaller in her white leotard, mimes the constraint of the student, then locates us in the 17th century schoolhouse. Her words startle. Even as we take in where we are, Pilar and Jen have moved on, inviting us on a brief history of education through movement punctuated by occasional phrases. Then we are in the present. They move in arcs across the room, dancing the pleasures of learning through discovery, the agonies of assessment, the inequities of schooling at the end of the 20th century. I no longer wait for their words to tell me where I am. I am completely gripped by the movement, by the physical sense of it.

Afterwards the dancers are again among us. We hardly know what to say. It is as if we are all audience, caught in a stunned silence, or all performers and just now taking in the physical sense of what we've learned this semester. Language seems predisposed to a certain view of relationship between ideas—one idea and then another, this time or that time, this person or that. This experience seems to deal differently with such notions, so that afterwards it feels difficult to name what happened in terms of components, but rather I sit with my body feeling something now about educational equity, about the gaps between educational theory and practice. And then at some point we do talk—articulate what we saw and felt, first tentatively and then more openly as we realize that our experiences of this dance are neither "correct" nor "incorrect" but only closer or farther from Pilar's and Jen's conscious intentions. I realize that many of us are re-learning the material, understanding it differently somehow, viscerally.

The third vignette offers the most dramatic example of embodied participation across the student midterms, in which words only punctuated the dance and the majority of the presentation took the form of bodily movement. In her reflection on the midterm, one of the dancers, Jen mused,

The facts would have come and gone but now that they're connected to movement my body will remember even if my mind doesn't. The hardest part wasn't the thinking in dance (that almost felt like cheating; it felt too right to be on a midterm) but trying to make sure that people who don't think in movement would understand what we were trying to say. We worried that we weren't good translators…

The inevitable imperfection of translation—that is, the struggle for expression and communication through an alternate venue—may well open the way for new questions,

tensions and syntheses. And in the case of making the body and physical ways of knowing central, we are jarred because we are unaccustomed to the body as medium of learning and expression in the classroom. We are also, however, deeply moved because, perhaps, we remember the bodily as a primary way of knowing and telling. This experience seems to us a rich and full form of re-membering, for which we subsequently feel compelled to find words.

WHAT WE RE-MEMBERED THROUGH EMBODIED TEACHING

As with our experience of the professional development workshop, we have found words to re-evoke the experiences of the student midterm presentations and to articulate and extend our understanding of their significance. But also, as with the professional development workshop, there are some understandings that remain with us primarily in our bodies. Alice's identification with the feeling of risk her student took in composing and singing a song; Alison's recollection of the inarticulateness she felt at not being able to express herself in musical notation; and Jody's initial nervousness and subsequent utter engagement as she watched her students dance—are all feelings re-evoked when we remember these midterm presentations.

CONCLUSION

When we first began to analyze the impact of the professional development workshop, we framed its power in terms of its demonstration of the relative thinness of our accustomed orientation towards education and of the tendency of this orientation to obscure the significance of embodied knowing. Thinking more deeply about embodied participation has led us to recognize how reflection and articulation can enhance what we learn through embodied participation. Thus rather than perpetuate the division between embodied learning and linguistic intelligence, we suggest that by rejoining movement and words we are able to remember ourselves better in learning and teaching. In finding language to tell stories of embodied learning experiences, as we have done in this essay, and letting those words exist alongside visceral memories, we argue for the integration of bodily and linguistic ways of knowing.

Bringing embodied knowing into both consciousness and language is what makes the work we describe here pedagogy. The evaluation points that mark most pedagogical encounters can be re-understood, not as moments when learners must offer disembodied, solely linguistic representations of their learning, but instead as occasions for lived and articulated experiences. The forms of embodied participation we render in the vignettes in this essay invite learners to embody understanding *and* find words to describe that experience. Through this conjoining, learners and teachers integrate our bodily experiences with our minds' understandings.

REFERENCES

Armstrong, R. (1994). *Multiple Intelligences in the Classroom.* Alexandria: Association for Supervision and Curriculum Development.

Boal, A. (1979). *Theater of the Oppressed.* NY: Urizen Books.

Bordo, S. (1993). *Unbearable Weight: Feminism, Western Culture, and the Body.* Berkeley: University of California Press.

Brecht, B. (1964). *Brecht on Theatre : The Development of an Aesthetic.* Edited and translated by John Willett. New York : Hill and Wang; London: Methuen.

Checkley, K. (1998). "The First Seven…and the Eighth: A Conversation with Howard Gardner" in *Educational Leadership*, **55** (1), 8-13.

Ellsworth, E. (1992). "Why doesn't this feel empowering? Working through the Repressive Myths of Critical Pedagogy" in Luke, C. and Gore, J. (Eds.), *Feminisms and Critical Pedagogy.* New York: Routledge.

Freire. P. (1990). *Pedagogy of the Oppressed.* New York: Continuum.

Gardner, H. (1999). *The Disciplined Mind: What All Students Should Understand.* New York: Simon & Schuster.

—. (1983). *Frames of Mind: The Theory of Multiple Intelligences.* NY: Basic Books.

—. (1993). *Multiple Intelligences : The Theory in Practice.* New York: Basic Books. Greenhawk, J. (1997). "Multiple Intelligences Meet Standards" in *Educational Leadership*, **55** (1), 62-69.

Griffin, S. (1978). *Woman and Nature: The Roaring Inside Her.* New York: Harper Colophon Books.

Haraway. D. (1988). "Situated Knowledges: The Science Question in Feminism and the Privilege of Partial Perspective" in *Feminist Studies*, **14** (3), 575-599.

Hatch, T. (1997). "Getting Specific About Multiple Intelligences" in *Educational Leadership*, **54** (6), 26-29.

Kondo, D. (1990). *Crafting Selves: Power, Gender, and Discourses of Identity in a Japanese Workplace.* Chicago: University of Chicago Press.

Moreno, J.L. (1987). *The Essential Moreno: Writings on Psychodrama, Group Method, and Spontaneity.* New York: Springer Publishing.

Palmer, P. (1987). "Community, Conflict, and Ways of Knowing: Ways to Deepen Our Educational Agenda" in *Change*, **19** (5), 20-25.

Rohd, M. (1998). *Theatre for Community, Conflict & Dialogue.* Portsmouth: Heinemann.

Stange, M. (1997). *Woman the Hunter.* Boston: Beacon Press

Sternberg, P. & Garcia, A. (1989). *Sociodrama: Who's in Your Shoes?* NY: Praeger.

Weedon, C. (1987). *Feminist Practice and Poststructuralist Theory.* Cambridge, MA: Blackwell.

How can prospective social studies teachers tap into their multiple intelligences in order to develop new kinds of knowledge? I don't mean to be facile, but I honestly think that a solution to this problem can be formed by establishing a new protocol, one that involves singing the blues, screaming, dancing, literally running around and boogieing down. Of course, there is a carefully calculated method in what must appear to be madness. Let us consider that method and see where the "madness" has a precise fit.

THEORETICAL RATIONALE

I teach an introductory methods course in social studies education, and its content consists of many of the classic theories in pedagogy already familiar to professional educators. Students who are new to the discipline, however, find much of the course content to be alien to what they have already learned. Paramount among my goals, therefore, is helping my students establish vivid schemes containing key elements of pedagogical theory. To reach this goal, I rely on the constructivist notions of John Dewey (1938) and Jean Piaget (1950). They inform my own teaching by reminding me how to provide appropriate learning experiences that can be understood and that stick.

I get help from Dewey by remembering how to engage my students in experiential learning activities. By structuring classroom episodes within the context of Dewey's mind/body paradigm (*Experience and Education,* 1938), I develop knowing and doing through auditory, kinesthetic, and visual modalities. I use this mind/body paradigm in order to enable students to assimilate ideas about teaching and learning social studies, schemes that they need to become successful in their majors.

Consequently, students create an operating system, which they can refer to as "the teaching/learning process." This is a scheme which, in Piagetian terms, will allow them to accommodate and assimilate previously unfamiliar knowledge and skills about teaching. My students literally construct new knowledge about classroom performance by experiencing the classic theories (Hyerle 1996). Classroom experiences engage students' auditory, kinesthetic, and visual capabilities as they build this new scheme called the teaching/learning process (Brooks and Brooks 1993).

This constructivist methodology in my classroom lets students appreciate a virtual encounter between Howard Gardner and Benjamin Bloom. Acquiring a comprehensive understanding of Bloom's Taxonomy (Bloom, Englehart, Furst, Hill, and Krathwohl 1956) is the highlight of my construction project, because Bloom represents a classic in pedagogy, one which sets the foundation of my students' new scheme. Yet Bloom's Taxonomy is theoretical and it needs to be made a living, breathing attribute of the teaching/learning process. Later, students can develop skills about teaching social studies which will span the range from theory to practice. My students need to view Bloom's

THE MISSING LINK: APPLYING MI THEORY TO ASSESSMENT STRATEGIES

FRED SAVITZ

hierarchy of learning as fundamental to articulating clear assessment strategies in the area of social studies.

THEORY TO PRACTICE

How to fit the domains of learning from Bloom's Taxonomy into a new scheme, then, demands the application of genuine, authentic experiences. For starters, I model contemporary practices in my own lessons, so I approach my presentation of Bloom's Taxonomy by engaging students in Multiple Intelligence experiences designed to encourage genuine learning (Gardner, 1983). Gardner's theory emphasizes authenticity in scheme construction. It is a theory that promotes addressing an array of seven distinct intelligences. Accordingly, students invoke their intelligences in music, personal and social interaction, linguistic skills, individual movement, mathematics, and spatial relations. When these are activated, students have a seven-fold opportunity to organize their teaching/learning process scheme shaped around Bloom's Taxonomy.

SINGING THE BLUES TO LEARN ABOUT BLOOM

In preparation for my methods class, I work on the kinds of strategies that demonstrate links between applying Gardner's theory and understanding Bloom's Taxonomy. It occurred to me that I could exploit my interest in blues music to assist in making that connection. In fact, I decided to compose an original blues tune, a tune that I would use

Using Frieirian Pedagogy to produce social consciousness in students is a way to vary the usual strategy/skill approaches found in basic writing and reading courses. At Harcum College in Bryn Mawr, PA, we found that when we implemented the social action principles of Freire (1990), not only did our students have more interest in the basic writing course, but their ability to write detailed academic essays improved significantly. The following is a description of the course and the student's reactions based on entries from the instructor's journal.

BACKGROUND

Most of the students in the basic writing course Reynolds taught in the Spring of 1997 were black or Asian women, which made them members of the social groups in our society that do not normally possess power. McLaren (1999) described our task and the status of our students when he explained how critical pedagogy entails a way of teaching that enables students to see how groups in power influence education. Bartholomae (1986) explained how people from groups without power can find the academic culture at college as foreign as another language. He pointed out that the student's position in society creates serious economic and personal problems which they must solve as they struggle to obtain an education.

We were particularly interested in Frieire's work with Brazilian villagers who became literate while working to improve social conditions (Wallerstein, 1987). Our students at Harcum also had personal problems produced by their economic position in society. Their social status created obstacles to their learning the academic modes of thinking described by Mc Laren (1999) and Bartholomae (1986). We teachers of basic writing courses had to devise a way to help our students overcome these obstacles.

PROBLEMS AS BASIS FOR INSTRUCTION

Wallerstein (1987) outlined Freire's fundamental method of making the problems in students' lives serve as the basis for instruction in literacy. Using a code, which can involve a picture or article, the teacher encourages the students to discuss their experiences and to see how the problems in their lives are part of major social issues in society. Then the teacher encourages the students to devise solutions to their problems and to act on the solutions.

To put Freire's theory into practice, we adapted Wallerstein's approach: We devised a basic writing course which required the students to choose a problem and to read and write about it. Since the students are from disempowered groups, we used the theme "underdogs in our society" from a course that Caldwell previously taught. We felt that even students from the traditional middle-class power groups could relate to the idea of being an underdog. Many teenagers in our society feel that they are not part of the main culture despite their ethnic or social background. The following will describe the students' reactions to the activities based upon entries recorded in Reynold's journal.

FREIRIAN PEDAGOGY, SOCIAL CONSCIOUSNESS, AND BASIC WRITING

PATRICIA R. REYNOLDS AND PENNY BURRALL

WRITING ABOUT UNDERDOGS

At the beginning of the course, the students were anxious because they had to write an in-class paragraph describing an experience where they were treated like an underdog. Harcum requires a writing sample at the beginning of the semester from all English students to make sure they are properly placed. Although Reynolds had a get-acquainted session after which she told them what they would be writing about in the next class, they seemed tense. Still they were able to write about situations where they suffered the pain of discrimination.

DISCRIMINATION IN KOREA

Soo talked about how women are treated in Korea. She said, "According to traditional customs in my country, all women were treated like an underdog by men…only women do housework, have few freedoms and wear skirts. I know that now-a-days our family's life changed a lot, but I'm also sure that the basic thing, treatment like an underdog, is not changed."

Beth talked about how it feels to be considered not as intelligent as other students. She writes, "When I was in elementary school, I was in private instruction. All the other children thought there was something wrong with me because I was not in their classes. They would look at me like I was dumb."

These and other students appeared to have no trouble thinking of situations where they considered themselves underdogs, so they were easily able to do the first assignment that centered on a song they chose—a song that they had heard outside the classroom and that describes an underdog. They had to write the words to the song and summarize the song. Then after listening to a few of the tunes presented by student volunteers, they had to write an academic paragraph in which they told why they liked their song. At first, they were reluctant to present their songs, but after Reynolds joked about old people liking the Rolling Stones, they laughed. Since the class consisted mainly of Japanese and African American women, the music chosen was very different. They laughed about this, but they did ask questions about songs they found to be very strange.

Often the lyrics of the songs not only expressed feelings of isolation, but also contained words of encouragement. Ji wrote "The song…['Candy Everybody Wants'] tells how there are equal rights for all people everywhere." She goes on to say, "If you want something, don't give up. Try to get it." Beth told how the song "Lean on Me" inspires her. She said, "The reason behind the song is so true. Just lean on me when you need a hand. This is a great song to listen to when you are down and need something to bring you up."

LONELINESS AND ISOLATION

The lyrics stimulated a discussion of the isolation and loneliness that being different can produce. The students were willing to discuss each song that had been chosen, but there was not enough time in the semester to permit this.

Besides academic writing assignments, the instructor gave them an opportunity to do free writing to showcase their abilities. This writing was graded only on the amount done. One page was a "B" and more was an "A". This gave the instructor a chance to respond to their ideas, and to provide the students a chance to try poetry or to share their lives. In the study Reynolds did for her dissertation (Reynolds, 1995), she found, like Kitagawa (1989), that responding to the students' creative composition in a supportive way creates a sense of audience and gives them confidence to work on their academic writing. As Bartholomae stated, such writing often constitutes a stifling experience for students who are not from the mainstream groups in society.

To help them complete the academic paragraph on their opinion regarding their songs, the instructor first gave them a chance to brainstorm and write any way they wished. Then she showed them the academic paragraph format. They found it confusing and had to struggle to make their original drafts conform to the thesis. Their writing was sketchy because they just wanted to state how the song affected them without referring to the actual lyrics of the song.

The instructor was able to help them in the Learning Laboratory. English 100 students were required to attend lab two hours a week. The purpose of the lab is to provide drills in the grammatical points that were often misused. Since the students were usually in small groups of five or less, the instructor could hold writing conferences and present individualized mini-lessons based on errors.

SUMMARIZING AND DOCUMENTING

After producing the argumentative academic paragraphs that stated their opinion of their song, the students had to read an article that presented old and unimaginative ideas on how to deal with the problems of an oppressed group in society. They then outlined the article, wrote a summary of it and a paragraph on how they would solve the problems. They had to use Modern Languages Association (MLA) documentation to report where they found the article.

This part of the course involved Freire's critical pedagogy. The students were drawn to articles that depicted social problems which concerned them. Many of the black women and one Japanese student chose to read about welfare reform. The Asian, white middle class, and some black students considered abortion. Other students chose to write about AIDS victims and gay issues.

SANTA'S SWEATSHOP

The instructor chose the article "Santa's Sweatshop" from *U.S. News and World Report* as a model to further the summarizing strategies. The article dealt with the treatment of children around the world who work in sweatshops to make the clothes people buy at the mall. She found that the entire class was shocked at the conditions in the factories and at first did not know what to do to help the children. After they discussed the brands mentioned in the article, they decided they would not buy clothes made by these companies.

As they dealt with exploitation of workers for profit, they also worked on basic reading and writing strategies. Since they had trouble finding the main ideas of "Santa's Sweatshop," the instructor had to show them that most of the time it was the first sentence in the paragraph. She also discussed the outline of the article and gave them a copy of one that she had made. Since students in basic reading and writing courses have trouble applying cognitive strategies to the assignments they have to do for their courses, the instructor allowed class time for individualized conferences. She helped each student find the main ideas of the article, produce an outline, and use it to write a summary.

EXPOSITORY PARAGRAPHS AND ON TO NOVELS

As the class moved to expository paragraphs in which they stated their opinion on how to help oppressed groups, the students' attitude changed. They had to talk about their opinions with a partner, and then interview their partner to learn about his or her opinion. They appeared to enjoy this activity as they spent the class session writing and talking. When the instructor told them they had to interview two or more people from different age groups, they responded well to the assignment. She felt this was a productive session.

Reynolds required her students to read a novel by an author of literary stature that dealt with the problems of a group considered to be underdogs in society. They had to write a summary and reaction for each chapter. Many of the black students chose Myra Angelou's works, and some of the Japanese students chose Yukio Mishima's novels. As they responded, most of them concentrated on describing how the novel helped them deal with prejudice in their lives.

Soo reacted to *The Woman Warrior* by saying, "It is not a real story, but it teaches me how to prepare the fight of life as a warrior." Chikage stated about Mishima"s *Confession of the Mask,* "When I finished this novel, I was sad. The author was always worried about his life and felt pain under oppression from people…I understood his life very well."

THE TUTOR SPEAKS

At this point in the course the instructor became concerned about some of the ESL students' writing because some of their sentences were still incomprehensible to her. She suggested that they find a tutor or make a native English speaker friend. They should have their peer tutor not write anything on the paper but rather tell them how a native speaker would say what they wrote.

This way, when they could choose from the ideas and words the tutor used to create the sentence that they needed, the writing became a combination of their words and the words they heard. Since this is a more tedious process than simply rewriting their sentences, they knew that getting a peer tutor was vital or else they could not learn how to write academic English fast enough to pass the course. Now the students were under pressure, but they seemed determined to work as hard as they could. They knew if they made any mistakes, they could keep rewriting any of their assignments until they earned the grade they wanted. Sommers (1982) and other researchers in revision stress the value of this arrangement.

As the class moved into changing an academic expository paragraph into an essay, the instructor found that being able to read the free writing of students provided a chance for her to reassure them that their writing was good even though it was not academic.

The topics of the free writing still reflected the problems in their lives. For example, Angelic thought about the number of children actually raised by two parents when she wrote "Nearly ten per cent of American children do not live in a house-hold headed by at least one of their parents. Of those who do, seventy percent live in two parent families and thirty per cent live in one parent families respectively." Beth reflected on the pain of going through a sexual harassment suit as she writes, "My lawsuit is over. The newspapers are writing articles about the outcome. It is a good feeling to know it is over, and that people can follow up about the lawsuit and find out that I was not wrong. It is great knowing that I can move on with my life. I also like the fact that some other girl will stand up for herself because she knows that there will be someone like myself to back her up."

Soo talks about the role of women in Korea: "According to my country's traditional customs, all women were treated like a underdog by men. Especially I can give some examples whenever women were treated differently through my family life…Whenever my father wants to drink water, I have to prepare the cup of water then give it to him…Women have just little freedom. I could not sleep outside even at the best friend's home, and I have to be back home at 9:00 p.m. when I go out with friends or whatever." These representative samples of my students' free writing show how they wrote about the prejudice they face in their lives. Although they knew they could write whatever they pleased to receive credit for the assignment, the students wrote about their lives as disadvantaged persons.

MASTERING THE ACADEMIC

To help them master the academic mode of writing, I used the five-paragraph essay format as a guide. I had to convince them it was a guide especially after several students asked if they had to have three examples or three reasons. Their main problem was conforming their brainstorming opinions to the academic form which requires a thesis sentence and reasons which explain why the reader should accept this thesis. Rose (1985) and Belenkey et. al. (1986) have found that basic writing students and women use logic which is different from the Aristotelian logic required in academic writing, which could explain why the teacher felt she was stifling their self expression. The writing conferences dealt with classifying their ideas into reasons and examples

Once they were completed, however, the essays were good examples of the academic format, and the students felt that they did express their own opinions. The set of essays from this group was one of the best sets the instructor has read in her career. After they understood that academic writing required them to go into detail about their ideas, the students were able to read other articles on their topics so they could add more examples. They used stories from their personal experiences to illustrate their reasons and included the experiences of the people they read about in the articles they found.

An important part of Freirian Pedagogy is that students take action to improve a particular social problem. In our class, the instructor required them to use their essay as a letter-to-the-editor of *The Philadelphia Inquirer*. If the editor chose their letter, only portions of their essays would be published. Therefore, the instructor encouraged them to summarize their entire arguement in the letter. She also provided samples of the business letter and envelope format they would use to send their letter. She required a typed copy of the letter, but she did not actually require them to send the letter. Some did so, but those did not appear in print.

SHORT STORIES AND JOURNALS

During the last few weeks of the semester, the class read short stories, which dealt with the problems women face in their personal relationships. The students had to write journal entries which contained facts from the story, their reactions, and any experiences the story evoked. This assignment was based on Bleich's (1975) heuristic. The class then discussed (1) their reactions to the men in the story and (2) the problems the women faced as Clifford (1986) and Fish (1980) suggest. *The Abortion* by Alice Walker produced a serious discussion. The white middle class women could not understand why a married woman would want to terminate a pregnancy, while the black women were able to provide reasons why a woman would want an abortion.

CONCLUSION

At the end of the semester, the students wrote an essay that gave their opinion of a character in the story and why they held that opinion. The instructor read these carefully and found that students had demonstrated a good understanding of the academic format. Supporting details were, however, thin. It was thought that the reason for this was the difference between the experiences of the characters and the students' lives. In general, Reynolds and Caldwell found that using Freirian Pedagogy in the basic writing course for the Developmental Program at Harcum College was exciting and rewarding. They planned to continue to use those methods as a vital way to help students develop reading and writing strategies needed to succeed in college.

REFERENCES

Bartholomae, D. (1986). "Inventing the University". *Journal of Basic Writing*. **5** 4-23.

Belenky, M. F.; McVicker-Clinchy, B.; Rule-Goldberger, N.; and Mattuck-Tarule, J. (1986). *Women's Ways of Knowing: the Development of Self, Voice and Mind*. New York: Basic Book, Inc.

Bleich, D. (1975). "Thoughts and Feelings" in *Reading and Feelings*. (pp. 7-19). Urbana: NCTE.

Clifford, J. (1986). "A Response Pedagogy for Nonconoconical Literature" in *Reader,* **Spring** 48-60.

Fish, S. (1980). "The Authority of Interpretative Communities" in *Is There a Text in This Class?*. Cambridge: Harvard University Press.

Frieire, P. (1990). *Pedagogy of the Oppressed*. New York: Continuum.

Kitagawa, M. M. (1989). "Letting Ourselves Be Taught" in Donna M. Johnson & Duane H. Ropen (Eds.), *Richness in Writing: Empowering ESL Students*. (pp. 70-83) New York: Longman.

Mc Laren, P. (1999). "A Pedagogy of Possibility: Reflecting upon Paulo Freire's Politics of Education" in *Educational Researcher*. **28** 49-56.

Macmillian, J. (1996). "Santa's Sweatshop" in *U.S. News and World Report*. December 16. 50-60.

Reynolds, P. (1995). *When Basic Writers Write about Literature: Self Expression or Self Destruction?*. Ann Arbor: University Microfilms International.

Rose, M. (1985). "The Language of Exclusion: Writing Instruction at the University" in *College English*. **47**. 341-359.

Sommers, N. (1982). "Responding to Student Writing" in *College Composition and Communication*. **33** (2) 148-156.

Wallerstein, N. (1987). "Problem Posing Education: Frieire's Method for Transformation" in Ira Shor (Ed.) *Freire for the Classroom: A Sourcebook for Liberatory Teaching*. (pp. 33-44) Portsmouth: Heinemann.

After a 10-year study of technology in classrooms, researchers in Apple Computer's Classrooms of Tomorrow Program described three distinct stages of teachers' use of technology (Sandholtz, Ringstaff, & Dwyer, 1997). The first stage is characterized by the teachers' mastery of the procedures of operating a certain technology—how to cut and paste in word processing or how to post messages and attachments on a discussion board. The next stage is when they use the technology to support their existing ideas about their subjects. Finally, and hopefully, teachers will begin the stage when they

reconsider and reconceptualize their subjects and education vis-á-vis whatever new technology they are employing. There is not a locked timeline for any of these stages nor is reaching the final stage a certainty. Yet a focus on this final stage can open up the possibilities for realizing the potential of distance learning. Although the type of reflective practice involved in reconsidering one's subject and profession does not need to be precipitated by the introduction of new technology, the interest in professional reflective practice over the last twenty years in the fields of education and organizational management—captured in the works of Donald Schön (1983) and Peter Senge (1990)—was prompted by the paradigm shifts in professional fields integrally affected by technological innovations.

An important component in reflective practice is the examination of mental models and preconceptions about a particular profession or practice. When examining our mental models, we look at our ideas about the systemic relationships of causes, effects, and rationales. A good place to begin in professional reflective practice is to examine the history of a profession or field: this involves a deep consideration of the path and cache of experience that has led to a particular state or perception. Unfortunately, current perceptions of distance learning are often tainted with suspicion. This should come as no surprise considering the overwhelmingly commercial character of many distance learning providers, as the following e-mail illustrates.

RE: University Degree Program

University Diplomas

Obtain a prosperous future, money earning power, and the admiration of all. Diplomas from prestigious non-accredited universities based on your present knowledge and life experience.

No required test, classes, books, or interviews.

Bachelors, Masters, MBA, and Doctorate (PhD) diplomas available in the field of your choice.

Call 24 hours a day, 7 days a week, including Sundays and holidays.

This type of shifty pitch does not simply give distance learning a bad name, but has created a deep distrust of distance learning as a credible method of education. This misapprehension inhibits distance learning's broad acceptance by educators, students, and the public. However, through a reflec-

DISTANCE LEARNING, REFLECTIVE PRACTICE, AND THE URBAN UNIVERSITY

CORDELIA R. TWOMEY
AND CHRISTOPHER SHAMBURG

EDITOR'S NOTE: *No collection that attempts to depict pedagogy in higher education today can omit at least a brief consideration of Distance Learning. The following essay presents a concise summary of the history and current practice of that rapidly developing sector, which seems decidedly American in nature. The concept discussed is a long way from the one-classroom Little Red Schoolhouse, but the main principle involved—that every individual has the right to an education—seems very close indeed. Because the authors are primarily interested in defining Distance Learning, they do not discuss the relationship between Multiple Intelligences and that approach to the delivery of lessons. Teachers might well find it interesting to discuss with their students the possible interactions between MI and Distance Learning.*

tion on the history, context, and function of distance learning, its role in the evolution of education and society can become clearer. By examining the themes and lessons of distance learning history, we can refine our own conceptions and mental models about its current and future role. By examining milestones in the field, we can find precedents that resonate with our current technologies, the mission of the urban university, and the social and educational demands of the 21st century. These examples give us a peer at the wealth of experience in the field and the role distance learning has had in evolutionary and revolutionary social changes.

A SELECTED HISTORY OF DISTANCE LEARNING

Even from a secular perspective, Saint Paul is considered one of the earliest recorded distance educators. An

Apostle and founder of the Christian church, Saint Paul sent and responded to letters from the earliest Christians. His 13 letters in the New Testament, believed to be a fraction of all he sent, instruct, unite, and bolster the burgeoning Christian community. From a secular perspective, the growing consensus about successful approaches to distance learning echoes many of the characteristics of Saint Paul's approach. Saint Paul was not only interested in instruction, but in building a diverse and geographically diffused community. His letters are characterized by a responsiveness to the particular concerns of his "students". Moreover, of special interest for the urban university, many scholars attribute Saint Paul's success to his life in cities (Metzger & Coogan, 1993). His urbane background had tooled him with a cosmopolitan sensibility and prepared him to deal with the diverse people and issues of his mission.

There are movements from the last 200 years that demonstrate the pedagogical and social significance of distance education. One of the most illustrative is Isaac Pitman's use of the mail to teach shorthand in 1837. His work was integrally related to the social, political, and national developments of mid-19th century England and the United States. Pitman began teaching shorthand by mail in England in 1837 and in the United States in 1852. His system became one of the most widely used in the world and was translated into 14 different languages.

Pitman's use of the mail is also a good example of the educational capitalization of a new technology, the Penny Post. The Penny Post revolutionized postage in England when Parliament passed the Uniform Penny Postage Act. The act paved the way for the adhesive penny stamp. Reliable and inexpensive postage was now a possibility in England—a major leap from the previous system that had been corrupted by political patronage and favoritism. The postage reforms were part of the wave of social reforms in England in the early 19th century, and effective mail delivery was a necessity for the expanding empire.

The text-based competencies of shorthand made it a natural subject for one of the first instructional uses of the Penny Post. Furthermore, the rising cultural wave of industry, commerce, and efficiency in the mid-19th century made England and the United States fertile ground for shorthand. Although the increased access to education via the Penny Post is fundamentally a liberating and democratizing movement, its fit into the spirit of the age could be seen by the ease that it could be imagined into the world of Dickens' Cratchit or Melville's Bartleby.

Another important milestone of distance learning occurred in the latter part of the 19th century when Anna Ticknor operated her Society to Encourage Studies at Home from 1873 to 1897. The organization had over 10,000 members and educated women of diverse class and economic backgrounds. Ticknor's work is especially relevant to the mission and goals of today's distance educators; she intentionally targeted a group that had been previously excluded or underserved by conventional education systems.

During the same time, William Rainey Harper was revolutionizing higher education at the University of Chicago by establishing the first college level correspondence courses. Distance learning complemented the mission and location of the University of Chicago. Established by John Rockefeller to be a Midwestern rival for the Eastern universities, the function of this outpost urban university in the broader rural landscape lent itself to a distance extension program.

One milestone from the 20th century that is worth mentioning is the establishment of the Great Britain's Open University in 1969. The Open University is notable because it was the first college distance learning program that was not just an extension program but a fundamentally new model of higher education. The Open University specifically targeted those who had been previously excluded from a college education. According to its promotional material, one third of its graduates would not have even been accepted to another college. It currently has 200,000 students and has served over two million.

There are certain themes and lessons that can be drawn from this selective history. From Saint Paul to the Open University, these ventures of distance learning can be characterized as both evolutionary and revolutionary. They are evolutionary in the sense that they were inextricably linked to the broader history of their times. They are revolutionary in the sense that the all radically challenged the existing educational and social structure. Both Saint Paul and Anna Ticknor had an overt, broader goal of uniting a community as well as instructing individuals, and all of these movements attempted to address underserved populations.

DISTANCE LEARNING AND THE URBAN UNIVERSITY

The current and projected state of distance learning in higher education and the prospective population who would most benefit from its implementation relate to the mission of urban universities. Distance learning programs are taking a powerful place in four-year colleges. In 2000, the Web-Based Education Commission, a bi-partisan congressional committee, projected that the number of college students enrolled in distance learning courses will triple between from 710,000 in 1998 to 2.2 million in

2002. The committee also reported an unprecedented number of the non-traditional students attending college and a related growth in the job market's demands for a college educated workforce. Today, more than 47% of college students are over the age of 25, a standard indicator of the non-traditional student. Moreover, in 2000, 85% of the jobs in the United States required education beyond high school—up from 65% in 1991. The distance learner was and will probably continue to be the non-traditional student, continuing his or her education due to pressure and incentives from the workplace. Urban universities have historically addressed this population—distance learning is a powerful extension of that mission.

ADDRESSING THE EVOLUTION OF A MISSION AND THE REVOLUTION OF INSTRUCTION

Reflective practice is a valuable way to address the opportunities and challenges that distance learning brings to higher education. The explosion of the Internet and Web-based distance learning over the last half decade has the potential to be an evolution of the mission of urban universities as well as a revolution of pedagogical challenges for professional educators. Creating courses online or adapting existing courses can be an overwhelming challenge for a teacher. This is where the process of reflective practice can be invaluable. Professional reflective practice urges a deep consideration of how, why, and what we are doing. It has often been referred to—looking at your area of expertise—with a 'beginner's mind'. In his germinal work on the subject *The Reflective Practitioner*, Donald Schön (1983), asserts that reflective practice can address "the mismatch between professional knowledge and the changing characteristics of situations in practice."

In the face of the changing technical and methodological challenges that web-based distance learning brings, reflective practice can guide us to that final stage of technological innovation that the ACOT researchers described—reconsidering and reconceptualizing our profession vis-á-vis the new technology. Schön's idea of reflective practice is to "criticize the tacit understandings that have grown up around the repetitive experiences…and make new sense of the situations of uncertainty and uniqueness." The parameters and conditions of Web-based distance learning would definitely qualify as one of the "situations of uncertainty and uniqueness" that Schön calls attention to. With his charge in mind and with a sense of the historic role of distance learning, we can begin to reform our current understandings about our profession vis-á-vis our changing landscape and these new opportunities.

PRACTICAL APPLICATIONS

Before you start to set up your distance learning course, there are two rules to remember:

1. The "anywhere, anytime" classroom translates into the "no where, no time" classroom.
2. The term "distance learning" has the potential to become meaningless.

With the first statement, the key point to remember is that discipline on the part of the student is the key to success. The image that "I can do this course at midnight in my bunny slippers" does not work. The student who completes the course and succeeds in learning is the student who sets aside a specific place and a set amount of time each week to work on the course.

In the second, your distance learning student could be the person living next door. Distance learning in America was set up for far different reasons than it was in places like Australia, where reaching people over large geographic areas was essential. In the US, it was designed to meet the needs of busy people who still want to enhance their lifelong learning.

In *Teaching Online,* William Draves clearly lists the differences between a traditional class and an online class:

A TRADITIONAL CLASS

- Is activity-based—students show up.
- Does not require a lot of advance technical work before the class starts.
- Is mostly oral.
- Is held at a given time—and only at that time.
- Has external discipline.
- Is a social experience.
- Is a more passive experience.
- Might be evaluated based on the instructor's "quality".

AN ON-LINE CLASS

- Content is delivered differently.
- There is a lot of advance technical work before the class starts.
- It is can be accessed at any time.
- Discipline is internal—and not everyone succeeds. Discipline is KEY.
- It is a much more active experience.
- The "quality" of the student's output is evaluated at the end of the course.
- Learning is outcomes and results oriented.

CHARACTERISTICS OF EFFECTIVE DISTANT INSTRUCTORS

As stated above, teaching in an on-line environment is far different from teaching in a traditional classroom. Not everyone is meant to teach online. Who make effective distance instructors? They are experienced classroom teachers who:

- Are goal oriented.
- Take charge of their learning experiences.
- Bring relevant life experiences.
- Cope with new professional demands
- Know that distance teaching is more than a new model of instruction delivery.
- Have excellent written communication skills.
- Have a high comfort level with technology.
- Have a willingness to invest large number of mentoring hours each week.
- Possess an excellent command of subject matter.
- Recognize that some learners gave a greater expertise in given areas.
- Have a high self-esteem.
- Possess a good sense of humor.

COMPONENTS OF AN ON-LINE COURSE

There are three basic components of an on-line course: content, interaction, and assessment.

1. Content—At our University, each syllabus must contain the following:

- Catalog Description
- Goals of the Course
- Instructional Procedures
- Course Content
- Evaluation Measures for Determining Students' Grades
- Bibliography with Required Text(s), Additional Required Readings, Supporting Bibliography/ Webliography, and Relevant Periodical Sources

2. Interaction—There are many ways to foster *interaction*, including:

- A threaded discussion forum (Remember: YOU initiate the topics.)
- Real time chat rooms
- E-mail

View each discussion as a dialogue. There are several "tricks" that you can use to stimulate interaction:

- If responses start to lag, behind the scenes get 2 or 3 students to stimulate conversation.
- When a question is posted, first compliment the question.

- Allow others to respond first.
- Make sure someone responds to every comment.
- Look for connections and "door openers."
- Be neutral and nonjudgmental.
- Help insecure learners.
- Have high expectations of your students.
- Help students who are frustrated.
- Encourage shy participants. Every single person must participate.
- Avoid negative reinforcement.

3. Assessment—There are many ways to assess students in an online learning environment. People say, "How do you know that the online student was the one who actually did the work?" How do you know that the student giving you the paper in class actually wrote that paper? The more you can customize an assignment and make modifications along the way, the more likely it will be that the student is doing his or her own work. There are many interesting way to assess your online student:

- Individual assignments
- Individual projects
- Group projects
- On-line project presentations
- Peer project assessment
- Research projects
- Tests

COURSE DESIGN

While you are designing your online course, consider the following:

- Would a prereading package facilitate learning and insure that all students had a common body of knowledge when entering the course?
- What expectations do you have?
- Does the course have content validity?
- Is the sequencing logical?
- Is the pacing appropriate to the level of the learners?
- Have you defined all terminology?
- Does your course foster higher order thinking?
- Did you provide cueing activities if students get stuck?
- Are there reinforcement activities?
- Are there enrichment activities?
- Does you test have validity?
- Is your test reliable?
- Have you used several types of assessment?
- Is there a "Help" area that students can go to?
- Is the course technically correct?

CURRICULUM DELIVERY ISSUES

There are times when curriculum delivery issues arise.

Have you:
- Considered synchronous and/or asynchronous course delivery?
- Helped students define "the learning place"?
- Posted the syllabus?
- Provided both individual and participatory assignments?
- Made the presence of the instructor known—frequently?
- Made students establish their presence—frequently?

SETTING TECHNOLOGY STANDARDS

Students must know that they have a responsibility, as well. They must have access to the technology needed to be active, viable members of that learning community. The excuse that "I didn't send any work because I didn't have Internet access for a month" is just not acceptable. You can help students by:
- Publishing the minimal technology requirements for distance participation.
- Listing technology tools to be used in the learning experience.
- Providing an on-line tutorial for essential technology skills.
- Maintaining a "helpline" for technology support.

PRESCRIPTIONS FOR FAILURE

There are several sure ways to insure that your distance learning course will fail:
- Take existing classroom materials and convert to web-based presentations.
- Not mastering the technology before the course begins.
- Let more than 48 hours lapse before responding to student inquiries.
- Allow negative or derogatory discussion to evolve online.
- Broadcast messages that should be private.

PRESCRIPTIONS FOR SUCCESS

On a positive note, there are things that can be done to insure that your distance learning course will be a success:
- Keep class size to approximately 20.
- Polish your syllabus before posting it.
- Do not change the rules in the middle of the course.
- Devise assignments that meet the needs of adult learners as described above.
- Make expectations realistic.
- Develop a community of learners for distant peer support.
- Assign collaborative and individual projects.
- Devise means for self-assessment.

- Devise means for online presentations.
- Publish online office hours and be there!
- Serve as a role model for excellence in distance teaching.

HINTS AND TIPS

There are a few guidelines that will help you along the way:
- Do not give Incompletes. Nationwide, the highest rate of non-completion is in online courses. Tell students the due dates and stick to them. Every course has a finite end.
- Clearly state how many times students are to post to the Web board, e-mail, etc.
- Set deadlines and stick to them.
- Have students send work to you that is in a format that is easy for YOU to open.
- If work arrives at 11:00 p.m. on Tuesday, students should not expect to have it returned on Wednesday at 10:00 a.m.
- Do not allow students to say, "I'm quiet. I'll just observe." Shyness is not allowed in on-line learning.
- Be careful about the use of humor. What might sound funny in a classroom, enhanced with inflection and facial gestures, might be misunderstood when written on the screen.
- Student photos are an excellent addition.
- Have students supply a short biography.
- Enhance your written presentations with photographs, streaming video and audio.

SUMMARY

Online teaching is an exciting, innovative experience. It allows us to "think out of the box" and try a new experience. If you enjoy interacting with students and working in your subject area, this takes teaching to a whole new level. The first time that you do it is the pioneer phase, but each time that you offer the course it will get easier and your confidence level will grow.

REFERENCES

Draves, W. A. (2000). *Teaching Online*. River Falls, WI: Learning Resources Network (LERN).

Metzger, B. M., & Coogan, M. D. (Eds.). (1993). *The Oxford Companion to the Bible*. Oxford: Oxford University Press.

Sandholtz, J. H., Ringstaff, C., & Dwyer, D. C. (1997). *Teaching with Technology: Creating Student-Centered Classrooms*. New York: Teachers College Press.

Senge, P. M. (1990). *The Fifth Discipline: The Art and Practice of the Learning Organization*. New York: Currency-Doubleday.

Schön, D. (1983). *The Reflective Practitioner*. New York: Basic Books.

Web-based Education Commission (2000). The Power of the Internet for Learning: Moving from Promise to Practice. Author: Washington, D.C. Available at http://interact.hpcnet.org/webcommission/index.htm

It is unfortunate that one cannot incorporate food and drink into a written paper, because I think the best way to begin to understand anything—especially a foreign language and culture—is with food and drink. So, I invite the reader of these lines to go get a cup of real, hot tea, sit back, and imagine the scene to be described. We are going to drink tea together Russian style. Culturally, it would be incorrect to call this a "tea party," because drinking tea with friends or family is such an integral part of everyday life and socializing in Russia. There are even sayings and proverbs about tea: *Tea isn't vodka: you can't drink a lot of it*; *Drinking tea isn't [as hard as] chopping firewood.*

During the nine months I lived in Russia and on subsequent visits, I rarely entered an apartment without being served tea. The same holds true when I visit Russian friends in New Jersey, New York, Boston, Illinois, California, Israel, and other places. The tea and the sweets offered are important, but still more important is the conversation (long-winded by American standards) that accompanies the tea. I believe that such events are significant cultural performances. I am not sure one could even begin to approach an understanding of Russian culture and Russian people without participating in at least a few such events. This is part of the reason that every semester of Beginning Russian at New Jersey City University starts with Russian tea. However, there's more to the story of how this became a class tradition. I'll get to that later, because now we have to set the table. As you receive an item or as I point to it, say what you have or what you see:

ta-RYEL-kuh	"plate"
LOZH-kuh	"spoon"
sal-FYET-kuh	"napkin"
CHASH-kuh	"cup"
CHAI-nik	"teapot"
chai	"tea"
pe-CHEN-iya	"cookies"
vah-REN-ie	"jam"
kahn-FYE-ty	"candy"
SA-khar	"sugar"

Oops! That "kh" sound in *SA-khar* "sugar" is giving you some trouble. Try laughing like Russians laugh: *Kha, kha, kha!* Pretend you're clearing your throat: *Kha, kha!* Try doing it again, LOUDER: *KHA, KHA, KHA!* You've got it; try *SA-khar* again now. *Khuh-rah-SHAW!* (Good; that was good!) Now, let me serve you:

Khah-TI-te chai?	"Would you like some tea?"
Da, spa-SI-buh, khah-CHU.	"Yes, thank you, I would."

Let me pour it now. First I take the porcelain Russian teapot and pour some dark, concentrated tea into your cup until it is 1/4 or 1/3 or 1/2 full, depending on how strong you like your tea. Then, I take the kettle and finish filling your cup with hot water.

STEALTH VERBING: MULTIPLE INTELLIGENCES IN LANGUAGE LEARNING

DONNA FARINA

Khah-TI-te pe-CHEN-iya?	"Would you like some cookies?"
Da, spa-SI-buh.	"Yes, thank you."
Khah-TI-te vah-REN-ie?	"Would you like some jam?"

Watch how some Russian people eat jam with their tea (I'll model it). Sometimes they put a spoonful or two of it in their cup, instead of (or along with) sugar. Sometimes they put quite a bit of it on a dish and proceed to eat spoonfuls as they drink their tea. That demonstration usually makes quite an impression on our students, who shudder at all that sweetness. Not all, though; some Cuban students have told how their relatives do the same thing right here in Jersey City or nearby Union City. The Polish students from Bayonne are not that surprised, either. It's a small world. Still, so far not one NJCU student has accepted to swallow a spoonful of the "raw" jam:

Spa-SI-buh, nyet. "No, thank you."

Okay, now it's time to practice with the person next to you at the table. It's your job to serve her tea. Practice your vocabulary; both of you should try to remember what the words are for everything you see on the table. Enjoy your tea and cookies! If you were studying Russian, when you came back to class the following week, you would repeat the whole tea party, though now the party would also be your first class quiz—an oral quiz. You would be required to offer your partner at least four things on the table: tea, sugar, jam, cookies; or maybe tea, sugar, cookies, candy. Your partner would have to respond appropriately to your questions, and then serve you.

MI and Russian Tea

Many of Howard Gardner's multiple intelligences are employed in this tea-sharing. Of course, the linguistic intelligence is used as students speak a foreign language. However, they are not just learning to repeat the words, "Do you want some tea?" The words are contextualized and accompanied by the appropriate real-life actions. Students use spatial intelligence as they look around at the offerings on the table, while they hear Russian words spoken. The students use the important bodily kinesthetic intelligence as they set the table; pour the right amount of strong tea for their partner before adding the hot water; and as they pick up the plates of sugar cubes, cookies, or candy to offer their partner. They use the interpersonal intelligence to interact with their partner in response to food and drink preference questions. While students might not be directly interacting with Russian people during this performance (unless the language teacher himself is from Russia), students are nevertheless using the interpersonal intelligence as they begin to internalize pieces of Russian culture through the tea; they are enlarging their understanding of the possible range of human behaviors and experiences. Here, I am using "understanding" in the sense that Gardner means it, as something you are able to do, to perform, to apply—and not just something that you may think you learned, passively. Last, I think that the students also use Gardner's intrapersonal intelligence during the tea performance: they learn about who they are (self-identity) and why they cannot stomach the idea of swallowing that spoonful of sweet jam along with their tea.

We know that research supports the use of the multiple intelligences in language learning. For example, vocabulary is learned best when a person touches the object while learning the word; looking at a drawing or photo of the object is not as good as touching the real thing but is still better than just seeing the printed word. I am a trainer of K-12 teachers who are getting certified in English as a second language or bilingual education. These teachers know about the multiple intelligences and instinctively create their lessons to tap into as many of them as they can, in order to reach pupils in urban schools with a wide variety of learning styles. One group of teachers did a demonstration in my graduate applied linguistics class that supports the notion that the more intelligences one uses in teaching, the better students perform. They presented groups of classmates with cues for remembering names: a print cue only (a card with the written name); a verbal cue (hearing the name spoken) plus the printed card; a photo of a person plus the verbal cue plus print. The group that received all three cues (visual, aural, and print) did the best in remembering the names; the group that only had the print cue did the worst.

Minimal MI in College

Despite the evidence that people learn better when teachers employ multiple intelligences, many of us working at the college level are lagging far behind my K-12 teachers in our approaches and techniques. Many of us are still stuck on print and lecture. We are not using visual aids as much as we should, we are not helping students improve interpersonal skills through well structured small-group activities, and we are not providing enough bodily-kinesthetic learning experiences. Sometimes this may be due to the misconception that these approaches are babyish and will insult our adult students, that we would be "talking down" to students if we used them. That this is indeed a misconception would be more obvious if we recall our own experiences at academic conferences. The brilliant professor who looks down at the lectern and reads his lecture for 30 minutes will not get through to us as much as the less-brilliant one who looks at us from time to time and has a decent handout or Powerpoint presentation to accompany her lecture. Our reluctance at the college level to employ more of the intelligences in our teaching also comes from habit; few of us were taught with multiple intelligences, and we teach by knee-jerking into what we previously experienced as students, what we saw our own professors doing.

I was a perfect example of how old habits can be hard to break. Though I am now in teacher education, I started out teaching Russian and French. I was well trained in foreign language pedagogy and had plenty of teaching experience. I knew about Communicative Language Learning and proficiency-based teaching. Yet, when I walked into my Russian class on the first day, I always did what I had seen from every Russian teacher I knew: immediately I would introduce print, the Russian alphabet.

When I first began taking Russian in the early 1980s, I spent four full semesters in classes where I rarely spoke any Russian! I took a lot of pencil-and-paper grammar tests and did well. I listened to tapes and pronounced words aloud at home to my parakeet. After two years of study, I couldn't even say who is in my family, or how many brothers and sisters I have. But I knew the Russian alphabet really well.

Now you understand what was behind my first-day teaching approach. If my students couldn't read the Cyrillic alphabet, the blackboard was not available to me as a tool in my classroom—I felt naked without my blackboard. My teaching decision was driven by what made me feel comfortable and what I was used to rather than what worked for the students. Moreover, the decision as to how to introduce the alphabet was not one I had ever really thought about. In my University, most foreign language classes that are taught in the evening meet only once per week. So invariably, I would get about two thirds of the way through the Russian alphabet in the first week. The second week, a few new people would show up who had registered late. Now, I'd have two groups, one starting from zero and another that needed to finish the alphabet and move ahead. This made me annoyed and frustrated with the students (of course not with myself!).

This vicious circle was broken when I attended the Conference on the Imagination in Language Learning that is held every spring here in New Jersey. A few years ago, Raul Vega Romero, a college professor of Spanish in California, told how he withholds all print from his college Spanish students for the first six weeks of the semester! The result, he said, is that they don't make the habitual pronunciation errors that English speakers make when learning Spanish, confusing "s" and "z" as well as other things. Why? Because many of these errors are print-induced errors. By the time his students finally do see print, they have already understood the correct pronunciations (in Gardner's sense of actually "performing the understanding") and therefore cannot be negatively influenced by the print.

DELAYED INTRODUCTION OF PRINT

For me this lecture was a light bulb above my head! I had been given permission to wait—at least a week, a lot more if I wanted—to introduce the Russian alphabet! So now, usually the only print the students are exposed to on the first day of Russian class (following the tea-drinking) are the words:

CHASH-kuh CHA-yuh   "a cup of tea"

The words appear on a poster that usually hangs in my kitchen but comes to class on the first day. It is a striking 1920s constructivist poster advertising a Russian film called "A Cup of Tea" with a drawing of a teacup in the center. Students learn to write these words and, if time permits, they may also learn to write their own names in Cyrillic. Instead of the decontextualized alphabetical order that I used to teach, students slowly and contextually learn to write. Visual, bodily-kinesthetic learning that taps into the students' experiences. My K-12 teachers could have told me this.

Any college teacher can learn to use the multiple intelligences, to teach any academic subject. It does require a willingness to be imaginative, to let go of old habits, and

to reflect more on the why's of what we do in the classroom. I no longer teach Russian, but the tea-sharing tradition lives on, because the adjunct instructor, Georgii Durman, easily learned how to use these techniques. At my presentation at the Urban Mission Conference, three undergraduate students from the Russian class were kind enough to demonstrate their skills and explain to the audience what they like about the tea lesson. Paulina Gryzewska, an undergraduate majoring in art, took Beginning Russian and came back for the second semester. She noted that the tea party makes you speak and really use the language; she remembers little that she learned from her Russian classes in Poland because it was taught so differently.

Richard Szuban began his study of Russian just before graduating. Although officially signed up for Russian I, he simultaneously completed the work for Russian II in the same semester, because he uses Russian in his customs job at Kennedy Airport in New York. At the end of one semester he was reading visa applications and headlines in Russian newspapers. For him, being able to acquire real Gardnerian understanding—even in the basic courses—was a necessity. Richard said that Prof. Durman's class was best when it did not rely on the book but on the real knowledge and experience Durman has of Russian language and culture. Marieli Vasquez, a transfer student, is majoring in computer science. Like Paulina and Richard, Marieli is already bilingual; Russian will be her third language after Spanish and English. In fact, usually in the Russian class a majority of the students are at least bilingual; that is a unique asset we have in our student body at the University. Marieli told the audience how she heard about the tea party even before she signed up for the class; this intrigued her. She expressed how much at ease she felt; it isn't like a class at all, because everyone is drinking tea and eating candy and cookies.

Because a foreign language takes a long time to learn, teachers often think about the performance of understanding as something that will happen far in the future: we'll teach them what Gardner might call an inert or passive understanding of all the present and past verb endings in Russian I, and then by the time they are in their third year of study they will actually be able to use the language. This approach to language teaching, the antithesis of the multiple intelligences approach, will most likely never lead to true understanding. Gardner talks about the pressure all teachers feel to finish covering all of "the material," the content: if we don't finish present and past tense in Russian I, how can we then finish motion verbs or perfective/imperfective (or whatever) in Russian II? College language teachers need to think about why 90% or more of students speak with their feet and never make it to a second or third year of language study. I believe that college students often understand better than their professors the importance of being able to perform the understanding over the importance of "covering the material."

SNEAKY LANGUAGE LEARNING

The title of this paper is meant to convey my view of what the role of grammar should be in language learning and teaching: it should have a very, very small role. Grammar should come in only when it is tightly linked, or interwoven, with a message students are trying to convey on a particular day. The message or meaning is a real communication, the performance of which eventually leads to understanding of grammar. For example, if students want to talk in Russian about where they live—Dallas, Texas; Weehawken, New Jersey; Jersey City—you probably have to explain a little (but very little!) to them about the prepositional case in Russian. If they want to talk about books or films that they like, you probably have to teach them something about a few (not all) Russian plural nouns. But, I think students should be taught those things in a sneaky, stealthy, devious, underhanded way.

The battle for a language teacher at an urban university or any university is to bring students into the classroom and then try to keep them there. Many of our urban students are already bilingual, bicultural, and globally aware. They know that it is useful to communicate in another language; they live every day among many cultures and realize also the importance of understanding other cultures. However, they are not interested in verb paradigms. I would venture to say that most human beings are not that crazy about verb paradigms, even in their native language; I think this is a healthy instinct. So college teachers need to catch up in their thinking with their students and with the multiple intelligences. If language teachers practice stealth verbing, and then students really learn how to use just a few verbs from day one—as in: "Would you like some tea?"—they could be on their way to an understanding of what language and culture mean. And unlike those pesky verb endings, this understanding might be with them for life.

The communication and entertainment industries are driving the growth of technology that enable us to get better internet access in remote areas. As a result, we are seeing a profound change in the delivery of cultural resources to students who wish to confront the human experience. This paper discusses the development of "Dynamic Web Integrated Learning Environment" (D-WILE) that can be relevant to the advanced study of music in the contemporary conservatory.

D-WILE offers learners the opportunity to experience the insights and wisdom that come from thoughts that are interconnected with a given piece of music, and to provide information that was not practical in the past. Why is it necessary for music students to have such an intellectual experience? The answer is that learning to perform a piece of music should not be seen as an isolated process. Mortimer Adler (1994) suggests that, to be an artist, one must become a spectator of all things. To be able to understand and perform a piece of music requires a systematic investigation of the cultural context in which it was created, and that information must be taken from a wide range of available sources. It is this very openness to a vast amount of materials, collected in a single learning environment, that will encourage students and help them to be truly innovative.

How can such knowledge about literature and other related fields assist musicians in developing their performance skills, specifically in its interpretation? All of the arts—music, painting, literature, etc.—are intellectual models of inclusive synthesis and abstract vision. They reflect the world at an altered angle, and offer a new way of seeing the past, the present and possibly, interpreting the future. Scolnicov (1988) suggests that art is inherently interconnected and interdependent with thinking about the world. Plato further suggests that emotion without knowledge or education can only produce an incongruent emotional expression of thought. To apply these ideas to musical performance, one can say that a performer's interpretation can be oversimplified if he is performing with an insufficient background knowledge of the piece of music at hand. The composition of a piece of music is based on carefully calculated structures and forms that express congruent ideas and emotion. Therefore, it is the performer's responsibility to express and communicate these ideas in an orderly fashion, just as the composer intended and as they are reflected in the composition. When a performer lacks sufficient cultural knowledge, he or she is likely to have an unbalanced understanding of a piece and to be unable to communicate an effective understanding of the emotional content of the piece.

In 1979, I wrote about my own personal experience in New York:

"I decided to learn about cultural background knowledge in my preparation of a large violin solo work by Eduardo Lalo, *Symphonie Espagnol*, which was to be

DEPTH IN MUSIC HISTORY VIA TECHNOLOGY

YOON-IL AUH

EDITOR'S NOTE: *Dr. Yoon-il Auh offers a broad critique of advanced music institutions and makes a strong suggestion for the use of the internet in finding new techniques of instruction, such as "D-WILE" which he developed to help his students.*

performed at Avery Fisher Hall in Lincoln Center. In order to find a definite structured idea at the heart of Lalo's work and to convey a specific emotional mood to the audience, I read related literature, visited museums to see artworks from the period of the composition, and discussed the piece with a music historian and musicologist at Juilliard, the conservatory where I was studying at the time. In the end, I was able to communicate with the audience much more effectively than I had ever imagined and they said so after the concert. Maybe the performance itself was better; maybe physically or psychologically I was in better condition than for some other performances. The fact remains that having both structured knowledge of the composition and a sense of the mood in which I wanted to communicate clearly made all the difference. Notably, it was not the background knowledge itself about Lalo's *Symphonie Espagnol* that helped me to perform better. It is, however, the influence of background knowledge that fulfilled a role by educating and enlightening me by presenting concrete models for imitation and expression."

The lesson to be learned here is that many cultural experiences and a good deal of cultural knowledge can be translated from one field to another, say from painting or literature to musical performance. When music is performed as it should be, that is, with an understanding of the whole

145

sphere of the composition, even a musically unsophisticated audience will feel what is happening and will feel a sense of suspense, a tension, and a deeper sense of art. One does not always need to impress the audience with superficial technical brilliance, which inevitably becomes boring if it is not accompanied by a palpable sense of human emotion.

This interconnectedness of distinct disciplines is true not only in the arts but in all fields. This is reflected in the current state of educational research where, in an attempt to solve problems in the last two decades, institutions and educators have turned to psychology, cognitive science, and new technologies in order to better understand the principles of innovative learning experience. Although such approaches might seem at first to diminish the importance of philosophical approaches to education in favor of more empirical methods of inquiry, philosophical problems continue to occupy the center of educational concerns, as educators and citizens are confronted with inescapable questions about the value, meaning, purpose, and justification of education (Scolnicov, 1988).

CURRENT CONSERVATORY MUSIC EDUCATION

In a typical four-year educational career at the music institution, the majority of students concentrate on the "technical outcome" of their playing. Most of the time, the private lesson session covers isolated facts and students invest the majority of their time attempting to memorize music for a mechanically perfect performance. A typical music institution divides students' time into five or more courses and distributes reading and listening lists for each course (Course Bulletin—Juilliard, Manhattan School of Music, Mannes 2000). For example, one course might focus on the time period of each important musical era, such as Baroque, Classical, and so on. Another course may be on rhythm, covering various meters used in music. A third course may focus on the teaching of music theory and harmony to gain familiarity and to memorize different types of scales, chord progressions, and rules of various cadences. This includes writing of different species of counter-points, and analyzing and writing four-part harmony. The fourth course may consist of memorizing historical facts, such as, those concerning works from various periods, styles, and tunes from choral and instrumental works, operas, symphonies, and many other odd combinatorial musical works. The fifth course is usually some form of a private lesson, meeting about one hour per week. Regardless of what students want to learn, a typical music institution would rotate the students within the courses described above, from geography to private lessons, again and again, year after year, with virtually nothing being altered.

After students have taken these courses, they will be tested. The tests may measure students' factual knowledge of dates and historical facts, or of rhythm and melody dictation. There may also be rote-listening tests of dozens of musical compositions. In the best of these learning scenarios, students may be asked to write a short essay about one of Beethoven or Mozart's work or to name a key composer in the first half of twentieth century and briefly explain why they are important. Finally, at the end of each school year, the students are tested for mechanical mastery of their musical instrument, not on how well they understand the work they are performing or how they have integrated the facts learned in classes into their performance, but on their technical outcome of their instrument.

COMPARTMENTALIZED CURRICULA

What is wrong with this method of teaching and the compartmentalized approach to learning it is based on? Jerrold Levinson (1990) explains that the crucial idea that art-work-hood is not an intrinsic exhibited property of a thing, but rather a matter of being related in the right way to human activity and thought. The initial goal of creating music, which is to intelligently interpret and perform a piece of music rather than acquire facts, is ignored. Specifically, this approach ignores the interdisciplinary and knowledge transferring that is needed for a student to become proficient at connecting knowledge to real-world applications. Instead, compartmentalized courses largely ignore the student's need to develop critical thinking and the need to connect worldly knowledge with the learned material. In addition to compartmentalized curricula, the main problem with courses taught at a typical music institution is that teachers hope or think that their students will develop a lifelong interest in what the teachers teach or a specific course offers.

If educators want to develop students' interests, it helps if students start with things they care about in the first place. It helps even more if students can see directly how what they are learning furthers their goals. A typical conservatory teaching method usually relies heavily on a fixed body of information. The pedagogical materials are often repetitive and cognitive activities are often limited—if not non-existent. That is, interconnectedness between harmony, analysis, and other social documents that may be related and would aid the students to attain a better awareness of a piece of music is virtually not emphasized. The distinctive theory and difficult-to-comprehend literatures seldom translate to solving pragmatic instrumental problems or to developing musicianship.

Today, this disconnection tends to be absolute; students and instructors seldom make an effort to relate relevant background information to the learning process. Therefore, it is found that the continuous problems of a conservatory-style education issues from the difficulty of synthesizing interpretation and theoretical studies while also focusing on and improving students' performance skills.

MULTIPLE INTELLIGENCES MAKE DIFFERENCES

The essence of uniformed schooling is the belief that every individual should be treated in the same way, same subjects in the same way and be assessed in the same way. This is a particularly unreasonable approach when in fact most music conservatory students are from abroad and therefore, bring to the institution the most diverse background of all fields of study, interest, and cultural knowledge and experience. In most cases, conservatories ignore these differences. Sometimes they are ignored because educators are either frustrated by the differences, or convinced that individuals are more likely to become members of a community if they can learn to be more alike. To the extent that the student and the teacher share that focus, the students who do well will consider themselves smart and be able to accelerate in such environments. However, if students have a fundamentally different kind of mind, they are likely to feel incompetent—at least while attending that school. For example, Debussy, Charles Ives, John Cage, George Gershwin, Igor Stranvinsky, to mention a few, had difficult a time intermixing with their colleagues and being able to meet the expectation of writing music during their time.

PROBLEMS OF MUSIC STUDIO:
TEACHING ADVANCED STUDENTS

Most of the time, much of the information presented in a private music lesson covers isolated facts that cannot be reliably recalled and used in other domains. Such a lesson rarely covers information relating to other fields of knowledge to expand the learning experience. Instead of spending the majority of their time attempting to memorize music for a technically perfect performance, these students should be encouraged to explore interdisciplinary studies. This may make well-rounded musicians and develop valuable skills in those who will not become professional musicians in the end.

For example, when a student is learning to play a musical composition by Franz Liszt, merely learning to play notes in the score does not complete the picture of performing Liszt's work. For example, Franz Liszt is the child of Beethoven, in musical sense. Liszt transcribed and performed all the Beethoven symphonies, and demonstrated fealty to his master by all inward and outward gestures. The legacy of Beethoven—developmental techniques, dramatic freedom, structural unity—can be heard throughout the

scores of Liszt (Sherman, 1997). Spiritually, Chopin made the strongest impression upon Liszt, in the sense of sanctioning and encouraging the mutual interests of music and poetry. In terms of virtuosity, Paganini made a major technical impression on Liszt, one that made him change the writing of his piano repertoire.

CAUSE AND EFFECTS
OF ILL-PREPARED PERFORMERS

In the last decade, educators have increasingly emphasized the importance of developing educational environments that enhance thinking and independent learning (Bransford et al. 1990; Bransford & Vye, 1989; Bransford & Johnson, 1972). One reason for this concern is that a field that is highly specialized in a narrowly defined area—such as learning to play the violin, piano or college athletetics—often tends to focus less on the ability to think and reason at the academic level. Therefore, it is found that critical thinking is often much less developed due to an excessive emphasis on technical measurements of the players.

The lack of interdisciplinary experience may give music students limited experience in critical thinking and in the mental processes of connecting worldly knowledge with the learning material. For example, similar to professional athletes, typical conservatory students concentrate on the "technical outcome," often a somewhat *ad hoc* affair that does not lead to the student becoming a self-evaluator. Furthermore, students with limited experience do not emphasize the self-assessment and self-actualization of their musical ability, which it would take to become a whole musician.

This artificial separation of the subjects on the theoretical level may have a direct impact on conservatory students' interpretation of a piece of music during live performances. A recent concert at Carnegie Recital Hall in New York City provided an example of this. Technically, the performance was acceptable; the musicians had rehearsed the piece itself adequately. However, the mood created and the emotional expression of the composition were unsatisfactory because the performers had only a very limited understanding of the cultural background of the composition. In particular, they had not researched the background of the work adequately. For example, it is possible that they had not listened to similar types of folk music (i.e., Irish or Welsh dances) or read relevant texts beforehand. As a result, the performance did not convey an adequate emotional understanding of this composition and left the audience unmoved.

THE EVIDENCE OF LIMITED WORLD KNOWLEDGE

A decline in the amount of world knowledge that music students possess is evidenced by the stories faculty exchange. A violinist, Yoon-il Auh, asked a group of advanced violin students at the Aspen Music Festival in his master class, "Who influenced the work of Paganini? "The students looked at their feet, the floor, or anything else to avoid embarrassing eye contact. A musicologist, Gustave Reese at New York University, asked his music class, "When was the Renaissance? When was the Roccoco period? How is Roccoco different from Baroque?" Finally, one brave student asked, "Who's supposed to teach us these things?" At this point, we have to wonder how students understand what they play and/or read when they do not have an instructor with a comprehensive education nearby to answer their questions.

Every music institution instructor has substantial anecdotal evidence, which shows that students do not know very much about general music history. This is not only the case in music. In other domains, there have also been a significant number of reports indicating that students have limited knowledge about the world. The National Endowment of the Humanities (NEH) report, *American Memory: A Report on the Humanities in the Nation's Public Schools,* cites data from a survey funded by the NEH that indicate that more than two-thirds of the American 17-year-olds were unable to place the Civil War within the correct half-century. The survey also demonstrated that the majority of students were unfamiliar with writers such as Dante and Chaucer, Dostoevsky, Whitman, Hawthorne, and Melville, to mention a few. The evidence of deficient background information and the inadequate readings that result from this deficiency is pervasive and alarming. When students lack world knowledge, their ability to read and their resulting facility for learning from text can suffer.

The point to be made here is that literacy—fully comprehending and capable adult literacy rather than the simple decoding of job applications, song lyrics, newspapers, and romance novels—requires background information. Whether one calls it "world knowledge," "cultural literacy," "non-visual information", or by its more generic name of "prior" or "background knowledge," the fact remains that all arts presuppose a degree of shared information between the artists and the listeners /viewers /readers.

CONSTRUCTING KNOWLEDGE

A typical music curriculum is already overcrowded with low-level information; teachers frantically race through required material, drilling students to memorize factual data to be regurgitated on mandated tests. Simply offering more information using the Web in existing educational settings would only make learning worse. Without skilled facilitation along with constructive assignments, students will flounder in a morass of unstructured data. Teachers must provide learners with educational experiences that enable learners to construct their own knowledge and make sense of massive, incomplete, and inconsistent information sources. Therefore, it is vital that educators to re-evaluate and augment current curriculum with collaborative, learning-through-doing activities based on linked, online materials and orchestrated across classrooms and community settings.

REFERENCES

Adler, M.J. (1994). *Art, the Arts, and the Great Ideas.* Macmillan Publishing Co.: New York.

Bransford, J. D. and Johnson, M.K. (1972). "Contextual prerequisites for Understanding: Some Investigations of Comprehension and recall" in *Journal of Verbal Learning and Verbal Behavior,* **11**, 717-726.

Bransford, J. D. and Vye, N.J. (1989). "A Perspective on Cognitive Research and its implication for Instuction" in L. B. Resnick and L. E. Klopfer (Eds.), *Toward the Thinking Curriculum: Current Cognitive Research.* Alexandria, VA: ASCD Yearbook.

Bransford, J. D.; Sherwood, R. D.; Hasselbring, T. S.; Kinzer, C. K.; and Williams, S. M. (1990). "Anchored Instruction: Why We Need It and How Technology Can Help" in D. Nix and R. Spiro (Eds.) *Cognition, Education and Multimedia: Exploring Ideas in High Technology.* (pp.115-139). Hillsdale, HM: Lawrence Erlbaum Associates.

Course Bulletin (2000). The Juilliard School.

Course Bulletin (2000). Manhattan School of Music.

Course Bulletin (2000). Mannes College of Music.

Gardner, H. (2000). *Foundation of Science and Values.* Symposium of the Tsuzuki International Scholarship fund.

Levinson, J. (1990). *Music, Art, and Metaphysics : Essays in Philosophical Aesthetics.* Cornell University Press.

Sherman, R. (1997). *Piano Pieces.* North Point Press: New York.

W hat follows is less a concrete plan for curriculum at the college level than a thought experiment. Possible? Probably not at present. Impossible? Definitely not, given the ongoing advances in computer technology.

BACKGROUND

In political theory classes, one of the most difficult concepts to convey to undergraduates is how government first arose. Government seems to be a universal. Wherever we find groups of humans, even in the most remote regions of the planet, government is present. Anthropologists tell us that even so-called primitive (or "preliterate") societies possess some form of conflict-resolution apparatus, even if it functions only intermittently. Clearly, the origins of government, which is to say an institution entrusted with the authoritative use of power to achieve various ends, are lost in prehistory.

Faced with the need to explain how government came into being, the Contract theorists–of whom the best known are Thomas Hobbes (1588–1679), John Locke (1632–1704), and Jean-Jacques Rousseau (1712–78)– invented what today might be termed a workaround: the "State of Nature." In his famous work *Leviathan*, Hobbes postulated a time when there was no government. In this "State of Nature," every man (read human being) was his own lawmaker, his own law enforcer, his own law interpreter: the analogy to legislative/executive/judicial powers is of course patent. The Hobbesian view is that humans are inherently selfish, and that where people come together, conflicts inevitably arise. In a state of nature, with no authoritative wielder of power, the prevailing situation becomes one of "war of all against all." In one of the most celebrated phrases in all of social science, Hobbes argues that in a state of nature life is "nasty, brutish, and short."

Hobbes and later Contract theorists contend that only a sovereign (powerful ruler) can provide the people the security needed for self-preservation. By willingly relinquishing the individual right to make, enforce, and interpret their own laws, the people in a state of nature form a body (Hobbes called it a commonwealth) that promotes the interests of all. The sovereign alone now has the powers previously enjoyed by each individual, but in exchange the people gain greater protection from the caprices and the unchecked violence of one another.

For political scientists, it is a given that even the worst form of authoritarianism is preferable to anarchy. This has resulted in neglect of examination of alternatives to the

<hr>

[1] Most attempts to deal with social systems based on other than traditional hierarchical structures (i.e., in essence, rulers and subjects, however democratically constituted) have understandably been in fictional form. One of the most carefully wrought examples of an effort to construct a believable albeit imperfect society based on anarchism (not anarchy) is Ursula K. Le Guin's award-winning science fiction novel *The Dispossessed: An Ambiguous Utopia* (1975).

STATE OF NATURE: A COMPUTER GAME YET TO BE BUILT

CLIFFORD E. LANDERS

EDITOR'S NOTE: *This paper was written before the Urban Mission Conference was conceived and in response to a request for innovative methods of teaching at the college level. Dr. Landers has imagined the striking learning possibilities of computer games that have not yet been constructed. It is almost visionary in the way it combines cybernetic characters with the principle by which human beings act together in order to survive. It encourages students to assess the commercially available computer games for a motivational and moral point-of-view. In its reliance on the imagination in university teaching, it is in keeping with the other papers in this anthology.*

existing decision-making process. In other words, the discussion begins *after* the creation of government rather than focus on how it came into being[1]. Yet theoretically the concept of government must presuppose its opposite—nongovernment. The game "State of Nature" would be a way of directing attention to this important but often overlooked aspect of political theory.

METHODS

Prior to beginning the simulation, students would be exposed to readings relating to issues of society-building, conflict resolution, and related problems. (Anthropological studies would also be brought in, providing an interdisciplinary facet to the course.) As hinted earlier, the necessary devices for effecting the proposed lesson are still in embryonic form and must await the emergence of technology adequate to the task. Nevertheless, the schemata essential to such a presentation can be offered.

1. *Computer Simulation.* In outward appearance, a traditional computer game in which players assume roles as interacting characters, State of Nature would allow various outcomes. Only one result, however, would maximize social utility for the largest number. The setting, whether on a primitive Earth or some hypothetical planet, is perforce a rustic one: forest, jungle, desert. Civilization, after all, comes about only after groups form and the state emerges. Technology, beyond simple tools such as axes and knives, is nonexistent. The physical manifestations of nature can vary, as in real life, from benign to hostile, sometimes changing in a short period of time. In general, resources are scarce and competition for them is inevitable. Geographic expansion is possible within limits imposed by time, climate, natural barriers, and animal power available for transport. Violence may occur in the game. Survival points are awarded in proportion to the amount of time a character manages to stay alive.

Just as in a true state of nature, the rules are nowhere expressed; players are forced to discover them as the game progresses. Some actions are rewarded, others punished. The pre-existing bias is toward cooperation and collaboration, while selfishness and egocentric behavior (usually but not always) bring negative results. A randomization factor is included in order to avoid predictability; outcomes are probabilistic rather than deterministic, but a given action will most often bring about a foreseeable result. That is, players can learn through observation that certain modes of conduct are more likely to have positive consequences than others. For example, players who pool their resources and exhibit solidarity have a better chance at survival than the stubbornly individualistic. The best outcome is experienced by those who form a coalition of reciprocal support–in effect, a nascent collective-security organization.

2. *Virtual Reality (VR).* Many of us have an exaggerated notion of the possibilities of VR from slick, state-of-the-art computer imagery on numerous science fiction programs and in films (a recent example, *The Matrix*, was especially striking). True character-based, multiplayer, interactive VR is still years, if not decades in the future. Nevertheless, for the purposes of this thought experiment, I can foresee a virtual-reality version of State of Nature. It might work something like this:

The VR State of Nature is played over the period of a semester, outside of class, presumably in the computer lab or its future equivalent (or perhaps online from one's dorm room), for at least an hour per week. Ideally, all students could be online simultaneously, thus ensuring interaction among the various players. Each participant assumes a role as a character; all start out with equal (rather minimal) resources. If the experiment is to be repeated in subsequent semesters, conditions can be modified to afford harsher or more benevolent environments. Or, by creating several different environments, there would be an opportunity to evaluate tentatively the relationship between environment and behavior.

Passage of time is simulated in a way that there is no "doomsday" assumption—that is, players have no idea how long the game will last. This provision should reduce last-minute, go-for-broke moves that might distort the verisimilitude of the exercise. Those killed or wiped out by natural forces will be resurrected to participate in another cycle—but starting from scratch and under a different identity; there will be no carryover. An entire cycle might encompass a period of pseudo-time ranging from at least five years to as long as two decades or more.

As in the more traditional computer version of State of Nature, players' strategies will vary. Some of the more obvious include:

ISOLATES OR HERMITS. As existing human societies in remote and inhospitable environments prove (the Inuit are an excellent example), isolation often equates with death. The group is a sine qua non for survival, and banishment is tantamount to capital punishment. Individualistic players will survive or perish, depending on randomly introduced exogenous events–meteorological, such as drought, a harsh winter, flash floods, or manmade, such as incursions by marauders. But the built-in bias toward cooperation ensures that they will not thrive.

POWER SEEKERS. Others will choose to pursue power as a way of guaranteeing their own safety, an approach that may lead to exploiting, enslaving, even killing other players. (Some may tie their fortunes to those of some ambitious would-be leader.) A very small number of such selfish players will prosper, but most will be eliminated by rivals or perhaps by the very tyrannicide that Locke espoused as being the inalienable right of the people.

LINKERS. These are those who, whether from instinct or reasoning, realize the need for cooperation among individuals for the collective good. A prerequisite to the emergence of any civilization, it presupposes the ability to surmount the daily struggle for existence that characterizes hunting-and-gathering cultures and create an agricultural surplus. Whether such linkers will emerge as a dominant element in any given game cycle is impossible to predict, but it is they who hold the best chance for creating a viable society. Efforts toward cooperation, while not always successful, are rewarded by the game, but random disasters can defeat even the best-laid plans.

EVALUATION

Every move in the game is recorded by the computer for later debriefing and analysis. At the end of the semester, the student turns in a journal relating the conclusions he or she drew from the experiment. The various outcomes are then compared in class, assessed and, one hopes, conclusions are drawn. In the post-mortem, various issues will be addressed stemming from the exercise:

- Could a state of nature actually exist in human society?
- Are any specific outcomes foreordained?
- What causes one society to evolve a different type of political system from another?
- What minimal needs of its members must a society meet to survive?
- What is the role of force in forging a society?
- Is democracy necessarily the best form of government for all societies?
- Is every society a priori capable of democracy?

For the purposes of this experiment, the evolution of society would not proceed beyond a stage roughly equivalent to the early civilizations in the Fertile Crescent. That is, a monarchy with some kind of organized class structure. Students wishing to investigate further the possibilities of nation-building may want to explore computer simulations such as the Civilization series that offer the opportunity to head a variety of cultures both historical and fictional.

CONCLUSIONS

This exposition, at best an outline rather than a finished design, may nevertheless raise issues useful to others seeking an innovative and imaginative approach to teaching. By making use of the constantly evolving area of computer simulation (and eventually, VR) we may find ways to stimulate student interest and enhance the learning experience.

An artist values simplicity. It is one of the criteria for creative excellence. Therefore I use simple language to communicate my ideas and hope you perceive this as the virtue I intend it to be. I do have a fundamental belief upon which all my teaching hangs. I believe that all human beings possess undeveloped creative competence and that arts have the power to unleash it to address the larger question of what it means to be a human being. This power is the basis of a dynamic technique of teaching that I call "Creative Lightning." Incorporating the principals of Multiple Intelligences (MI), it places the student directly in the midst of interactive learning experiences. In the first part of this article, I discuss the importance of creativity in my organization, "Artsgenesis" and then I illustrate the way I get students to participate in a theatre-based approach to the Civil War. Next, I talk about the use of the arts in leadership training for school principals in Connecticut. I close by giving an account of my response to my daughter's question, "Where do the arts come from?"

UNLEASHING CREATIVE COMPETENCE

KATHLEEN GAFFNEY

ARTS IN EDUCATION

I entered the field of arts-in-education after I had a direct experience of how the arts—theatre, dance, music and the visual arts—can transform a child's life and ability to learn. Now, I speak across the country on the subject of arts applications that stimulate learning across the multiple intelligences. I am a great fan of Dr. Howard Gardner and his work. And my first experience in MI Theory was from the perspective of a parent. My own child had been rescued from autism through the arts.

My daughter, Kerrianne, was perfectly normal at birth but eleven months later she was diagnosed with cancer of the eye. Five weeks after her operation for retinoblastoma, she received an MMR shot (measles, mumps and rubella). Within twenty-four hours she contracted measles, then meningitis which led to profound neurological damage. My husband and I consulted many specialists but our baby was pronounced autistic and severely developmentally disabled. At this juncture, I discovered early intervention and enrolled my daughter in three very innovative programs requiring one of the parents to attend school with the child every day. I attended school with my daughter five days a week for two years.

THE SONG ON THE AUTOHARP

Kerrianne and I worked with physical therapists, occupational therapists, and pediatricians of every ilk, developmental psychologists, cognitive specialists and my true heroes in life—special educators. Our daughter's remarkable story has been told on CBS and PBS television programs, has been featured in *The New York Times*, and is the subject of another book *Exceptional Path* due out in December. Specialists had been working with Kerrianne for two years with almost no results. Then the music therapist brought out an autoharp. Roughly triangular in shape, made of wood, it has many piano type strings and makes a beautiful sound when strummed. At the first session, the music therapist just plucked a few strings and I saw my child's hands flicker. The next week they placed the autoharp on her lap and played an entire song with the vibrations entering her body. Now her hands moved toward the instrument. The next week they placed the pic between her thumb and forefinger and helped her to strum. Then my child who had not held a toy in over two years began to strum the instrument all by herself over and over as if she was possessed. When they took the pic away she cried.

A month later when I looked at Kerrianne, she looked right back at me. Six weeks later when I hugged her, she hugged me back. I called it a miracle. The developmental psychologist called it "spontaneously extending her limits." I witnessed music, visual arts, theatre, dance miraculously reclaim her mind and spirit. I wanted to understand how and was led to Dr. Howard Gardner's book *Frames of Mind: Theory of Seven Intelligences*. Some of the programs designed for Kerrianne used an MI method of stimulating learning by creating bridges from a dominant intelligence to another area that needed development.

I became a passionate investigator of learning theory. My husband, Roger Shea, and I raised funds and opened an agency to help people develop.

THE WISDOM IN THE ARTS

Although I have been a practicing artist, playwright and actress for twenty years, I am constantly amazed to find the most profound wisdom about the arts in the simplest of demonstrations. Let me share a true story that happened in 1995 when I was one of the facilitators for a conference on Inclusion for the State of New Mexico. The conference participants were divided into four groups: political, human resource, advocates, and the arts. I facilitated the arts group of about two hundred individuals. In my group were artists, arts administrators, representatives from the National Endowment for the Arts, and the leaders of the five nations—Oglala, Black Foot, Lakota, Pueblo and Navajo tribes. I began the session with some prepared remarks to focus the gathering on the work ahead and used the word "art" several times as I spoke.

NO WORD FOR "ART" IN THE LANGUAGE OF THE BLACK FEET

I had been speaking for only ten minutes when from the back of the audience a man rose. He was Black Bear, the leader of the Black Feet, and he spoke very loudly and slowly with respect. "Excuse me, I mean no disrespect, but we of the Black Feet have difficulty every time you say the word 'art.' For in our language there is no such word. For us, what you call art is in everything we are and everything we do. You Anglo's—and I mean no disrespect—have taken art out of everything and put it over there." He pointed far away. "But for me, what you call art is in my clothing, my healing, my cooking, my spirit, it is as close to me as my skin." Those words have rung in my mind ever since. Art has been taken out of teaching and must be put back.

There has long been an argument about the appropriate role of the arts in education with many passionate proponents believing in arts for art's sake. I believe this also, and I believe—like Black Bear—that the arts have been taken out of everything and must be woven back into the very fiber of teaching and learning in our schools. Dance, music, theatre, visual arts and literary arts provide vibrant opportunities to stimulate learning across the intelligences providing emotional learning as well as helping a student remember the facts. Whether we address the Civil War, the westward expansion or immigration through Ellis Island, we will create more wisdom by using the arts to teach. In their wonderful book, *Understanding by Design*, McTigue and Wiggins drive home the importance of sharing with students an overall "big idea" into which a student may place facts, the reason for the facts and where learning results in understanding.

CIVIL WAR TAPESTRY

Educators and students who participate in the Artsgenesis Civil War Tapestry become the families from both North and South who lived through this time period in America's past. The families and their struggles are stunningly brought to life through recreating scenes of ordinary and extra-ordinary events and the questions of the Voice of the Ages. Through these improvised scenes of

family life and relationships, those who are participating experience life in the United States from 1861 to 1863. They write, create characters, and are interviewed; they create spontaneous dialogue and monologues, exchange and perform their own letters. Through the lens of these ordinary people speaking directly about their life and times, a living emotionally moving tapestry emerges. So many participants say they felt like it was real.

Teachers practice theatre processes that work in accordance with the National Theatre Standards while they learn the underlying reasons responsible for the war. Facts of the Battle of Gettysburg, facts of the life of the time such as average human life span, what books were commonly read, what job people held are made personal. Then the facts are woven seamlessly throughout the texture of this newly created person's life. But beyond this, participants understand first hand the incredible toll in human life and suffering brought about by this war and the profound change it had on the future of the United States. A cover article written by a participant from Oregon describes what it is like to learn about the Civil War this way.

A ROOM FULL OF PRINCIPALS AND STUDENTS

"It is 1863. Your 16-year-old son has signed up to fight in the war between the North and the South. As you stand just off your front porch, you hear his regiment approaching. Be brave, he cannot see you cry. As he joins his unit, you wave goodbye. And a room full of principals, teachers, and artists waved goodbye. So began Civil War Tapestry, the first day of a three-day *Arts for Learning* workshop held this past October at McMenamins Kennedy School in Portland Oregon. I flew in from New York with a host of creative drama "tools" to use with the *Arts for Learning* teachers, and artists in Oregon (some 100 people) in a unique curriculum immersion experience. I set only two rules for their work together: say "yes" to your creative ideas and say "yes" to the creative ideas of others.

I randomly assigned participants to families of the Civil War and left each to their own creativity to design a name, ethnicity, place of origin, status and political alignment. As within all families, there emerged the individual identities, complex dynamics, and secrets—all fodder for these educators as they plunged themselves into the experience.

"How many pairs of shoes do you own?" "What did you have for breakfast this morning?" I questioned. "I hear your family is hungry, and I can see that your sister has no shoes. I will give you $350 right now, more money than you've ever seen in your life, if you'll go to a town in Pennsylvania called Gettysburg. You have four seconds to decide because the train is leaving now." Identities were born, family histories unfolded, plots developed. Each participant was forced to confront and empathize with history.

These families were together for a full day. Through this powerful program weaving the arts and history, these educators lived as a six-year-old slave girl, the Scottish patriarch of a rum-running clan, or a brave, young farm hand. Their intertwined stories were the weft and weave of an intensely moving and informative tapestry. It was an emotional and highly creative event, giving teachers and artists the chance to become learners in a powerful way. But wait.

"The postal carrier is here—he will take this bag of mail to Gettysburg, but he leaves in four minutes." The room scrambles as families jot off as much as they can for a letter to the loved ones gone to battle—some with confessions of unmatched love, some clearing up feuds, many praying for a homecoming. "But," my character sighs, "these letters do not arrive in time. Will all of your family members at the Battle please stand along the back wall. In formation please, as if we are posing for a photo." Then, with a gentle wave of the hand, I designate who did, and did not, survive the Battle of Gettysburg. As the casualties take their seats, now permanently removed from their family groups, gasps and groans are heard in an otherwise quiet room. There are few dry eyes.

All teachers reported feeling emotionally involved. As human beings take possession of their own creativity, they witness amazing results. Music is added as a background, just like a movie is scored. Our kids today know when to pay attention because the music gives so many clues. Using music in our classrooms can help us orchestrate student energy and interest. I wouldn't want to teach without my CD player and CD's.

LEADERSHIP TRAINING FOR PRINCIPALS

I have conducted leadership training for principals in Connecticut Commission's HOT Schools program and have always added the techniques I developed.

In dealing with leaders, since they tend to be very bright, they will often anticipate what is going to happen so they can better control it. My job was to keep the upcoming parts of the workshop surprising so they could stay in the learning moment. The first part of the leadership training focused on How Effective Principals think.

The participants were divided into small working groups of four to five. One person was chosen to act as a recorder for the group, another was to act as observer to the group dynamic, and all were to participate in answering the question. Everyone was given a 3x5 card. They were asked to give an individual response to this question: "What are the three most successful strategies used by Effective principals?"

They answer on the card. (Most cannot limit themselves to only 3 strategies—this is important later). Then they go around their group and discuss everyone's three answers. Many are similar some very insightful. Then the group decides which three they will recommend to the entire group.

Reporting out begins. The three recommendations of each small group are captured on a flip chart. They are interviewed not only about what they do but also why it succeeds. By the time the fourth group reports, there is repetition but the concepts are described using different words. There is discussion around whether these are the same concepts or are the apparent variations really a different tactic. Usually there is agreement that the variations are extremely useful. Discussions about tactics and the well-known Chinese War Strategy book *The Art of War* ensue.

Now we get to the observer's comments on how the group dynamics functioned. This debriefing demonstrates another important facet of leadership—human resource management. We discuss insights here with an emphasis on motivation, inspiration and dealing with the prickly personalities, entrenched behaviors and other difficult human resource issues. Usually it is agreed that there are no absolutely right or wrong answers, but instead some solid approaches. We underline how this reflects how an artist actually creates. We use solid guideposts but the art comes from the individual interpretation and expression of those guideposts.

A JOURNAL OF VISUAL SYMBOLS

But by comparison, the experience in the afternoon named "Symbol Journal" was a deeper more comprehensive view into each individual's problem-solving techniques. It focused not only on what they thought but also on what they felt. Principals were asked to review their year both professionally and personally using symbols to represent various facets. Each one was given an enormous sheet of paper and chose two markers. They were instructed to divide their page into 12 segments. There was some amazing creativity displayed in this simple task. No one divided his or her sheet the same. Horizontal orientation, vertical lines, sloping hill like structures, cubes, diagonals, folding like a fan, folding into tiny squares demonstrated better than any speech the variety of approaches that can be taken in every task. Participants had to put a month symbol on each segment then reconstruct what happened during that time with visual symbols. Some efforts were very organized, orderly and small; other free, brightly colored, some chaotic. There was a good deal of laughter and release as the principals re-created their year. But the greatest value came in the individual sharing.

As they shared, I chose not to remark on the organization, orderliness or color of their journals. That spoke volumes by itself. Each principal came to the front to explain how he or she interpreted their year. The symbols add humor and sometimes uncover devastating challenges. For example one principal had sketched only a lidless toilet for the month of August.

When this principal shared, there was hearty laughter until she explained that the former principal, whom she replaced in August, had taken every stick of furniture, every chair, even the toilet seat with her when she left. A great feeling of compassion swept across the group. The principal presenting her journal knew her problem had been understood by her peers, and relief spread over her. She knew she was with empathetic colleagues. There were many instances of strong feelings being released and affirmations for having survived the year. Participants were also able to mock or send up difficult experiences and laugh at them from a new perspective. Comparing the two approaches to leadership training in their evaluations, the principals all stated they learned on more levels in the afternoon when creative interpretation was used.

CREATING A MYTH

Even a discussion with your own child can provide an opportunity. My youngest daughter Kasey was only four years old when she asked me, "Mommy, where do the arts come from?" I compressed thousands of years into a brief myth. I told her, "Long, long ago, when we lived in caves and counted time in moons, before we spoke in words, we wondered just like you are wondering today. We wondered why the sun rose and set. We wondered why the river flooded only sometimes. Every day we wondered what we would eat. We wondered about our beginning and our end, but it was difficult to think about things that had no names. So we began to name what was in our experience. We gave ourselves and others names. The names separated us. Names represented an edge, a boundary. I am this and you are other.

As time passed we found it safer to live together and tribes collected. From these tribes there emerged leaders who could command respect for notable deeds or by looking out for the entire tribe's safety. Now we had leaders. Soon it occurred that it would be more efficient to divide up the tasks. We learned to organize. Some leaders began to plan and so developed the skill of thinking ahead and trouble-shooting developed. Memory and experience became valuable. We had discovered learning and wanted more of it. But we had to rely on only what a person could remember. How could we capture all we needed to remember outside of one individual's brain? So we encoded the

memories in stories, pictures, dances and music. The arts were the way we recorded who we were and what was important to us.

Meanwhile, the leaders became so busy leading that they could spend very little time wondering. So the task of wondering fell to others, often those gifted with wonderful questions. The wonderers became elevated in the tribe since the leaders went to the wonderers for advice. The leaders were called chief; and the wonderers, shaman. Shaman searched for tools to help them. The early tools were bones and herbs and smoke. But then the Shaman looked at how the people used stories and pictures and dances and music to remember, and thought these same things could help them wonder better. So they began visualizing, drawing, moving and making sounds and questioning always questioning. Shaman and chiefs tried to provide answers for their tribe. Many times they were right and the tribes began to thrive and organize themselves further. As years passed both chief and shaman found better tools. Leaders helped fashion codes (rules) of civilized behavior. They fashioned spears, bows and arrows for safety and to procure food. Shaman refined colors, symbols, visions, stories, and chants into ceremonies and rituals. And the people thrived.

Hundreds of years later the role of the shaman had become so big it had to be divided up. Parts of the job became what we now call healers, philosophers, teachers, scientists, inventors, doctors, mystics and artists. All of us are people who wonder and try to remember. Musicians, singers, painters, sculptors, poets, actors, dancers wonder and remember with their bodies, their designs with their rhythms, their voices and their words. The arts are all paths to wisdom, to understanding the mystery of our life on this earth.

Two roads diverged in a wood, and I—
I took the one less traveled by,
And that has made all the difference.
Robert Frost

It was the summer of my fourteenth year. My family had rented a small bungalow in West Saugerties, New York. West Saugerties was a tiny hamlet whose chief attraction was a fierce and cold mountain stream that spilled into a delightful swimming hole—before it continued its way down the rugged mountain. There was a road that almost everyone used to reach their favorite place. On the morning after I arrived, I made up mind to go swimming. Out the back door I went but instead of heading in the direction of the usual road, I decided to explore the forest behind our bungalow to see if it might lead me by another way. That morning I came upon a growth of high grasses. Rather than skirting them, I pushed my way through them. Some twenty or twenty-five yards further I suddenly heard voices coming from the pool. Every day that summer I took my clandestine route, so much so that by the end of August I had worn down the high grasses and created my own path.

ALL ARE BOTH TEACHER AND STUDENT

What moves me to recollect this half-forgotten memory from another time and another place? It serves as a metaphor for a missing element in the search for what teaching and learning are about. There is an inescapable priority that must lie with the teacher's path to knowledge and learning. Every class that I teach includes the Latin term *auto didact*. It can be translated "self-taught" and I use the term to signal to my students that the responsibility for learning rests with each of them. But I wish to carry it further. I wish to identify myself as a student and as such, subject to the same commitment to learning. What takes place in the classroom is not a teacher talking to some students or students talking to a teacher. It is a conversation in which all are both students and teachers.

The philosophers like to speak of "facticities". These include all those happenings, all those experiences, all those memories that compose an individual life. It would include the genes we inherit as well as the people who nurture our way: parents, teachers and friends. It would also certainly include all those books, films and conversations that point the way or speed the journey. At any moment we depend on these realities—we are these realities.

THE INEVITABLE CHOICE

But always present along with these is the freedom of choice. We make choices that determine the road we will take, the way we will go. Just as we cannot ignore the many

A ROAD NOT TAKEN

JOSEPH DREW

givens of what we have received, it would be foolhardy to belittle the power of free choice.

There is an intriguing story from the Arthurian legend. Arthur is sitting with his knights. Gawain, his nephew, asks that they vow together to go in pursuit of the Grail. They so vow. And then Gawain suggests that they begin the search in the dark of the forest where there is no path. And so they do. Joseph Campbell interprets this as an inner need to determine one's own life. As children we needed to follow the directions of others who have the strength and wisdom to succor us. But as adults, we reach the time of life where we set these aside.

The Arthurian legend keeps reminding us that there is a darkness and uncertainty to our lives that cannot be removed. Colleges and Universities have traditionally forgotten the lesson that mystery begets wisdom. We have worshiped at the altar of rationalism, giving to the intellect a dominance that it could not and should not assume. We have created our own sacred figures: Plato, Aristotle, Descartes; we have had a succession of enlightenments that have brought neither light nor peace of mind. The answer is not to discard reason and its votaries.

ROADS NOT TAKEN REMAIN OPEN

Rather, it is to find room for other things. It is to build a home that welcomes mystery. It is to find a place for each person's free choice. It is to realize that the road not taken, the many roads not taken, lie open to the weary traveler. They may just make "all the difference."

PAMELA ANN ATCHISON is principal of the Kent County Secondary Intensive Learning Center associated with the Capital School District in Dover, Delaware. Previously, she was a teacher of special education at the same school. Ms. Atchison's interest in Multiple Intelligences stems from her experience with students who have exceptionalities.

DR. YOON-IL AUH is the director of Distance and Distributed Learning at Central Michigan University. He has also taught at the Juilliard School and at Columbia University and is author of a computer programming book, *A Guide to the Programming Process,* published by Intrepid Pixels Technology Inc.

DR. NINAH BELIAVSKY is an assistant professor at the Institute of ESL at St. Johns University, Queens, NY. She holds an M.A. and a Ph.D. in applied linguistics from Northwestern University and a B.A. in linguistics and psychology from the University of Wisconsin in Milwaukee and Madison. Dr. Beliavsky's primary areas of interest are bringing music into the classroom and studying child language acquisition.

DR. CHERYL BLUESTONE is an associate professor of psychology at Queensborough Community College, which is part of the City University of New York. She is the principal investigator for a National Science Foundation grant to revise social science courses offered at QCC. In addition to her interest in developing curriculum, Dr. Bluestone is conducting research related to social class and stress as they may influence mothers' and fathers' behavior.

PENNY BURRALL is a reading specialist at the Belmont Charter School, Philadelphia, PA. She acted as the Director of the Developmental Program at Harcum College for 12 years and taught reading and writing courses for ESL and under-prepared college students. Ms. Burrall writes poetry and children's books. She frequently directs writing workshops for K-8 teachers and is a regular presenter at the International Reading Association's national conventions.

ABOUT THE AUTHORS

DR. GERALD CARPENTER is professor of history at Niagara University where he began teaching after earning graduate degrees at Tulane University. He teaches a variety of courses related to American business and labor history. In 1994, he won his university's Excellence in Teaching Award, largely because of the insights discussed in this book.

DR. JODY COHEN serves as Lecturer in Education within the Bryn Mawr/Haverford Education Program. Both her teaching and her research focus on students' and teachers' perspectives on schooling. Recently, she co-authored an essay with a middle school teacher and students for *In Our Own Words: Students' Perspectives on School.*

JANICE MARCHUT CONRAD is a Lecturer in the Biological Sciences Department at Plattsburgh State University of New York. She has more than 30 years experience in teaching, including assessment of General Education learning outcomes, and research in academic and industrial laboratories. She was awarded a National Science Foundation grant in1996 for "Improvement of Undergraduate Biology Laboratories."

DR. PETER L. CONRAD is a professor and chair of the Department of Biological Sciences at Plattsburgh State University of New York. He is the recipient of two National Science Foundation grants that supported innovative curriculum design in undergraduate science education at Plattsburgh. He is a plant biologist, has served as a senior research scientist in an industrial laboratory and is a Vietnam-era veteran.

DR. ALISON COOK-SATHER is assistant professor and Director of the Bryn Mawr/Haverford Education Program. Recent publications include "Authorizing Student Perspectives: Toward Trust, Dialogue, and Change in Education" (*Educational Researcher,* **31**, 4, 2002), "Between Student and Teacher: Teacher Education as Translation" (*Teaching Education,* **12**, 12, 2001) and *In Our Own Words: Students' Perspectives on School* (co-edited with Jeffrey Shultz, Rowman & Littlefield Publishers, Inc., 2001).

DR. CHRISTINA CRAIG, professor emeritus at the College of New Jersey, taught undergraduate methods courses, supervised student teachers, and served as advisor and coordinator of the Art Education Program during her 29-year tenure in the Department of Art. Currently, she divides her time between her studio and serving as a consultant in visual arts through Young Audiences of New Jersey.

DR. ROBERTA DAVIDSON received her doctorate from Princeton University, where she specialized in Medieval literature. While in graduate school, she developed an interest in Gender Studies, and subsequently helped to establish the first-ever program in Gender Studies and a minor in the field at Whitman College, where she is currently an associate professor. She also taught individually or in a team with John Kerwin at the Washington State Penitentiary.

DR. JOSEPH DREW (late) cultivated a love and pursuit of those subjects that involve humanistic areas—history, philosophy and literature. His doctorate in philosophy was from New York University. His career in higher education included such interesting assignments as ombudsman at Queens College of the City University of New York, chief student life officer at Rutgers, the State University of New Jersey, and academic vice-president at New Jersey City University. He also studied film at The New School for Social Research.

DR. DIAN D. DUDDERAR is an assistant professor in the teacher education program at St. Mary's College of Maryland and incorporates the study of MI in all of her courses. In addition, she is the coordinator of an innovative student teaching program in Costa Rica.

DR. DEBORAH ELDRIDGE is an associate professor at Hunter College of the City University of New York and coordinates the Masters in Literacy Program. She researches, presents, and authors work in the area of the teacher preparation and is currently writing a reading methods textbook for pre-service teachers of urban elementary school classrooms.

DR. DONNA M. FARINA teaches graduate courses for teachers seeking certification in ESL or bilingual education, in the Department of Multicultural Education at New Jersey City University. She has also taught undergraduate French and Russian at NJCU. Presently, Dr. Farina is directing a two-year grant funded by the U.S. Department of Education entitled "Reaching across Borders: Internationalizing Students in K-12 Urban Teacher Education." Dr. Farina's main research interests are lexicography and censorship.

CARMEN FERRÁNDIZ is an assistant researcher for the Spanish Ministry of Education and graduated in Pedagogy from Murcia University. She is doing her Ph.D. in Multiple Intelligences. Prof. FERRÁNDIZ has been in Yale University working with Professor Robert Sternberg in Tacit Knowledge and Triarchic Intelligence Theory. Prof. Ferrándiz has published articles about gifted and talented children, creativity, multiple intelligences and learning styles. She and Professor Prieto have published the book entitled *Multiple Intelligences and the School Curriculum.*

DR. PATRICK K. FREER is assistant professor of choral music education at Georgia State University. He has been the Director of Choral Activities at Salisbury University (MD), the Education Director of Young Audiences of New Jersey, and, for eleven years, taught public school music at all grade levels. Dr. Freer holds BM and MM degrees from Westminster Choir College of Rider University, and an Ed.D. from Teachers College, Columbia University.

KATHLEEN GAFFNEY is president and co-founder of Artsgenesis, Inc., which designs and delivers innovative interdisciplinary arts integrated programs for teachers and students in New Jersey, New York and Connecticut.

DR. HOWARD GARDNER, a leading developmental psychologist, was educated at Harvard University where he now teaches. He is most highly recognized for his theory of Multiple Intelligences, which is a critique of the notion that there exists but a single human intelligence that can be assessed by standard psychometric instruments. The author of eighteen books and several hundred articles, Gardner and his colleagues have been working on the design of performance-based assessments. Most recently, he has helped launch the "Good Work Project" which is concerned with work that is both excellent in quality and also exhibits a sense of social responsibility.

JENELLE GILBERT is an assistant professor in the Department of Kinesiology, California State University at Fresno where she teaches at both the graduate and undergraduate levels. Her research interests include mental training, girls and women in sport, as well as athletic stress and coping.

DR. EDVIGE GIUNTA is associate professor of English at New Jersey City University, where she teaches memoir as well as other literature and writing courses. Her critical work—which deals primarily with Italian American women writers and filmmakers— her poetry, and her memoirs, have appeared in many journals and anthologies. She is the author of *Writing with an Accent: Contemporary Italian American Women Authors* (Palgrave/St. Martin's Press 2002), and co-editor, with Louise DeSalvo of the anthology *The Milk of Almonds: Italian American Women Writers on Food and Culture* (Feminist Press, 2002).

DR. KATHLEEN GORMAN-CARTER is assistant vice president for academic affairs at The Richard Stockton College of New Jersey. She was formerly an associate professor in an NCATE-accredited teacher education program. Dr. Carter's interest in multiple intelligences is in the identification of MI in pre-service teachers and adult learners.

JOHN KERWIN began his career as a producer/director/writer for NBC News and later went on to found his own production company, Kerwin Communications. After many years in the business, he received his Masters in Communications from Washington State University and turned to teaching. He taught full-time at the Washington State Penitentiary for eleven years, and is now an Assistant Professor of Communications at Pennsylvania State University.

DR. ANSLEY LAMAR is professor of psychology and the founder of the Urban Mission Conference series at New Jersey City University. At the time of the "Conference on Innovative Methods of Teaching in Higher Education," he was the Dean of the College of Arts and Sciences at NJCU. As the Chairman of the Executive Committee, Dr. LaMar played a key role in the planning and realization of the Conference.

DR. CLIFFORD E. LANDERS taught political science at New Jersey City University from 1972 until his retirement in 2002. A Fulbright exchange professor in the Dominican Republic in 1981-82, he has translated some 14 novels from Brazilian Portuguese including works by Jorge Amado and Rubem Fonseca. He received the Mario Ferreira Award in 1999. His book *Literary Translation: A Practical Guide* was published by Multilingual Matters Ltd. in 2001.

DR. JOHN D. LAWRY is professor of psychology at Marymount College of Fordham University. He obtained his Ph.D. in educational psychology from Fordham University in 1972. He is the author of *Guide to the History of Psychology* (University Press of America, 1991), *May You Never Stop Dancing: A Professor's Letters to His Daughter* (St. Mary's Press, 1998) and *College 101: A First-Year Reader* (McGraw-Hill, 1999).

DR. ALICE LESNICK serves as lecturer in education within the Bryn Mawr/Haverford Education Program, where she oversees the minor in educational studies. Her research focuses on the integration of students' field experiences with academic study, and on the nature and role of reflective writing in students' learning.

DR. CHARLES LYNCH, an assistant professor of English at New Jersey City University since fall 1996, is a poet and member of the Baha'i faith. He is heartened by the ways ethnic and cultural diversity inspire young adults to share knowledge and experiences to transform life in the United States for the better. "They certainly deserve more credit than the mass media gives them," he said.

DR. CYNTHIA MORAWSKI is an associate professor in the Faculty of Education, University of Ottawa where she teaches and supervises in both the undergraduate and graduate programs. Her research interests include social-emotional factors related to the learning process, reading and language arts, women and education, bibliotherapy, and reflective teacher education.

An educational researcher by training, **DR. GRIFFIN MUSSINGTON** is associate professor at Delaware State University. She earned a Ph.D. from The Ohio State University in Curriculum and Instruction and Professional Development. She has the distinction of being the first Holmes Scholar from The Ohio State University. A consultant to several school districts around the nation, she conducts in-service workshops for teachers on discipline and classroom management, learning style, teaching style and pedagogy for today's classrooms.

DR. KATHLEEN PEARLE is a research associate at Rowan University's Center for the Advance-ment of Learning. She received her Ed.D. from the Department of Educational Leadership at Rowan. Her dissertation, "Metacognition as Vehicle for Organizational Change: How 'Thinking about Thinking' and Intentional Learning Break the Mold of 'Heroic' Teaching in Higher Education," is an action research study of organizational change using the Interactive Learning Model at Foothill College.

DR. SUSAN M. PERLIS is an assistant professor of graduate education at Marywood University in Scranton, PA. She holds a Bachelor of Arts degree in Elementary Education, Psychology and a Master of Science in Education in Curriculum and Instruction Supervision from College Misericordia, and a doctorate in Educational Leadership and Policy Studies from Temple University with a specialization in Higher Education Administration.

DR. LOLA PRIETO is a professor of educational psychology in the University of Murcia (Spain). She graduated in Pedagogy and Psychology from Valencia University. She specialized in Learning Potential Assessment with Dr. Reuven Feuerstein in Jerusalem. Prof. Prieto has also worked in Triarchic Intelligence Theory at Yale University with Professor Robert Sternberg. She has published several books and articles focusing on learning strategies, education of gifted children, multiple intelligences, and intellectual styles.

DR. PATRICIA REYNOLDS is an Urban Education and reading instructor who also directs the Learning Center's writing program at Penn State University's Delaware County Campus. In the nineties, she taught English Composition at Harcum Junior College where she, with Penny Burrall, the head of the Developmental Program, modified the basic writing course.

DR. DINA ROSEN is an assistant professor with the Department of Early Childhood and Elementary Education at Montclair State University. She has been a teacher and school technology director in preschool–eighth grade settings. Dr. Rosen has published research concerning early childhood and elementary education, technology, and assistive technology.

DR. CHRISTOPHER SHAMBURG is an assistant professor of educational technology at New Jersey City University. He has published and presented on issues of reflective practice, language arts education, vocational education, teacher preparation, and educational technology.

Dr. Fred Savitz is professor of education at Neumann College, Aston, Pennsylvania, where he engages the intelligences of his teacher education students in classes in *Educational Psychology* and *Social Studies Methods.* He finds inspiration in singing and playing the blues with a blues/funk/rock band named Sterlin Colvin and the Improv.

 **Dr. Holly Seplocha** is an assistant professor of early childhood education at William Paterson University. Beginning as a preschool teacher, she has been in the field for over 25 years as a teacher, administrator, researcher, and adult educator. She has extensive experience throughout the nation providing seminars for teachers and supervisors.

 Dr. Constance Sica's varied background as a free-lance writer, art editor, production/ stage designer and T.V. producer/writer/host has greatly influenced the development of her multiple interactive teaching approaches in the classroom. Her articles have appeared in various publications including *The New York Times* and *The Academic Forum.* Dr. Sica is an assistant professor at New Jersey City University.

 Dr. Janis Strasser is an assistant professor of early childhood education at William Paterson University. She has taught at public and private schools for over 25 years. Dr. Strasser has published research on literacy, multicultural education, and the arts and is frequently invited to speak at local and national conferences.

 Formerly a Fulbright Scholor in Modern German Drama, **Dr. Christine Lilian Turczyn** is a poet, educator, and freelance writer. She has taught critical and creative writing at William Paterson University, Binghamton University, and the University of Wisconsin, among other post-secondary institutions. Dr. Turczyn has received various prizes for her poetry, including first prize at the Allen Ginsberg poetry awards and was a recipient of a fellowship from the Geraldine R. Dodge Foundation.

 **Dr. Cordelia R. Twomey** is an associate professor and chairperson of the Master's Degree in Educational Technology program at New Jersey City University. She is the co-author of a microcomputer textbook, many articles and technical manuals, and is involved in urban education issues on the state and national level.

 **Dr. Heidi Upton** received the B.M. and M.M. degrees from The Juilliard School and the D.M.A. degree from Manhattan School of Music. Associated with Lincoln Center Institute since 1998, Dr. Upton was asked in 2001 by the Institute to be one of its first full-time teaching artists.

 **Dr. Jon A. Yasin** is a professor of English at Bergen Community College in Paramus, New Jersey. He is a 2000-2002 fellow with the National Academy of Education/Spencer Postdoctoral Fellowship. He has taught linguistics at the United Arab Emirates University, and he was Le Responsible au Centre D'Animation Rural in N'gabou, Senegal.

Ron Bogusz is Director of Publications and Special programs at New Jersey City University. He is also the designer of this book and its cover. The effort to make everything fit and work well is enormous and requires exceptional talent. His contribution to this book is clearly on a par with the writers. (EDITOR'S NOTE)